PREFACE

PREFACE

As editor of this book, I need to confess that it feels partially autobiographical. Not in the literal sense, but in terms of representing the culmination of my career to date. Don't get me wrong, I'm far from done. But, in many ways, the last 20 years have led to this book.

My passion has always been figuring out ways to help children who have difficult peer relationships, especially those kids who don't tend to get attention or intervention from adults. They may be picked on, teased, left out, and in other ways miserable, but they don't get services because they don't act up or draw attention to themselves. Helping these children is really the impetus for all the work I do. So, maybe understanding how I got here may help put some context around the information shared in this book.

In the 1990s, I began my academic career working with schools to investigate the types of peer problems children experience and how these negative social interactions impact outcomes such as academic success and emotional and behavioral health. The end goal of this research has always been to inform treatment. If we can better understand the underlying causes of these social phenomena and the factors that increase versus decrease risk for a given child, then we can build interventions that effectively remediate or even prevent negative outcomes.

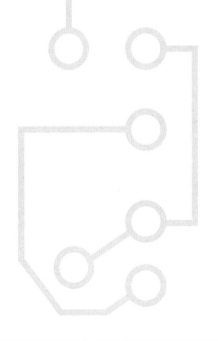

But, as repeatedly stated throughout this book, effective assessment is necessary for effective intervention. This is especially true for the underserved, socially rejected, or isolated child who doesn't make a fuss at school. Early in my career, it became clear that relying on data from adults— say, teachers or parents—was not sufficient for identifying the majority of children who suffer significant peer problems. For example, in 2004, I compared teacher-report of peer problems with peer nomination data for 1,204 3rd to 5th grade students. Unfortunately, I found that teachers failed to identify 83% of the children who were actually highly disliked and rejected by their peers. In many ways, this disconnect makes sense. Teachers have limited access to information about children's social relationships. Embarrassment over social problems—along with a belief that adults can't help anyway—often leads children to keep their problems to themselves. Telling an adult may also make things worse—you may be seen as a "teacher's pet" or "tattletale"—resulting in more bullying and ostracism. Also, as discussed in this book, we would expect some disagreement between teacher report and peer nomination—adults' expectations for children's behavior tend to differ from those of peers. However, a miss-rate this high is truly problematic because we know:

- The best results come from early intervention;
- We can't intervene with kids we can't identify; and
- Peer problems typically get worse without intervention.

In fact, teachers were more accurate when peer problems were more extreme. For example, teachers were able to accurately identify about 70% of children who were extremely rejected by their peers (greater than three standard deviations above the mean). But, from a prevention and intervention perspective, it's not good policy to wait until problems become extreme. More money and time will be needed because now intervention efforts will need to be greater. Chronic and more severe problems are more difficult to treat, so likelihood of success is lower. Plus, there's likely to have been all kinds of collateral damage—escalating disruption in the classroom that undermines learning for all students; entrenchment of reputational biases in the peer group that will work against the child who tries to change his social behavior; corrosion of the child's academic performance as social anxiety distracts him from learning; and so on and so on.

OK, I realize I'm on a soapbox and preaching to the reader, so I'll stop now, but the fact that I couldn't rely on teacher report to identify children in need of intervention was alarming to me in my early career. So, I set out to find a solution.

Teachers failed to identify 83% of children who were actually rejected by their peers.

First Try at Improving Social Skills Assessment Through Technology

In the mid-2000s, I and Jim Thomas developed the SCAN (Sociometric Collection and Analysis) software to streamline the sociometric data collection and analysis process. The most accurate means of assessing peer problems—of any type—is peer nominations or sociometrics (see Chapter 9). In my career, I've repeatedly used sociometrics to identify children for social skills intervention, particularly those who are victimized by peers, socially anxious and withdrawn, or socially rejected. Many times, teachers have questioned my selection of children, saying things like "but she's a great student," or "but he's quiet and well behaved in class," or "but she never causes trouble" as reasons why I must be wrong. These children each had significant peer problems—and benefited from social skills intervention—but would have suffered in silence without an independent, objective assessment method to identify them. The intent with SCAN was to bring the peer nomination assessment method into schools for everyday use. We tested the software in schools, and got great feedback from users saying that SCAN significantly improved the process and decreased the barriers to using sociometrics. However, SCAN— just like sociometrics more generally—is still primarily used by researchers, not school providers. Even after SCAN minimized the time and training needed to collect and analyze the assessment data, it wasn't enough to make peer nominations doable for schools.

> Effective assessment is necessary for effective intervention.

Time for Something Completely Different

Intelligent game platforms for education and health have grown over the past decade. It occurred to me that we could take advantage of these emerging technologies and the societal shift towards technology—both in schools and more generally—to integrate social skills assessment (SSA) directly into gameplay for children. I reviewed the commonly used SSA rating scales, looking at the types of issues that were indicative of particular social problems. I became familiar with interview methods that assess the quality of children's social problem solving skills for dealing with presented social situations. I also consulted with computer scientists who had created intelligent tutoring systems (ITS) with embedded assessment—such as Dr. James Lester of North Carolina State University—in order to learn about how these systems work.

This foundational work—along with considerable grant funding from the National Institutes of Health and the U.S. Department of Education—has enabled me and 3C Institute to build the first ever software engine for an intelligent *social* tutoring system (ISTS). This ISTS defines the underlying game mechanics, user interface parameters, pedagogical approaches, and data collection and analysis methods for social problem solving situations presented within a virtual game environment. *Zoo U*—which is the focus of Part III of this book—is built on this engine. The means by which *Zoo U* translates gameplay into social skill metrics—and the ways that game-based SSA can overcome the barriers that plague traditional SSA methods—are well described in this book, so I won't review them here.

What is important to emphasize is that our research findings with children, parents, and school professionals—for *Zoo U* as well as 3C Institute's other game applications—confirm that games are the solution I've been looking for. Intelligent games offer unparalleled capabilities to create individualized, dynamic, and engaging assessment and intervention tools that can be delivered at low cost to youth and families across the globe. By lowering time, training, and financial barriers—while simultaneously maximizing engagement for children—games for assessment and intervention are truly the wave of the future.

The Next Step

As mentioned earlier in this preface, my end goal has always been to use assessment to inform and guide treatment. So, the end goal for *Zoo U* is not to provide just an effective, feasible, and engaging social skills assessment tool, but rather an effective social skills intervention that uses data to intelligently guide children toward targeted social learning goals. As discussed in Chapter 17, 3C Institute has created the *Zoo U Intelligent Social Tutoring System (Zoo U ISTS)* which integrates the *Zoo U* assessment and then goes further by embedding intelligent, data-driven pedagogical assistance and progress monitoring of skill development as children participate in this social intervention.

But I'll leave that story for the next book…

Games lower implementation barriers, increase engagement, and yield powerful SSA data.

CONTENTS

Preface ii

Introduction 2

Part I: Understanding Social Skills

Part I Overview 10

Chapter 1: Defining Social Skills 11

Chapter 2: Pivotal Developmental Changes 29

Chapter 3: Impact of Social Skills on Adjustment 47

Part II: Traditional Social Skills Assessment

Part II Overview 70

Chapter 4: Goals of Social Skills Assessment 73

Chapter 5: Guidelines for Evaluating SSA Options 89

Chapter 6: Using Behavioral Rating Scales for SSA 93

Chapter 7: Using Behavioral Observations for SSA 107

Chapter 8: Using Interview Methods for SSA 119

Chapter 9: Using Peer Nominations for SSA 131

Chapter 10: Traditional Best Practices for SSA 151

Part III: Game-Based Social Skills Assessment

Part III Overview 160

Chapter 11: Using Games for SSA 161

Chapter 12: *Zoo U* Game Platform for SSA 173

Chapter 13: *Zoo U* Scoring Metrics 187

Chapter 14: *Zoo U* Assessment Reports 199

Chapter 15: *Zoo U* Foundational Studies 211

Chapter 16: Advantages of Games Over Traditional SSA Methods 225

Part IV: Moving from Assessment to Intervention

Part IV Overview 238

Chapter 17: Scaffolded Social Tutoring 241

Chapter 18: Assessment as a Component of Intervention Planning in Schools 257

Chapter 19: Bridging to Home 271

Chapter 20: Informing Treatment of Children with Autism Spectrum Disorders 283

About the Editor 300

About the Contributors 304

Acknowledgments 308

INTRODUCTION

INTRODUCTION

WHAT'S IN THIS BOOK

In this book, we explore how game-based platforms can be used to assess children's social skills, and we present a concrete example of this new best practice in the form of the *Zoo U* assessment (http://www.3cisd.com/marketplace/catalog/202/Zoo-U-Social-Skills-Assessment). To lay the foundation for this discussion, the authors first review the social skills literature underlying social skills assessment (SSA), and then provide a comparative evaluation of the various traditional SSA approaches. We conclude the book with a discussion of how game-based SSA can serve as a springboard for intervention in schools and at home.

This Book is Separated Into Four Parts:

PART I reviews the social skills literature—the theory and research underlying any social skills assessment. **Chapter 1** defines the various types of social skills—engaging, inhibitory, and solution-focused—and examines how these social behaviors, attitudes, and attributes influence the quality of our social relationships. In **Chapter 2**, we explore the developmental shifts that occur in social skills and social relationships from early childhood through young adulthood. Then, **Chapter 3** describes how social skill deficits translate into specific social troubles with peers and how these relationship problems can lead to academic, behavioral, and emotional adjustment problems for children and adolescents.

PART II examines how children's social skills and social functioning are traditionally assessed. **Chapter 4** defines the common goals for SSA: screening to identify children with social skill deficits, monitoring a child's progress during the course of an intervention, and evaluating the impact of an intervention for helping a child achieve particular outcomes. **Chapter 5** presents specific criteria that can be useful when evaluating whether a SSA approach is right for you—feasibility, utility, accuracy and engagement—

and also describes the rating scale used in this book to evaluate each of these criteria. **Chapters 6 through 9** then evaluate the traditional SSA methods—behavioral rating scales, behavioral observations, interviewing, and peer nominations—highlighting the benefits and limitations of each. **Chapter 10** is a summary chapter in which we compare the relative strengths, weaknesses, costs, and benefits of traditional SSA approaches.

PART III explores the ways that game-based assessment can move SSA beyond the limitations of traditional SSA methods. **Chapter 11** presents the evolution of computerized assessment methods and shows how games can be particularly powerful for generating social skill data. **Chapter 12** introduces the *Zoo U* social skills assessment platform and discusses the theory and research behind development of its social problem solving scenes. In **Chapter 13**, we define the underlying scoring metrics used to assess social skills through *Zoo U*. In **Chapter 14**, we present the ways in which assessment data gathered through *Zoo U* is translated into customized reports and intervention recommendations. **Chapter 15** summarizes the iterative development and testing process that was used to establish the *Zoo U* software and its underlying scoring rubric. Then, in **Chapter 16**, we evaluate the strengths and weaknesses of a game-based approach to SSA—applying the same rating scale as used in Part II—and compare game platforms with traditional SSA methods.

PART IV turns attention to how game-based SSA can be used to improve the effectiveness of social intervention with children. In **Chapter 17**, the authors discuss how the gaming environment can be extended to an individualized, adaptive social tutoring tool with data continually informing and personalizing instruction for maximum learning. **Chapter 18** presents how game-based SSA data are a perfect fit for the Response to Intervention (RtI) and Multi-Tiered Systems of Support (MTSS) approaches that schools use to implement and assess social and behavioral interventions with children. **Chapter 19** discusses how schools can use the data generated through *Zoo U* to extend social interventions into the home environment. Then, in **Chapter 20**, we consider the ways that games can be useful for assessment and intervention specifically for children with autism spectrum disorders who often experience severe social skill deficits.

Part I

Social skills literature

Part II

Traditional social skills assessment

Part III

Game-based social skills assessment

Part IV

Social skills assessment and social intervention

HOW TO USE THIS BOOK

Our intent is that you use this book to make informed decisions about which SSA method(s) to use in your situation to answer your assessment questions. Every child is different and every situation is different. By clearly defining and presenting the pros and cons of each SSA method—game-based and traditional—this book should help you select the SSA tools that best fit your specific needs. While the authors clearly and strongly believe in the benefits of game-based SSA, we also believe that a thorough assessment protocol typically requires a mix of complementary methods in order to gather a full and complete picture of a given child's functioning. We hope that the information in this book will shed light on how game-based platforms can be a viable and potentially powerful method to include in your assessment toolbox.

After reading this book, the reader should expect to achieve the following **learning objectives:**

- identify those social skills that fall into the three broad categories (engaging, inhibitory, and solution-focused);

- identify the developmental shifts in social skills and social relationships from early childhood through adolescence;

- recognize how social skill deficits impact social relationships as well as academic, behavioral, and emotional functioning;

- recognize the ways that SSA can be used to guide the intervention planning process (screening, monitoring, and evaluating);

- identify the four commonly used traditional SSA methods (behavioral rating scales, behavioral observations, interviewing, and peer nominations);

- be familiar with how games—particularly Zoo U—can be used to collect and report social skills assessment data;

- identify the relative pros and cons of different SSA approaches, including historic methods and innovative game-based technologies; and

- recognize how game-based SSA can be used to inform and enhance social intervention in schools and at home.

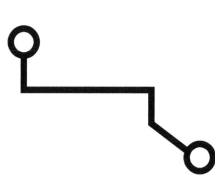

SCOPE OF BOOK

The topics discussed in this book could fill volumes. The authors elected to focus their discussion in order to provide the background needed to meaningfully discuss game-based SSA and the implications for social intervention. However, as noted in chapters throughout this book, we did not—and could not—cover all relevant related topics in detail. For example, while the role of parents in social skill development is pivotal, a discussion of the huge literature detailing how parents impact their child's social development is beyond the scope of our book. However, if you're interested in pursuing any of these topics further, we've provided citations and additional information in the **Chapter Notes** section for each chapter.

OTHER CONSIDERATIONS FOR THIS BOOK

As you read this book, the authors would like you to keep a couple other points in mind.

Focus on Peer Relationships

This book focuses almost exclusively on considerations of peer relationships. However, social skills impact all social relationships—with parents, with siblings, with teachers, with coaches, with new people you meet every day. While each relationship brings slightly different social demands and expectations, these nuances do not take away from the critical role of social skills. We encourage the reader to think beyond peer relationships and explore—perhaps through reading references provided in the Chapter Notes—the role of social skills in social interactions more broadly.

The Role of Culture

It's also important to keep in mind that the topics discussed in this book are based on research primarily with children in the United States. Unfortunately, few studies have explicitly tested how these social dimensions vary across cultures or even across subcultures within the U.S. As such, our understanding of children's social development is subject to **cultural relativism**. In other words, children's social competence is a relative term defined by the structures and goals of their particular culture. Let's look at a couple examples of how cultural relativism has implications for the conclusions that can be drawn from this book.

First, in Hispanic/Latino cultures, social competence involves the ability to cooperate with others to work toward the collective good.[1,2] In this collectivistic view, children experience much greater contact with and interdependence among family members, making social competence more closely tied to familial relationships than is the case in individualistic cultures such as the United States. The prominence of family social relationships in collectivistic cultures is likely to impact developmental trends discussed in Chapter 2, such as the shift from parents to peers as primary providers of key relationship functions. While there's limited research to draw on here, there's evidence to support this hypothesis. In a study by the editor that compared Costa Rican and American children, Costa Rican parents continued to be the primary providers of all positive relationship functions across childhood, while peers surpassed parents for the American children by the time the children were in late elementary school.[3] In addition, teachers and relatives such as grandparents were found to play a more important role for children in Costa Rica. In this collectivistic culture, there was little evidence that family members, especially parents, become less important for any relationship function during middle childhood.

Second, the collectivistic and interdependent nature of Asian cultures results in development of social skills and social competence specific to the values and expectations of those cultures. For instance, Japanese children are socialized to attend to and fit in with others so as to increase the quality of social interactions and promote social cohesion.[1] As a result, there's emphasis on social skills that result in reduced social friction and confrontation, including deference and respect to parents and authority figures, social responsibility, modesty, cooperation, and pride in one's social group rather than in one's personal achievements.[4] Moreover, culturally-relevant behavioral cues may send different messages during interpersonal interactions. Avoidance of eye contact may signal respect or deference in Japanese culture, whereas such behavior suggests inattention, rudeness, or shyness in the United States.[5]

Children's social competence is a relative term defined by the structures and goals of their particular culture.

Cultural differences in the nature of interpersonal interactions and understanding of one's relation to others result in differing social expectations for acceptable and normative behavior.[6,7,8] Individualistic cultures, such as the United States, tend to value individual skills and achievement whereas collectivistic cultures tend to stress the importance of the group. Children from collectivistic cultures receive a higher level of social pressure for conformity and cooperation, whereas individualistic cultures more easily tolerate conflictual and competitive behavior. Significantly different cultural scripts for sex roles—how boys and girls should behave—are also evident across these differing cultures.[9]

Just as our social developmental theories need to be adjusted to allow for cultural variations, **ecological validity of SSA** needs to be considered as well. Current assessment tools measure children's social skill levels by establishing cut-offs for high, borderline, and poor performance scores compared to a 'normative' score (a score expected of children of the same age) (see Chapter 4). These norms are largely based on research studies with children in the United States. We need to raise the question of how true or valid a given assessment measure is relative to a child's culture or subculture. While we lack the research to fully understand how cultural differences impact children's social skill development, it's important to keep these differences in mind when conducting an SSA. This is particularly true given the increasing diversity of U.S. schools. Subcultural differences—while perhaps not as pronounced as cross-cultural differences—need to be taken into consideration when interpreting scores generated from any SSA tool.

Don't assume that all purported social skills games actually yield accurate and informative data!

Not All Games are Created Equal

Our hope is that this book will help clarify how games can be used to benefit children—not only for engaging, effective SSA, but also for engaging, effective social intervention. But, don't assume that all purported social skills games actually yield accurate and informative data.

As with any new hot trend, expect to get inundated with an increasing number of games that claim to be effective for social skills assessment and/ or social intervention. Do your homework! Make sure that any game you employ for SSA is based in solid research that demonstrates its validity and reliability. Do not lower your standards for psychometric soundness just because of a game's flashier packaging. You must hold games to the same accuracy standards as you do any other SSA approach or you'll just be collecting data that actually undermines your intervention planning goals. Similarly, before using a game for social intervention, make sure that that game has solid research backing up its claims of efficacy. Look for rigorous research—specifically randomized clinical trial studies—demonstrating that the game positively impacts children's social behavior and relationships. Then, you'll not only be saving time and money, but also maximizing the likelihood of positive change for participating children.

INTRODUCTION NOTES

1. Markus, H. R., & Kitayama, S. (1991). Culture and the self: Implications for cognition, emotion, and motivation. *Psychological Review, 98,* 224-253.

2. Triandis, H. C., Marin, G., Lisanksy, J., & Betancourt, H. (1984). Simpatia as a cultural script of Hispanics. *Journal of Personality and Social Psychology, 47,* 1363-1375.

3. DeRosier, M. E., & Kupersmidt, J. B. (1991). Costa Rican children's perceptions of their social network. *Developmental Psychology, 27,* 656-662.

4. Rivera, B. D., & Rogers-Adkinson, D. (1997). Culturally sensitive interventions: Social skills training with children and parents from culturally and linguistically diverse backgrounds. *Intervention in School and Clinic, 33,* 75-80.

5. Sue, D. W., & Sue, D. (1977). Barriers to effective cross-cultural counseling. *Journal of Counseling Psychology, 24,* 420-429.

6. Ogbu, J. U. (1981). Origins of human competence: A cultural-ecological perspective. *Child Development, 52,* 413-429.

7. Chen X., & French, D. C. (2008). Children's social competence in cultural context. *Annual Review of Psychology, 59,* 591-616.

8. Halbertstadt, A. G., Denham, S. A., & Dunsmore, J. C. (2001). Affective social competence. *Social Development, 10,* 79-119.

9. Lindsey, L .L. (1997). *Gender roles: A sociological perspective.* Upper Saddle River, NJ: Prentice Hall.

PART I

UNDERSTANDING SOCIAL SKILLS

UNDERSTANDING SOCIAL SKILLS

OVERVIEW

*What do we mean when we use the term 'social skills?'
It's one of those commonplace terms that can mean very different
things to different people. However, in order to assess something
accurately, you must first be able to clearly define what you're
measuring—otherwise, you could be gathering data that has
little relation to what you thought you were assessing.*

*So, in this section of the book, we—the authors—define exactly
what we mean by the term 'social skills,' how we conceptualize
the impact of social skills on the quality of children's social
relationships, and how we see social skills being tied to children's
adjustment more generally, including their academic
performance and mental health. Where possible, we also explore
the role of development and gender on the definition
or expression of these skills.*

*In the first chapter of this section, we describe the various types of
social skills, their form and functions, as well as examine how they
are interconnected. We also discuss social behaviors, attitudes,
and attributes that influence the quality of our social relationships
with key social network members. In the next chapter, we explore
the developmental shifts that occur in social skills and social
relationships from early childhood through young adulthood. In
the third and final chapter of this section, we examine what we
know about how social skill deficits translate into specific social
problems with peers and how these relationship problems can lead
to academic, behavioral, and emotional adjustment problems for
children and adolescents.*

Defining Social Skills

by: Melissa E. DeRosier, Ph.D.

DESCRIPTION

Social skills help us form and maintain social relationships with others as well as navigate a multitude of interpersonal situations.[1-3] In this chapter, we define the various types of social skills, their form and functions, as well as examine how they are interconnected with one another. We then discuss social behaviors, attitudes, and attributes that influence the quality of our social relationships, particularly with key social network members. In the last two sections, we explore how possessing particular social skills is necessary, but not sufficient for achieving positive social connections. Our confidence in the application of those social skills impacts our level of social success, as does our underlying social intent towards others.

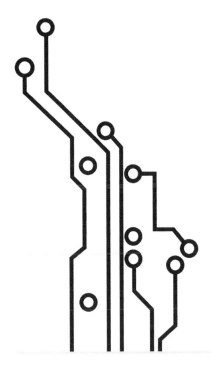

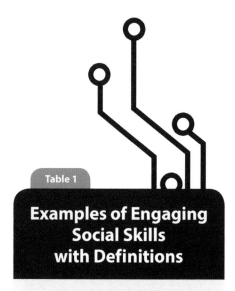

Table 1

Examples of Engaging Social Skills with Definitions

Verbal Communication

WHAT we say; the content of our message; the words we use to communicate our thoughts or feelings; examples include talking, writing, sign language, and Braille

Non-verbal Communication

HOW we say something; communicating what we think or feel without using words; examples include tone of voice, body language, facial expression, and eye contact

Listening

Hearing what others have to say; finding out what the other person is thinking or feeling through listening and asking questions; not interrupting or putting someone down

Perspective Taking

Ability to see a situation from another's point of view; knowing what another is thinking or feeling

Empathy

Ability to understand the thoughts and feelings of another; ability to feel what another person is feeling

Social Initiation

Taking the first step to begin playing or talking with another person; joining with one or more people for a social activity or conversation

TYPES OF SOCIAL SKILLS

A wide array of specific behaviors and abilities are included under the umbrella term of 'social skills.' From a broad perspective, social skills typically fall into one of three categories: engaging, inhibitory, or solution-focused.

Engaging Social Skills

Certain social skills are used to *engage* others. The underlying purpose of such skills is to build, repair, or strengthen social relationships. You use these skills to actively engage with the other person in a social interaction; you can comfort someone who is feeling down (**empathy**), ask someone to join you (**social initiation**), or confide your thoughts and feelings to another (**communication**). In **Table 1**, we define six key social skills for engaging others: verbal and non-verbal communication, listening, perspective taking, empathy, and social initiation. Individuals who struggle with engaging social skills are often seen as passive, withdrawn, timid, or solitary.

Engaging social skills can flow in two directions—outward towards another or inward from another. In each case, you're actively seeking to fortify your social relationship, but the focus of a given social interaction may either be on you or on the other person. For example, you can help others understand what you think and feel (**communication**) or you can try to understand what others think and feel (**listening**). You can show compassion for others or accept compassion from others (**two directions of empathy**). This idea is similar to receptive versus expressive skills in the language arts. Receptive language skills allow you to *take in and understand* written or spoken language while expressive language skills let you *express yourself* through written or spoken language. Similarly, you can use engaging social skills to understand and participate in activities with others (**receptive**) or to initiate conversations with others and help them understand you (**expressive**). As with language abilities, receptive and expressive social skills tend to go together; however, people can vary in their receptive versus expressive ability levels. For example, you may be able to accept an invitation to join a group, but have difficulty inviting others to join you.

Both expressive and receptive methods of engaging others are critical for social success. Being able to approach someone, start up a conversation, and share things about yourself are all important aspects of establishing a new relationship. Once a relationship has begun, however, receptive skills for listening, understanding, and joining with the other person are necessary for maintaining that relationship. Ultimately, individuals who excel at both receptive and expressive engaging social skills are most adept at reciprocity in social interactions (for example, being able to give and take in conversation) and therefore, are best able to create and maintain social relationships over time.

Inhibitory Social Skills

With inhibitory social skills, you inhibit internal impulses to say or do something that could potentially damage your relationship with another person. This is also an active process whereby you purposefully control, censor, or prevent a given action (verbal or physical). A primary inhibitory social skill is **impulse control**, also termed **'Stop & Think'** in the social skills training literature. Acting without thinking about the possible impact on others often leads to unintended hurt feelings and conflict. Impulse control is the ability to stop and consider the situation, even for just a moment, before acting. In that moment, you weigh likely positive and negative consequences of saying or doing what your impulses are driving you towards and consider whether that action will further your social goal. This process enables you to make an informed decision about what to do or say in that situation. For example, imagine you see a group of people playing a game and you want to join in. Your immediate impulse may be to just jump in and start playing. However, acting on this impulse will likely irritate the other players and may lead to conflict. If you fail to 'Stop & Think' in this situation, you'll actually sabotage the likelihood you can achieve your end goal of playing with this group. If, on the other hand, you waited by the sideline, watched the group patiently—perhaps smiling or making an encouraging comment on their game play—and waited for them to acknowledge you, you would be much more likely to then be invited into their group to play.

Attention Deficit/Hyperactivity Disorder (ADHD) is the classic example of poor inhibitory social skills. People with ADHD have particular difficulty controlling their behavioral responses so they often say or do things impulsively without evaluating possible consequences.

» STOP AND THINK ABOUT

• Positive Versus Negative Consequences

• Short and Long-term Consequences

• Social Goal

Self-awareness
+
Self-control
=
Emotion Regulation

In essence, impulse control helps you stop and think about both the short-term and the longer-term consequences. A certain behavior may feel good in the short-term—getting to play a game is fun or hitting someone who calls you a name may help you blow off steam—but then result in negative longer-term consequences—it could lead to conflict or hurt feelings, it could create an enemy or get you in trouble. You must be able to take a moment to weigh the various positive and negative short- and long-term consequences of your different options in order to make an informed decision. To do this, you must have good impulse control.

It's much more difficult to 'Stop & Think' when we're emotionally charged—we all struggle with impulse control when our emotions are triggered. In fact, emotions actually short circuit this rational process of weighing consequences; essentially our judgment of what to do and say in a situation becomes emotionally hijacked.[4] For example, if someone accuses you of doing something wrong, your immediate emotional response is likely to be defensive, hurt, and angry. If you impulsively act on those emotions, you're much more likely to say something mean and hurtful in response. The end result of this exchange will be much more damaging to the relationship than if you had been able to control your emotions in the heat of the moment.

Recognizing and managing the feelings underlying your behavioral impulses is called **emotion regulation**, another key inhibitory social skill. The first step in emotion regulation is self-awareness. You must be able to recognize when your emotions are intensifying, which requires paying attention to any changes in your internal reactions or physiology during the course of a social interaction. Then, you can use that physiological data to help you identify what emotions you're feeling. If your jaw is clenched, your heart is racing, and you feel hot, then you're probably getting angry. If you have a sinking sensation in your stomach and your heart rate slows, then you're probably feeling sad or hurt. The key here is recognizing and identifying your emotional responses *as they are happening*. It does relatively little good to recognize that you lashed out at your friend because you were embarrassed after you've already hurt her feelings.

Once you're aware of your underlying emotions, it's then possible to control your behavioral responses in that situation. This is the second step in emotion regulation: actively controlling the impact your emotions have on your behavior. As with 'Stop & Think,' emotion regulation requires you to purposefully break the flow of a social interaction. The intent of this break is to calm down and interrupt the emotional hijacking that is affecting your judgment. It is very difficult, if not impossible, to engage in the logical process of weighing behavioral responses when emotions are heightened. Therefore, the inhibitory social skill of emotion regulation enables you to break this cycle and calm down before acting. Depending on the volatility of the situation, this could mean taking a momentary break in the flow of conversation (you can take a breath and count to 10 before responding) or actually postponing the conversation. Regardless, the key to emotion regulation is the conscious decision to inhibit behavioral responses that are fueled by emotion.

Solution-focused Social Skills

The third category of social skills is actually a set of meta-social skills that require integration of various engaging and inhibitory social skills in order to achieve a specific goal. **Table 2** provides examples of solution-focused social skills with their overarching social goal. The focus of each of these skills is on the successful navigation of an interpersonal problem or opportunity. Solution-focused social skills require higher-order reasoning for planning, analysis, and evaluation of social interactions. Individuals who excel at solution-focused social skills think through a given situation, consider alternative social problem-solving approaches, select specific engaging and inhibitory social skills, and then coordinate their use in that situation. For example, imagine you want to join a group of people who are talking together. An assumption runs through your mind that they're probably busy with one another and don't really want to talk to you. To figure out whether your assumption is true in this instance, you employ the skill of **'Check-it-out'** (see Table 2) to approach the group (**social initiation**), wait to be acknowledged (**an inhibitory skill**), listen (**receptive communication**), and ask questions (**expressive communication**). Once you have accurate information (one way or the other), you can then act accordingly in that situation. If, on the other hand, you had simply acted on your assumption and avoided initiating with that group, you likely would have missed out on a positive social opportunity, but more importantly you would not have learned anything to inform your social problem solving in similar situations in the future.

Table 2

Examples of Solution-focused Social Skills

Assertiveness

Goal is to stand up for yourself in the face of pressure by or conflict with others; being able to accomplish your goal without being aggressive with others or withdrawing

Cooperation

Goal is to accomplish a task by working together with others, such as completing a project at school or playing a team sport

Compromise

Goal is to negotiate a mutually agreeable solution to a problem or conflict, such as deciding what to do when you each want something different

'Check-it-out'

Goal is to discover the 'truth' about a given situation, such as investigating whether a rumor or an assumption is true

Social Action Planning

Goal is to figure out the steps needed to reach a personal social goal, such as making friends or dealing with a bully

This example underscores an essential aspect of solution-focused social skills—the ability to evaluate the success of a selected approach for achieving a social goal. It's not only necessary to plan and execute a series of social steps, you must also evaluate how that plan worked. The most socially adept individuals are those who continually engage in social problem solving from planning, to execution, to evaluation, and back again.[5-7] Data gathered through social experiences—successful or not—forms a social database that then serves as a point of reference you can draw on to help navigate and adapt to future social situations.

THE INTERPLAY OF SOCIAL SKILLS

Social skills involve a complex interplay of behavior, cognition, and emotion. The historical evolution of research regarding social skills training (SST) programs with children illustrates the power of this interplay. For many years, SST programs focused almost exclusively on behavior, teaching children what to do or not to do in a given social situation and then practicing those behaviors through role plays and other hands-on activities. Not surprisingly, research on these behaviorally-centered SST programs found only marginal treatment benefits for those who participated and these effects were typically short-lived.[8] There are two main reasons for this failure. First, behavioral skills learned in a restricted, safe, and structured intervention setting often fail to generalize to messier, riskier real-life settings. If you learn, for example, *"when someone calls you a name, you ignore them and walk away,"* that may work in real life and then again it may not. Similarly, maybe in real life, others don't accept your invitation to play quite as easily as they did in the intervention setting. If a child tries a behavioral strategy learned in SST and then it doesn't work, it's likely that the child will dismiss the strategy as a failure and not try it again. This is basic learning theory; if a behavior is punished or not reinforced (for example, the teasing doesn't stop or they don't let you play), you're less likely to engage in that behavior in the future.

Second, it's impossible for an SST program to provide practice in all possible permutations of a social situation that a child might face. If you focus instruction only on what to do or not to do in a given circumstance, the child will be left at a loss when he faces a situation that was not explicitly taught. It's not enough to simply teach the child a set of possible behavioral responses, the child must be able to evaluate the pros and cons of different possible behavioral responses for a given situation and then understand why one may work better than another; children need to engage in the cognitive process of social problem solving. It's like the Chinese proverb: *Give a man a fish and you feed him for a day. Teach a man to fish and you feed him for a lifetime.*

Around the 1980s, cognitive-behavioral therapy was becoming the mainstay for effective treatment across many clinical conditions, and SST programs began integrating cognitive social skills into their training.[9,10] A significant addition to SST was the concept that our thoughts—which are often automatic or unconscious—directly impact our ability to navigate social interactions.[11-13] This understanding of how a negative cognition (expectation or assumption) can result in a maladaptive response for a social situation was pivotal. Cognitive social skills such as 'Check-it-out' were increasingly integrated into SST as a way to help children identify and alter these types of dysfunctional thought patterns. SST programs also began to focus equally on both *stop* and *think* by teaching children how to identify and weigh possible consequences before selecting a behavioral response.

In general, cognitive-behavioral SST programs show more success for participants than do solely behavioral ones.[10,14-16] By teaching children the process of how to think through a social situation—evaluating the pros and cons of acting in a particular way, challenging dysfunctional expectations and assumptions, and using this social information to inform social choices— cognitive-behavioral SST programs better prepare children to navigate social situations in the real world. A further benefit of teaching cognitive social skills in SST programs is to help children understand not only *how* to behave prosocially but also *why* behaving in a prosocial manner will be good for them. SSTs that include

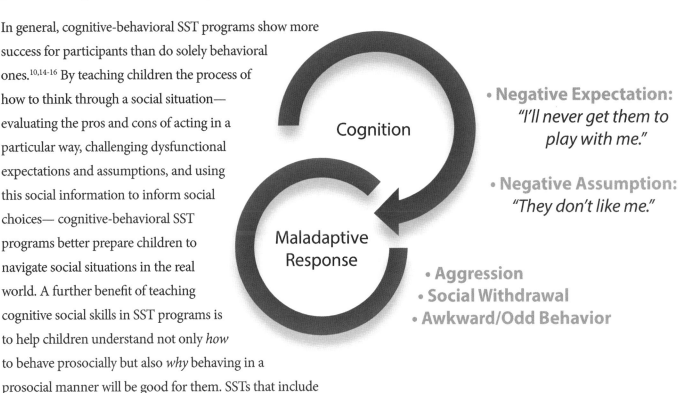

Give a man a fish and you feed him for a day. Teach a man to fish and you feed him for a lifetime.

Cognition

Maladaptive Response

- **Negative Expectation:** *"I'll never get them to play with me."*

- **Negative Assumption:** *"They don't like me."*

- **Aggression**
- **Social Withdrawal**
- **Awkward/Odd Behavior**

a cognitive component can teach children that good social skills can help them make friends, decrease the likelihood that other kids will tease them, and earn them the respect of others. Increasing this cognitive process of **social motivation** is critical for achieving long-term change in social behavior.

Social skills related to emotions have lately been gaining attention and a number of SST programs for emotional skills training have emerged in recent years. There are emotional literacy programs to build children's ability to identify and label their emotions, and emotion regulation programs to help children manage and control their emotions in the moment (such as relaxation training for anxious children).[17-20] While specialized emotion-focused interventions are increasingly available, emotional social skills continue to be underrepresented within broader SST programs.

This omission is unfortunate given the vital role emotions play in determining our thoughts and behaviors during a social encounter. For example, emotions provide valuable clues to inform social problem solving for a given situation. Imagine you start to feel anxious when thinking about joining a group of people you don't know. Awareness of this feeling can help you identify an underlying negative assumption (such as *"they won't like me"*) that is negatively influencing your social behavior. Emotions can also derail your ability to use social skills effectively. Imagine you feel defensive and hurt during a conversation when someone criticizes you. These emotions then drive thoughts of all the things you could say in your defense, so that you don't really hear the rest of what the other person is saying. In essence, these emotions undermine your ability to be an effective listener. Self-awareness and emotion regulation skills are critically important for avoiding unwanted social consequences as well as for optimizing your ability to be socially successful.

No one skill area is more important than another, but rather behavior, cognition, and emotion are inextricably tied with one another. Research supports SST programs that teach and practice all three social skill areas—behavioral, cognitive, and emotional—as most effective for improving the social skills and relationships of participants.[21,22] This more integrative approach to SST better prepares children for navigating the complexities of human social interactions by helping them learn about, explore, and practice social skills across these three areas.

RELATIONSHIP FUNCTIONS AND SOCIAL SKILLS

Social support and connectedness are critically important for our health and well-being.[23] As discussed in detail in Chapter 3, social connections fill a basic, essential human need.[24] When we're able to establish close, supportive social relationships with others, we're much more likely to be physically and mentally healthy, as well as successful in our school, work, and personal lives. While relationships can serve many purposes, the relationship functions listed in **Table 3** have been repeatedly supported in the research literature as core functions of social relationships.[25-30] It's possible for a member of your social network to provide just one of these functions or all of them, depending on the relationship. A teammate may be a very important companion with whom you spend a lot of time. A tutor may provide valuable guidance to you for learning a specific skill. Your best friend may be fun to hang out with as well as helpful for listening to you and caring about you when you need it.

Not all relationship functions are positive; as you can see in Table 3, conflict is also considered a core relationship function. In fact, close social relationships always involve some level of conflict. Conflict shows that you're invested enough in the relationship to have an opinion and to care strongly about something. Relationships with no conflict tend to be shallow and superficial. While it's true that too much conflict in a relationship is dysfunctional, a moderate level of conflict is not only typical, but healthy. When individuals are able to engage in conflict and move past it to resolution, their relationship tends to become stronger and closer.[31,32]

Social Skills Foster Relationship Functions

The quality of your social skills directly impacts the quality of your social relationships. For example, the social skills involved in conflict resolution and problem-solving (such as negotiating a compromise) are essential to maintaining a healthy balance of positive versus negative functions within a relationship. Positive social skills enable you to not only provide key relationship functions to others, but also to receive those relationship functions from others.

Table 3

Core Relationship Functions

Companionship

Hanging out, having fun, and spending time together; doing activities together

Intimacy

Talking about private thoughts and feelings; confiding things others don't know

Reliable Alliance

Being a trustworthy, predictable ally who can be counted on, even in difficult times

Guidance

Teaching how to do something; providing assistance or aid; helping get something done

Caring

Expressing affection, caring, and concern for the other's thoughts and feelings; affirming the other

Conflict

Getting mad at; getting into arguments or fights; antagonizing, nagging, or criticizing the other

Individuals who exhibit positive social skills will find it easier to establish new relationships and continue those relationships over time. **Table 4** provides examples of specific skills, behaviors, and attributes that have been found to foster versus undermine each core relationship function.[25,33-36] This is not an exhaustive list and many of these items impact multiple relationship functions. For example, being bossy and domineering makes others less likely to want to hang out with you (undermines companionship), but also means they may be less likely to confide in you or seek you out for assistance (undermines intimacy and instrumental aid). When an individual exhibits positive skills, behaviors, and attitudes, she is much more likely to benefit from a stable social support network with healthy, positive social relationships. Conversely, individuals who consistently exhibit the types of negative attributes listed in Table 4 will have great difficulty giving and receiving these functions in their relationships with others and the quality of their social network will suffer.

> The number of people included in your social network is much less important than the quality of your relationships with these network members. A handful of close, supportive relationships will be better for your health and well-being than a large number of shallow, mediocre relationships.

ROLE OF CONFIDENCE

While possessing social skills is a necessary ingredient for social success, the role of confidence cannot be understated. Confidence is comprised of two complementary attitudes: **self-efficacy** and **outcome expectancy**.[37] In the realm of social relationships, self-efficacy is the belief that you *can* perform a social act, such as saying 'hi' to someone you don't know. Outcome expectancy is the belief that if you act in a given way, you'll be successful in achieving your social goal. For example, if you say 'hi' to someone you don't know, they'll say 'hi' back. Confidence comes from both believing in your own social abilities (self-competence) and believing that your actions will produce the desired results (optimism).

Social skills training programs are often good at increasing children's sense of self-efficacy by providing participants with a toolbox full of specific behavioral, cognitive, and/or emotional social strategies along with opportunities to practice those strategies in the intervention setting.

Table 4

Skills, Behaviors, and Attributes that Foster and Undermine Core Relationship Functions

Fosters Companionship

Is cooperative, engaged, friendly, imaginative, creative, outgoing; shares interests; has a good sense of humor

Is bossy, domineering, disruptive, intrusive, impulsive, aggressive, mean, timid, withdrawn, sullen, awkward

Undermines Companionship

Fosters Intimacy

Is interested, open, sharing, at ease, respectful, a good listener

Interrupts; is disrespectful, dismissive, blaming, closed

Undermines Intimacy

Fosters Reliable Alliance

Is honest, trustworthy, reliable, predictable, loyal

Is dishonest, manipulative, unreliable, a 'backstabber', a 'tattletale'

Undermines Reliable Alliance

Fosters Guidance

Is responsive, flexible, humble, knowledgeable, talented

Is non-responsive, rigid, blaming, a braggart; has low cognitive skills

Undermines Guidance

Fosters Caring

Is respectful, affectionate, kind, supportive

Is disrespectful, insulting, demeaning

Undermines Caring

Fosters Conflict Resolution

Compromises, negotiates; is calm, predictable, a good problem-solver

Is aggressive, demanding, explosive, unpredictable; has restricted problem solving skills

Undermines Conflict Resolution

However, children's sense of outcome expectancy typically comes with experience, as they try out these new strategies in real-life social situations and see how they work.[38-40] As children use their nascent social skills and experience social success, their outcome expectancy grows. This transition period of social skill experimentation and consolidation is essential for building confidence, but it's also a risky time when social failure can undermine outcome expectancy and erode self-efficacy. For example, research shows that reputational biases impact how peers respond to children's attempts to change their social behavior. If a child has a reputation for being aggressive and mean, his peers are likely to ignore, rebuff, or even punish that child's attempts to act prosocially.[41-44] Over time, if the child continues to act prosocially despite this lack of social reinforcement, his reputational bias within the peer group can change.

This research underscores how expectations are an essential component of confidence.[45-48] The optimism underlying outcome expectancy is not idealistic, but rather realistic. Individuals with high social confidence understand that sometimes they'll be successful and sometimes they won't, and that's okay. Social failure does not translate into hopelessness or feelings of ineptitude. If unsuccessful, socially confident individuals try a different strategy or move on to the next social opportunity. They do not give up nor stop believing that they can be successful; they demonstrate high social resilience.

The phenomenon of the 'self-fulfilling prophecy'[49,50]—a prediction that directly or indirectly causes itself to become true—also illustrates the pivotal role of expectations. If you know what to do in a social situation, but believe your efforts will be fruitless, then you're probably right. Negative expectations in a social situation often generate feelings of anxiety which then translate into saying or doing awkward, intrusive, or inappropriate things which, in turn, decrease the likelihood that other people will respond positively to you. On the other hand, if you know what to do in a social situation and believe that you'll be successful, then you're much more likely to actually be successful. Attitude has as much to do with social success as social skill level. In fact, even if your social skills are less strong than someone else's, if your confidence is greater, you're more likely to be successful.

> Just because I was unsuccessful with this particular person or in this particular situation doesn't mean I won't be successful with a different person or in a different social situation.

Relation Between Confidence and Self-esteem

While confidence and self-esteem are clearly related, they are not synonymous. Self-esteem is conceptualized as your belief in your own self-worth, overall or in a specific area, such as *"I'm good at math," "I'm a good person,"* or *"I deserve to be treated fairly."* In the social realm, self-esteem reflects how positively you evaluate your current social relationships or social functioning, such as *"I'm popular with other kids at school," "I'm easy to get along with,"* or *"I can make friends easily."* In this way, self-esteem is an *indicator* of how good you currently feel about yourself socially. Confidence, on the other hand, is much more action-oriented; it's believing you can and will be socially successful. Confidence, along with social skills, drives the quality of your social interactions which then moves the meter of your social self-esteem higher or lower. When you experience social successes, your self-esteem will be higher. When you experience social failures, your self-esteem will be lower. Self-esteem simply reflects your current perceived level of social functioning. In contrast, cognitions underlying self-efficacy and outcome expectancy (such as expectations, assumptions, and interpretations) are not simply correlational with social adjustment, but rather directly influence your social actions, and thereby, the quality of your social relationships.

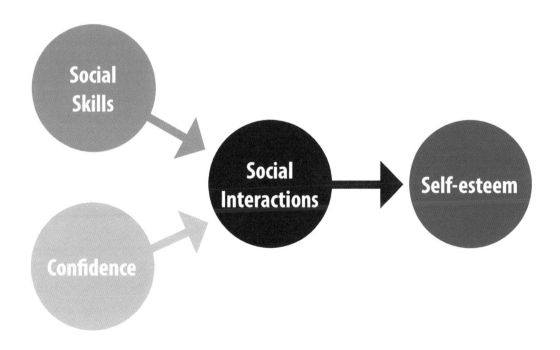

PROSOCIAL VERSUS ANTISOCIAL INTENT

When discussing social skills, there's often an assumption that high social skills equals behaving prosocially. To be prosocial means to act with positive intent towards others: to be kind, caring, unselfish, and otherwise altruistic. While high social skills and prosocial behavior generally go together, there are instances when individuals with high social skills use those skills with antisocial intent. For example, research on children's social status has identified two groups of students who are 'popular' within their peer group at school.[51,52] One group fits the classic popular persona of being highly liked by lots of peers and demonstrating attributes such as friendly, kind, honest, and caring. However, another group, termed 'perceived popular' in the research literature, are socially skilled, but seen as selfish, mean, or otherwise antisocial towards other children. Perceived popular children are just that—generally assumed to be popular, but actually not well liked by many in the peer group. These students are more akin to the Hollywood version of popular—the student who leaves others out, spreads rumors, and bullies or teases those who aren't in their clique of friends.

Implications for Social Skills Assessment

Fortunately, this Machiavellian brand of socially skilled individual is relatively rare. However, the fact that some highly skilled individuals use their social skills in an opportunistic manner to manipulate and deceive others in order to get their way presents a challenge for social skills assessment. Most, if not all, social assessment tools quantify skills along a continuum of poor to excellent. There are few tools to help distinguish prosocial from antisocial motivations for socially skilled children. As discussed in Chapter 9, collecting peer nominations to identify children within the perceived popular social status group is useful in this regard, but the time and staffing costs associated with this assessment method make its regular use impractical. Relying on teacher- or other adult-report is more feasible, but also more likely to be inaccurate because skilled antisocial individuals are very good at concealing their true intent from adults. One suggestion for how to tease apart these sub-groups comes from the self-esteem literature. Research indicates that prosocially popular children tend to be modest when assessing their social self-esteem, actually underestimating the degree to which they're popular or socially successful.[53] In contrast, antisocial children tend to report an overinflated sense of social self-esteem and a confidence level bordering on arrogance. Combining social skills assessment with a self-report self-esteem measure may be helpful for distinguishing between prosocial and antisocial intent.

Implications for Social Skills Training

The role of prosocial versus antisocial motivation for social behavior also has implications for how SST programs are designed. Children who act antisocially (with low or high social skills) typically do so, in part, because their behavior has been successful for achieving a social goal. Therefore, it's important for SST programs to help children see how behaving prosocially can be an alternative—or even a more productive—way to achieve that same social goal. For example, bullies often engage in aggressive, domineering behaviors in an attempt to earn respect from others. When others do what you say and listen to you, that looks and feels like respect. So, the bullying behavior is reinforced and the bully is more likely to continue to act in these antisocial ways in the future. SST can be used to help bullies see that their behaviors are actually producing fear—not respect—and that prosocial alternatives can be more successful in earning them the respect they want. As discussed earlier in this chapter, increasing social motivation will help children actually use the prosocial skills learned through SST in real-life situations. Keying in on the child's social motivation is likely to be far more successful for changing his antisocial behavior than simply telling him that being a bully is bad.

While using social skills to purposefully deceive, control, or harm others is antisocial, it's not inherently wrong or evil to behave prosocially because it leads to positive outcomes for you. Pure altruism is a rare thing and is not a standard that we should set for our children. Rather, SST programs can help motivate children to behave prosocially by explicitly teaching and letting them practice prosocial attitudes that drive intent. Helping children understand that acting with mutual respect, responsibility, and honesty can produce a win-win (positive outcomes for them as well as for the other person) can increase the likelihood of their using prosocial means to achieve their social goals.

CHAPTER 1 NOTES

1. Asher, S. R., & Renshaw, P. D. (1981). Children with friends: Social knowledge and social-skill training. In S. R. Asher & J. M. Gottman (Eds.), *The development of children's friendships* (pp. 273-296). New York, NY: Cambridge University Press.

2. Beauchamp, M. H., & Anderson, V. (2011). An integrative framework for the development of social skills. *Psychological Bulletin, 136,* 39-64.

3. Coie, J. D., Dodge, K. A., & Kupersmidt, J. B. (1990). Peer group behavior and social status. In S. R. Asher & J. D. Coie (Eds.), *Peer rejection in childhood* (pp. 17-59). New York, NY: Cambridge University Press.

4. Goleman, D. (2005). *Emotional intelligence: Why it can matter more than IQ.* New York, NY: Bantam Books.

5. Greenberg, M. T., Kusché, C. A., & Riggs, N. (2004). The PATHS curriculum: Theory and research on neurocognitive development and school success. In J. Zins, R. Weissberg, & H. Walber (Eds.), *Building school success on social and emotional learning.* New York, NY: Teachers College Press.

6. Kam, C., Greenberg, M. T., & Kusché, C. A. (2004). Sustained effects of the PATHS curriculum on the social and psychological adjustment of children in special education. *Journal of Emotional and Behavioral Disorders, 12* (2), 66-78.

7. Suveg, C., Southam-Gerow, M. A., Goodman, K. L., & Kendall, P. C. (2007). The role of emotion theory and research in child therapy development. *Emotion and Child Treatment, 14,* 358-371.

8. Durlak, J. A., Weissberg, R. P., & Pachan, M. (2010). A meta-analysis of after-school programs that seek to promote personal and social skills in children and adolescents. *American Journal of Community Psychology, 45,* 294-309.

9. Curran, J. P., & Monti, P. M. (1982). *Social skills training: A practical handbook for assessment and treatment.* New York, NY: Guilford Press.

10. Sweet, A. A., & Loizeaux, A. L. (1991). Behavioral and cognitive treatment methods: A critical comparative review. *Journal of Behavior Therapy and Experimental Psychiatry, 22,* 159-185.

11. Crick, N. R., & Dodge, K. A. (1994). A review and reformulation of social information-processing mechanisms in children's social adjustment. *Psychological Bulletin, 115,* 74-101.

12. Crick, N. R., & Dodge, K. A. (1996). Social information-processing mechanisms in reactive and proactive aggression. *Child Development, 53,* 1146-1158.

13. Dodge, K. A. (1993). Social-cognitive mechanisms in the development of conduct disorder and depression. *Annual Review of Psychology, 44,* 559-584.

14. Guerra, N. G., & Slaby, R. G. (1990). Cognitive mediators of aggression in adolescent offenders: II. Intervention. *Developmental Psychology, 26,* 269-277.

15. Herbert, J. D., Guadino, B. A., Rheingold, A. A., Myers, V. H., Dalrymple, K., & Nolan, E. M. (2005). Social skills training augments the effects of cognitive behavioral group therapy for social anxiety disorder. *Behavior Therapy, 36,* 125-138.

16. Herbert, J. D., Rheingold, A. A., & Goldstein, S. G. (2002). Brief cognitive behavioral group therapy for social anxiety disorder. *Cognitive and Behavioral Practice, 9,* 1-8.

17. Webster-Stratton, C., & Reid, M. J. (2003). Treating conduct problems and strengthening social and emotional competence in young children: The Dina Dinosaur Treatment Program. *Journal of Emotional and Behavioral Disorders, 11,* 130-143.

18. Joseph, G. E., & Strain, P. S. (2003). Comprehensive evidence-based social-emotional curricula for young children: An analysis of efficacious adoption potential. *Topics in Early Childhood Special Education, 23,* 62-73.

19. Greenberg, M. T., Kusché, C. A., Cook, E. T., & Quamma, J. P. (1995). Promoting emotional competence in school-aged children: The effects of the PATHS curriculum. *Development and Psychopathology, 7,* 117-136.

20. Izard, C. E., Trentacosta, C. J., & King, K. A. (2004). An emotion-based prevention program for Head Start Children. *Early Education & Development, 15,* 407-422.

21. Asher, S. A., Parker, J. G., & Walker, D. L. (1996). Distinguishing friendship from acceptance: Implications for intervention and assessment. In W. Bukowski, A. Newcomb, & W. Hartup (Eds.), *The company they keep: Friendship in childhood and adolescence* (pp. 366-405). New York, NY: Cambridge University Press.

22. Payton, J. W., Wardlaw, D. M., Graczyk, P. A., Bloodworth, M. R., Tompsett, C. J., & Weissberg, R. P. (2000). Social and emotional learning: A framework for promoting mental health and reducing risk behaviors in children and youth. *Journal of School Health, 70,* 179-185.

23. Rubin, K. H., Bukowski, W. M., & Parker, J. G. (2006). Peer interaction, relationships, and groups. In N. Eisenberg (Vol. Ed.), W. Damon & R. M. Lerner (Series Eds.), *Handbook of child psychology: Vol. 3. Social, emotional, and personality development* (6th ed., pp. 571-645). New York, NY: Wiley.

24. Baumeister, R. F., & Leary, M. R. (1995). The need to belong: Desire for interpersonal attachments as a fundamental human motivation. *Psychological Bulletin, 117,* 497-529.

25. Buhrmester, D., & Furman, W. (1987). The development of companionship and intimacy. *Child Development, 58,* 1101-1113.

26. Demaray, M. K., Malecki, C. K., Rueger, S. Y., Brown, S. E., & Summers, K. H. (2009). The role of youth's ratings of the importance of socially supportive behaviors in the relationship between social support and self-concept. *Journal of Youth and Adolescence, 38,* 13-28.

27. Laursen, B. (1993). Conflict management among close peers. *New Directions for Child and Adolescent Development, 60,* 39-54.

28. Laursen, B. (2001). A developmental meta-analysis of peer conflict resolution. *Developmental Review, 21,* 423-449.

29. Chase-Lansdale, P. L., Wakschlag, L. S., & Brooks-Gunn, J. (1995). A psychological perspective on the development of caring in children and youth: The role of the family. *Journal of Adolescence, 18,* 515-556.

30. Parker, J. G., Rubin, K. H., Erath, S. A., Wojslawowicz, J. C., & Buskirk, A. A. (2006). Peer relationships, child development, and adjustment: A developmental psychopathology perspective. In D. Cicchetti & D. J. Cohen (Eds.), *Developmental Psychopathology, Vol. 1: Theory and method* (pp. 419-493). Hoboken, NJ: Wiley.

31. Hanzal, A., & Segrin, C. (2009). The role of conflict resolution styles in mediating the relationship between enduring vulnerabilities and marital quality. *Journal of Family Communication, 9,* 150-169.

32. Bodenmann, G. (1999). Dyadic coping and its significance for marital functioning. In T. A. Revenson, K. Kayser, & G. Bodenmann (Eds.), *Couples coping with stress: Emerging perspectives on dyadic coping* (pp. 33-49). Washington, DC: American Psychological Association.

33. Buhrmester, D., Furman, W., Wittenberg, M. T., & Reis, H. T. (1988). Five domains of interpersonal competence in peer relationships. *Journal of Personality and Social Psychology, 55,* 991-1008.

34. Shaver, P., Furman, W., & Buhrmester, D. (1985). Transition to college: Network changes, social skills, and loneliness. In S. Duck & D. Perlman (Eds.), *Understanding personal relationships: An interdisciplinary approach.* (pp. 193-219). Thousand Oaks, CA: Sage Publications.

35. Gifford-Smith, M. E., & Brownell, C. A. (2003). Childhood peer relationships: Social acceptance, friendships, and peer networks. *Journal of School Psychology, 41,* 235-284.

36. Fehr, B. (2008). Friendship formation. In S. Sprecher, A. Wenzel, & J. Harvey (Eds.), *Handbook of relationship initiation* (pp. 29-54). New York, NY: Psychology Press.

37. Ollendick, T. H., & Schmidt, C. R. (1987). Social learning constructs in the prediction of peer interaction. *Journal of Clinical Child Psychology, 16,* 80-87.

38. DeRosier, M. E. (2004). Building relationships and combating bullying: Effectiveness of a school-based social skills group intervention. *Journal of Clinical Child and Adolescent Psychology, 33,* 125-130.

39. DeRosier, M. E., & Marcus, S. R. (2005). Building friendships and combating bullying: Effectiveness of S.S.GRIN at one-year follow-up. *Journal of Clinical Child and Adolescent Psychology, 34,* 140-150.

40. Harrell, A., Mercer, S., & DeRosier, M. E. (2009). Improving the social-behavioral adjustment of adolescents: The effectiveness of a social skills group intervention. *Journal of Child and Family Studies, 18,* 378-387.

41. Dodge, K. A. (1980). Social cognition and children's aggressive behavior. *Child Development, 51,* 162-170.

42. Dodge, K. A., & Frame, C. L. (1982). Social cognitive biases and deficits in aggressive boys. *Child Development, 53,* 620-635.

43. Hymel, S., Wagner, E., & Butler, L. J. (1990). Reputational bias: View from the peer group. In S. R. Asher & J. D. Coie (Eds.), *Peer rejection in childhood* (pp. 156-188). New York, NY: Cambridge University Press.

44. Dodge, K. A., Lansford, J. E., Burks, V. S., Bates, J. E., Pettit, G. S., Fontaine, R., & Pride, J. M. (2003). Peer rejection and social information-processing factors in the development of aggressive behavior problems in children. *Child Development, 74,* 374-393.

45. Seligman, M. E. P., & Csikszentmihalyi, M. (2000). *Positive psychology: An introduction.* American Psychologist, 55, 5-14.

46. Seligman, M. E. P. (2007). *The optimistic child: A proven program to safeguard children against depression and build lifelong resilience.* New York, NY: Houghton Mifflin.

47. Seligman, M. E. P. (2002). Positive psychology, positive prevention, and positive therapy. In C. R. Snyder & S. J. Lopez (Eds.), *Handbook of positive psychology* (pp. 3-12). New York, NY: Oxford University Press.

48. Gillham, J. E., Shatté, A. J., Reivich, K. J., & Seligman, M. E. P. (2001). Optimism, pessimism, and explanatory style. In E. C. Chang (Ed.), *Optimism & pessimism: Implication for theory, research, and practice* (pp. 53-75). Washington, DC: American Psychological Association.

49. Madon, S., Willard, J., Guyll, M., & Scherr, K. C. (2011). Self-fulfilling prophecies: Mechanisms, power, and links to social problems. *Social and Personality Psychology Compass, 5,* 578-590.

50. Lee, J. (1986). Self-fulfilling prophecies: A theoretical and integrative review. *Psychological Review, 93,* 429-445.

51. Litwack, S. D., Aikins, J. W., & Cillessen, A. H. N. (2010). The distinct roles of sociometric and perceived popularity in friendship: Implications for adolescent depressive affect and self-esteem. *The Journal of Early Adolescence, 32,* 226-251.

52. Hymel, S., Closson, L. M., Caravita, S. C. S., & Vaillancourt, T. (2011). Social status among peers: From sociometric attraction to peer acceptance to perceived popularity. In P. K. Smith & C. Hart (Eds.), *Handbook of childhood social development* (2nd ed., pp. 375-392). New York, NY: Wiley-Blackwell.

53. Marcus, S. R. (2006). *Continuity and change in middle elementary students" popularity and social preference* (Unpublished doctoral dissertation). University of North Carolina at Chapel Hill, Chapel Hill, NC.

Pivotal Developmental Changes

by: Melissa E. DeRosier, Ph.D.

DESCRIPTION

Across the lifespan, our social connections fulfill an array of core human needs, from companionship to instrumental aid to intimacy to affirmation. However, the structure of our social network shifts over time, as our social needs and social circumstances evolve. In this chapter, we explore the types of social opportunities and challenges that children face from early childhood through young adulthood. We also describe developmental shifts in social cognition, including pivotal periods when developmental delays can place children at greater risk for social relationship problems.

This chapter is intended to provide a review of developmental trends generally seen for social relationships and social skills based on what we know from the research literature. Where possible, we include a discussion of gender differences in these developmental trends. When you're conducting a social skills assessment, it's important to take gender as well as development into consideration. For example, a moderate level of aggressive behavior would be considered normative for a 6-year-old boy, but that same

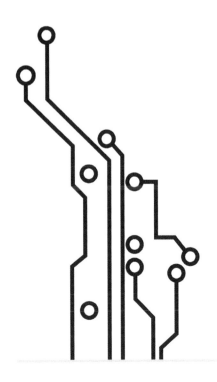

level of aggression would be considered highly atypical for a 15-year-old girl. You need to ensure that the scores resulting from your social skills assessment measure take normative developmental expectations into account.

However, it's also important to keep in mind that there will always be exceptions to the common trends described in this chapter. A child may develop a given social skill faster than average, have a lower social need than others, or face non-typical environmental stressors (such as living in an abusive home) that can impact his social skill development. When administering a social skills assessment, it's important to bear in mind the individual factors that influence the child's development, as well as his skill level relative to normative expectations. These considerations will impact the specific types of interventions that you recommend as most helpful for that child.

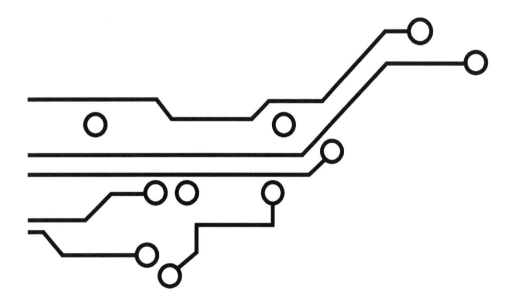

SHIFTS IN SOCIAL NETWORK

Your social network consists of a variety of important social relationships, including those with parents, siblings, peers, and romantic partners. As we discussed in Chapter 1, these social network members serve crucial relationship functions. These are the people you hang out with and do fun things with. You turn to them in times of need, confiding your innermost thoughts and feelings. They help you solve problems, learn things, and feel better about yourself. Across the lifespan, the size of your social network typically expands, branching out from a handful of close relatives in early

Where do we learn our social skills?

The beginnings of social skills lie in early childhood experiences when children try out many new behaviors and get feedback on what is and is not acceptable. Parents and other key social network members play a vital role in establishing the child's underlying social foundation. These are the social skills that children then take with them to school and into interactions with peers outside the family. If the foundation is solid, children are much more likely to be socially successful.

A wealth of developmental research describes how parenting styles, early childhood experiences, and environmental characteristics impact the life trajectories of children. A detailed discussion of this research is outside the scope of this book. However, we'd like to briefly highlight two fundamental social learning processes that impact social skill development, beginning in early childhood and continuing across the lifespan: behavior reinforcement and modeling.

Behavior reinforcement is based in learning theory. Positive reinforcement of a behavior increases the likelihood that that behavior will occur again in the future. For example, if you praise a child for politely asking for something, he's more likely to be polite when asking next time. Punishment or absence of positive reinforcement of a behavior decreases the likelihood that that behavior will occur again. For example, if you remove a child from a play date because she took the other child's toy away—and explain clearly why you're putting her in time-out—she's less likely to grab things from others in the future. When you're rewarded for prosocial behavior and disciplined appropriately for antisocial behavior, prosocial behavior will increase over time and antisocial behavior will decrease over time. As you engage in this process of acting on the world and receiving feedback, you begin to decipher the social rules that dictate social interactions. This understanding provides you with a compass to better navigate future social situations.

In addition to what you learn from direct interaction with others, social rules, consequences of actions, and interpersonal expectations are learned by watching others. Social network members provide role models for how people treat one another. If parents show respect to each other, the child comes to expect that people in the world should respect one another. If the child's sibling hits her and isn't disciplined, she learns that being aggressive is okay. Even from a very early age, children watch the social interactions around them and adopt those interaction styles and attitudes for themselves. In fact, the more close the relationship, the stronger impact modeling has for determining the child's social behavior.

childhood to include peers, romantic partners, and other key relationships during adolescence and early adulthood. As the membership of your social network changes, so does the relative importance of particular members for serving the various relationship functions.

In early childhood (ages 0 to 5 years), relationship functions are primarily provided by parents and other caretakers who ensure the child's health and well-being on a daily basis. Children in this age range spend most of their time with these caretaking adults, and are generally dependent on them to determine where they go and what they do during the day. Siblings, cousins, or other children they regularly interact with can also be important sources of companionship and instrumental aid.

Once children enter grade school, they engage with same-aged peers all day long, during structured class time as well as free play. Plus, as children mature, they participate more and more with peers in extracurricular activities such as sports, clubs, and social events. As their social world expands, children become increasingly interested in other children their age, making these relationships more meaningful and motivating for them. At the same time that peers are becoming more influential, parents are becoming less so. **Figure 1** illustrates these relative shifts in the roles that

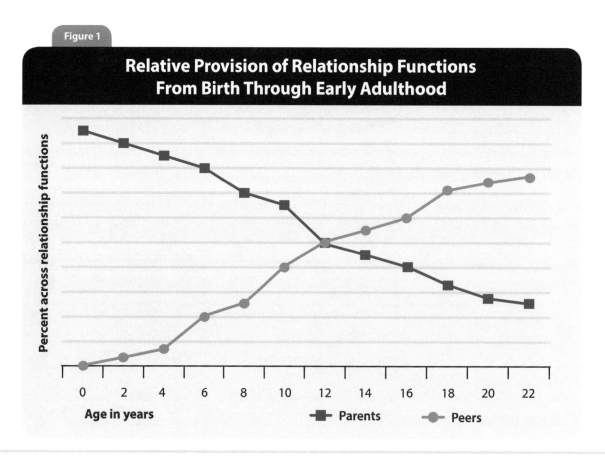

Figure 1

Relative Provision of Relationship Functions From Birth Through Early Adulthood

caregivers and peers play in the provision of core relationship functions. This graph reflects general patterns in the data across a variety of research studies on this subject[1-5] and is intended for illustration purposes only. These trends can, of course, vary considerably for individual children and families.

Across the school years, peers become increasingly important providers of key relationship functions, including support, advice, companionship, and affirmation.[2-6] Parents become less involved in their child's day-to-day activities and less privy to their child's social interactions with other children. Parental involvement at school and with homework also declines as children become increasingly independent and self-sufficient.

This is not to say that parents cease to influence their children nor that they stop being core social network members. In fact, parents, siblings, and other close relatives continue to provide essential relationship functions throughout a child's lifetime, often increasingly so, as the child progresses through middle adulthood. However, across the childhood and adolescent years, peer influence typically comes to match and even exceed that of family members. The shift in relationship functions from parents to peers tends to escalate at four developmental periods:

1. **Entrance into grade school**: Young children who attend daycare and preschool settings have more opportunities to meet and play with other children; however, it's typically not until children enter grade school that same-aged non-relative peers become substantive providers of social support.

2. **Late elementary school years**: Between 3rd to 5th grades, social cognitive skills grow rapidly and major changes in the peer social structure occur which make peer interactions significantly more important to children and therefore more influential.[7-9]

3. **Middle school years**: The social environment drastically changes from elementary to middle school when children move from smaller, more protective settings to much larger, diverse, and competitive social groups.[5,10-11] The social anxiety produced by this transition coincides with other major biological and academic changes. As hormones rage and academic demands rise, social support by peers becomes paramount.

4. **High school years**: The importance of peer relationships escalates again between 9th and 12th grades when adolescents struggle for and attain greater independence.[12-14] In the process of an adolescent becoming a young adult—

driving herself around, planning for life after high school graduation, and entering into romantic relationships—she purposefully distances herself from her family in an effort to define who she is as an individual. In this transition period, adolescents increasingly look to their peers to help them solve problems, feel good about themselves, and figure out who they want to be.

SHIFTS IN SOCIAL NETWORK

As children grow and mature, their peer relationships also evolve. The relationship functions provided within a friendship shift over time, as does the relative importance of particular social skills for building and maintaining positive peer relations.

Companionship

During early childhood, the primary relationship function that friends provide is companionship. Social interactions are mostly activity-focused in this age group—playing video games, jumping rope, riding bikes, eating lunch together—for both boys and girls, though the specific activities they engage in may differ considerably. Participating in activities with friends helps children learn and understand the importance of social skills for sharing, cooperating, and compromising during play activities. Activity-based companionship remains a primary function of peer relationships across childhood and adolescence (and adulthood), but, as children mature, time spent together increasingly involves conversation-based companionship. Friends talk and share information with one another through phone calls, texting, Skype, email, and in-person communication progressively more as they enter the late elementary and middle school years. Conversation-based companionship is an important element of any friendship, and it is especially integral to friendships for girls.

Intimacy

As friends begin to share their thoughts and feelings with one another, the social skills of communication (verbal and non-verbal), listening, empathy, and perspective taking become increasingly needed. Children with strong skills in these areas will be able to effectively share personal information with their friends, and accurately receive personal information from their friends. As a result, feelings of closeness and mutual understanding can grow so that that peer relationship becomes an important source of the social function of intimacy.

Reliable Alliance

The sharing of private information necessitates that you be able to keep your friend's information confidential, so the social skill of impulse control becomes critically important. Children learn that if you reveal someone's thoughts, feelings, or actions without their permission—either purposefully or through a 'slip of the tongue'—you will not have that person as a friend for long. You must use impulse control to prevent revealing this information and, in so doing, you demonstrate loyalty and trustworthiness which, in effect, fortifies the relationship. Serving as a reliable ally becomes critically important for maintaining friendships as children enter adolescence, particularly for girls.

Guidance

In times of need, children turn to their peers more and more, looking to them for help solving problems and getting things done. This guidance and assistance may focus on more practical problems, such as help in playing basketball or understanding a homework assignment. However, as intimacy and reliable alliance in a relationship grow, guidance starts to include assistance with social problems as well. Solution-focused social skills for 'Check-it-out' and social action planning are especially important for helping others effectively deal with social problems. In addition, assertiveness skills may be needed. You may need to be assertive with your friend—sticking by what you believe even if she may disagree—or you may need to help your friend be assertive and stand up for herself in a social situation. As you're able to help others—providing effective, useful advice without putting them down or making them feel bad—the more your friends will come to trust your opinions and seek you out for advice.

Caring

While caring is an important function for social relationships across the lifespan, its expression is closely tied to developmental shifts in other relationship functions. For example, when social interactions focus on activities, caring can be expressed by asking what the other person would like to do. When social problem solving becomes a more prominent part of a friendship, caring can be expressed by asking how the other person is feeling. Further, as social interactions increasingly center around more sensitive and personal topics, friends are more likely to reveal information about their true inner thoughts and feelings. Because you risk rejection each time you share something real about yourself, it can be very scary for the person sharing. Effective use of engaging and inhibitory social skills during these social exchanges fosters your ability to express affection, care, and concern, so your friend is more likely to feel accepted and supported. Mutual expressions of caring help affirm your relationship and deepen the quality of that relationship.

Conflict

As discussed in Chapter 1, conflict is a central function of social relationships. Conflict occurs within close social relationships at all ages, though the source of conflict varies depending on developmental age. For example, an argument over possession of a toy is more likely for younger children, while an argument over a perceived social slight is more likely for older children. At any age, however, it's how you manage that conflict which determines whether it undermines or strengthens your relationship. All of the different social skills can be of help in a conflict situation, but emotion regulation, compromise, and listening are the most critical skills for moving a conflict to resolution. Being a predictable, calm, and competent problem-solver when there is conflict with your friend makes the relationship feel more secure and actually brings you closer.

SOCIAL COGNITIVE DEVELOPMENT

Imaging studies of the brain demonstrate how significant neurological maturation occurs across childhood and adolescence,[15,16] particularly in the prefrontal cortex of the frontal lobe. This area of the brain is responsible for executive functions—the CEO of the brain—which coordinate, plan, and control behavior in social situations. As this brain region matures and develops, children are increasingly able to focus their attention, engage in problem solving, formulate plans, and inhibit their impulses. These changing cognitive capacities not only bring significant, and sometimes rapid, development in social skills, but also directly impact how children perceive, interpret, and understand their social world.

Social Comparison

Since Leon Festinger introduced the concept of social comparison in the 1950s, social psychology research has repeatedly shown that people have a strong desire or need to evaluate their own abilities and that they look to others as comparison.[17-19] It's thought that you compare yourself to others in order to better understand yourself in a given area. This clarity for where you stand relative to others impacts how you feel about yourself (self-esteem), helps you define what areas you need work on or improve (motivation), and enables you to better predict how others will behave toward you (expectations). Social comparison applies to every aspect of your life— how attractive you are, how smart you are, how well you play tennis—and there's a large body of research describing how these processes function under different circumstances.[17] For our purposes, we're most concerned with comparative processes within the social realm—how you evaluate and understand your social standing relative to others in your peer group.

Young children's cognitions are what Piaget called 'egocentric,' meaning that the young child is unable to distinguish his own subjective perceptions of the world from those of others.[20,21] The ability to understand that others may have beliefs, opinions, and desires different from your own is necessary in order to engage in social comparison. This capacity for abstract reasoning develops over the course of childhood and early adolescence and, as it develops, so does social comparative thinking (not to mention empathy and perspective taking).

In middle childhood, typically between the 2nd and 4th grades, children's capacity for social comparison emerges.[22] During this time, children start to take notice of their place in the peer group in every conceivable area from academic skills, to athletic skills, to looks, to social status. Children become increasingly aware of their social acceptance. They formulate beliefs about how popular they are, and peer problems start to have more meaning for them.

However, social comparative reasoning evolves over time, with some children able to discern the social structure at a young age and others not developing this cognitive skill until well into adolescence.[23] As a result, children's views of their social standing can vary widely from objective reality,[24-26] and the accuracy of these perceptions influences their peer relationships.[26-30] Research shows that developmental delays in social cognitive abilities place children at risk for peer problems, poorer social skills, and lower social status.[31,32] For example, children who have difficulty interpreting social cues correctly are less popular with peers whereas children who are more accurate in their social perceptions are more likely to experience positive peer relationships.

The value of social comparative reasoning for guiding and managing your peer interactions is clear. If you're able to understand the social expectations of others and predict their behavior in a given situation, you're at a significant advantage when negotiating social situations.[31,33] For example, imagine you need to pair up with another child to complete a class project. If you know who in the class is close to you in social standing (or power), you'll be better able to predict which children are likely to want to work with you. As a result, you're better able to target your invitation and more likely to get a positive response (gaining a partner and avoiding the embarrassment of rejection).

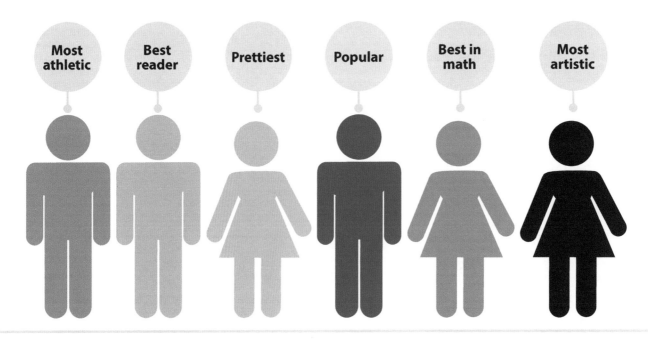

Social comparative reasoning also decreases the likelihood you'll commit a social faux pas, and therefore be better able to avoid negative social consequences. For example, imagine you believe that you're popular, but you're not, and a group of other children on the playground rejects your social approaches. Without an understanding of your place within the peer group, you'll be confused by this rejection and frustrated. This frustration may lead you to act out against those who rejected you, which, in turn, will further undermine your social standing.[5, 34-36]

SHIFTS IN PEER SOCIAL STRUCTURE

We're using the term 'peer social structure' to refer to the social map of a peer group—who plays with whom, what are the ties linking individuals, and what is the hierarchy or 'pecking order' across individuals in this group.

In the early elementary school years, the peer social structure is quite fluid and open, with roles frequently changing and members moving in and out of social sub-groups.[37] Best friends one day may be replaced the next without anyone's particular notice. At this age, social groups tend to be large and diverse; children of different races and backgrounds are as likely to be friends as are boys and girls at this age.

As children mature, their social relationships become much more stable and the peer social structure becomes more rigid and restricted.[38] Children form fewer friendships and concentrate their social interactions on a smaller set of peers. However, while the number of relationships may decline, the friendships that are established tend to be longer lasting and more likely to persist over time and across situations compared to those of early childhood. The quality of these friendships also tends to evolve, becoming more close, caring, and intimate over time.[5,39-41]

Along with changes in the number and quality of friendships, the overall peer social hierarchy morphs into a more complex and fixed social structure. As children's cognitive capacity for social comparative reasoning grows, a social pecking order emerges where there's an implicit understanding within the peer group of who is more popular than whom and who has more social power than someone else. Social interactions get more competitive as children recognize this social hierarchy and become motivated to move up this pecking order, or at least not fall down it.

As social competition escalates, children become increasingly motivated to fit in socially and be accepted. Similarity starts to drive friendship selection.[42-45] So, you're much more likely to be friends with someone who looks like you, comes from a similar background, and is the same gender as you. So starts the migration towards social sub-groups—also called cliques—that are increasingly homogeneous.

In late elementary and middle school years, as this pecking order and friendship selection process plays out, the social map for a peer group becomes progressively more defined (see **Figure 2** as an illustration). Members of a clique tend to spend most of their time interacting with other members, with few, if any, social interactions with members of other cliques. These interaction patterns make it increasingly evident who does and does not belong to a particular social group, and this differentiation process escalates as sub-group members start to dress alike and act like one another more and more.

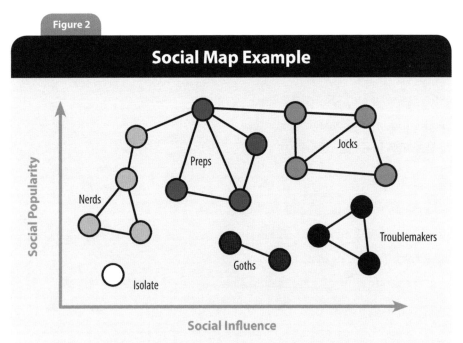

Figure 2

Social Map Example

There's no set number or type of cliques included in a social map. Over time, depending on the particular collection of children within the larger peer group, cliques start to form and become identified (implicitly or explicitly). Common present-day sub-groups include 'nerds,' 'jocks,' and 'preps,' but other more specialized sub-groups can form, such as 'hipsters,' 'goths,' or 'stoners.' Children with no sub-group affiliation may receive any number of negative labels from peers, but we'll use the term 'isolates.'

As labels are assigned and the social status hierarchy is defined, 'Us versus Them' group dynamics begin to flourish.[46] Children increasingly treat one another according to their clique identification, rather than their personal characteristics. They favor or prefer those in their own sub-group while avoiding, shunning, or dismissing those outside their clique. A wealth of psychological and sociological research demonstrates how group dynamics polarize our social interactions and attitudes throughout our lifetime.[47-51] Male versus female, white versus black, southern versus northern, Democrat versus Republican, football fan versus soccer fan . . . the list goes on and on. You can identify with any number of sub-groups, and there are real benefits to these affiliations. In particular, group identification helps you feel that you belong, that there are people you can trust, learn from, and depend on, and that you're safe. On the other hand, these group dynamics escalate competition between sub-groups.[51-53] In the school social setting, teasing, bullying, and ostracism of those in cliques different from your own become commonplace across the school years, and those children who don't fit into any sub-group— 'isolates'— are at particular risk for these types of negative social interactions.

In adulthood, we have a high level of control over our group affiliations—we can change social groups if we want, we can keep our affiliations private, and we can affiliate with different types of social groups in different settings. In the school peer group environment, children and adolescents have much less control over their social status and group affiliation. This relatively closed and restricted social environment tends to highlight and reinforce sub-group assignment. Transition points that disrupt the social structure for a time, such as the transition to middle school or from middle school to high school, are the best opportunities for changing your social affiliations. However, once the map is drawn (or re-drawn) within the school environment, it's more difficult for children to move from one sub-group to another, or even affiliate across multiple sub-groups, and there can be significant negative social repercussions for trying.

Another complicating matter in the peer social structure is the emergence of romantic relationships. As puberty hits, opposite-sex peers start to notice one another again and the awkward dance between adolescent boys and girls begins.[54-56] Cliques often expand beyond same-sex members to include opposite-sex peers, particularly during high school, and rivals for romantic targets emerge within and across cliques. Your place within the peer social structure is now determined by who you date as much as who you're friends with. As social competition intensifies, romantic and sexual factors become ripe fodder for teasing, bullying, and ostracism.

IN-GROUP vs. OUT-GROUP

You view members of the other group as fundamentally different (and inferior to) those in your group

SHIFTS IN SOCIAL NORMS

As a child's social world becomes more complex across the elementary, middle, and high school years, he needs increasingly sophisticated social skills to successfully navigate peer interactions with same- and opposite-sex peers. This is true partially because the social situations themselves are becoming more complicated, but also because society's norms and expectations are shifting over this same time period. What is and is not considered socially appropriate behavior changes across childhood and adolescence and these expectations differ somewhat for boys versus girls. In order to be socially successful, children need to recognize these changing norms and adapt their social behavior accordingly.

Aggressive Behavior

Expectations for aggressive behavior is one example of a changing social norm.[57] Physical aggression includes hitting, shoving, kicking, slapping, and any other means by which you physically harm another. Verbal aggression includes arguments, calling names, teasing, and insulting someone either in person or through other communication, such as email, phone calls, and written notes. In children's younger years, overt forms of aggression, such as physical or verbal fights, are more tolerated and less severely punished. However, society becomes much less tolerant of open conflict as children move through the elementary school years; this is particularly true for girls. In middle school, incidents of openly aggressive behavior decline and this trend continues into the high school years. That's not to say that aggression among children stops. Rather, in response to changing social norms, children start expressing their aggression through more indirect and concealed methods, such as making sure they bully at a location away from prying adult eyes, using exclusion from the group to hurt someone, and spreading rumors behind someone's back. Some research suggests that girls are more likely to engage in these indirect forms of aggression than are boys.[58] However, it's clear that expressions of aggression by both boys and girls increasingly take these hidden and veiled forms as they move through childhood and into adolescence.[59,60]

Expressions of Feelings

Another example of a changing social norm is the degree to which expressions of feelings by boys are accepted in society.[61-63] After boys enter elementary school, they are much less likely to express their feelings—such as hurt, distress, and caring—and this decline continues throughout childhood and adolescence. Teachers and other adults are much less tolerant of emotional displays by boys, such as crying, compared to girls. In fact, when a boy hurts himself on the playground, teachers show less compassion and spend less time consoling him than they would if he were a girl. Societal expectations for what it means to be masculine—being tough, in charge, in control—impacts the development and expression of key social skills for boys, including communication, empathy, and emotion regulation.

CHAPTER 2 NOTES

1. Hartup, W. W. (1979). The social world of childhood. *American Psychologist, 34,* 944-950.

2. Nickerson, A. B., & Nagle, R. J. (2005). Parent and peer relations in middle childhood and early adolescence. *Journal of Early Adolescence, 25,* 223-249.

3. Bokhorst, C. L., Sumter, S. R., & Westenberg, P. M. (2009). Social support from parents, friends, classmates, and teachers in children and adolescents aged 9 to 18 years: Who is perceived as most supportive? *Social Development, 19,* 417-426.

4. Rosenthal, N. L., & Kobak, R. (2010). Assessing adolescents' attachment hierarchies: Differences across developmental periods and associations with individual adaptation. *Journal of Research on Adolescence, 20,* 678-706.

5. Rubin, K. H., Bukowski, W. M., & Parker, J. G. (2006). Peer interaction, relationships, and groups. In N. Eisenberg (Vol. Ed.), W. Damon & R. M. Lerner (Series Eds.), *Handbook of child psychology: Vol. 3. Social, emotional, and personality development* (6th ed., pp. 571-645). New York, NY: Wiley.

6. Furman, W., & Buhrmester, D. (1992). Age and sex differences in perceptions of networks of personal relationships. *Child Development, 63,* 103-115.

7. Hartup, W. W. (1992). Peer relations in early and middle childhood. In V. B. Van Hasselt & M. Hersen (Eds.), *Handbook of social development: A lifespan perspective* (pp. 257-281). New York, NY: Plenum.

8. Lewis, C., & Carpendale, J. (2004). Social cognition. In P. K. Smith & C. H. Hart (Eds.), *Handbook of social development* (pp. 375-393). Malden, MA: Blackwell Publishing.

9. Ladd, G. W., Buhs, E. S., & Troop, W. (2004). Children's interpersonal skills and relationships in school settings: Adaptive significance and implications for school-based prevention and intervention programs. In P. K. Smith & C. H. Hart (Eds.), *Handbook of social development* (pp. 394-415). Malden, MA: Blackwell Publishing.

10. Gifford-Smith, M. E., & Brownell, C. A. (2003). Childhood peer relationships: Social acceptance, friendships, and peer networks. *Journal of School Psychology, 41,* 235-284

11. Zarbatany, L., Hartmann, D. P., & Rankin, D. B. (1990). The psychological functions of preadolescent peer activities. *Child Development, 61,* 1067-1080.

12. Allen, J. P., & Land, D. (1999). Attachment in adolescence. In J. Cassidy & P. Shaver (Eds.), *Handbook of attachment theory, research and clinical applications* (pp. 319-335). New York, NY: Guilford Press.

13. Noom, M. J., Dekovic, M., & Meeus, W. H. J. (1999). Autonomy, attachment and psychological adjustment during adolescence: A double-edged sword? *Journal of Adolescence, 22,* 771-783.

14. Nelis, S. M., & Rae, G. (2009). Brief report: Peer attachment in adolescents. *Journal of Adolescence, 32,* 443-447.

15. Blair, C. (2002). School readiness: Integrating cognition and emotion in a neurobiological conceptualization of children's functioning at school entry. *American Psychologist, 57,* 111-127.

16. Nelson, C. A., & Luciana, M. (Eds.) (2001). *Handbook of developmental cognitive neuroscience.* Cambridge, MA: MIT Press.

17. Corcoran, K., Crusius, J., & Mussweiler, T. (2011). Social comparison: Motives, standards, and mechanisms. In D. Chadee (Ed.), *Theories in social psychology* (pp. 119-139). Oxford, UK: Wiley-Blackwell.

18. Suls, J. M., & Miller, R. L. (1977). *Social comparison processes: Theoretical and empirical perspectives.* Oxford, UK: Hemisphere.

19. Suls, J., & Wheeler, L. (2011). Social comparison theory. In P. A. M. Van Lange, A. W. Kruglanski, & E. T. Higgins (Eds.), *The theories of social psychology: Volume 1* (pp. 460-482). Thousand Oaks, CA: Sage Publications.

20. Piaget, J. (1954). *The construction of reality in the child.* New York, NY: Basic Books.

21. Piaget, J., & Inhelder, B. (1956). *The child's conception of space.* London: Routledge & Kegan Paul.

22. Ruble, D. N. (1983). The development of social comparison processes and their role in achievement-related self-socialization. In E. T. Higgins, D. N. Ruble, & W. W. Hartup (Eds.), *Social cognition and social development: A sociocultural perspective* (pp. 134-157). Cambridge, England: Cambridge University Press.

23. Eccles, J. S., Midgley, C., Wigfield, A., Buchanan, C. M., Reuman, D., Flanagan, C., & Mac Iver, D. (1993). Development during adolescence: The impact of stage-environment fit on young adolescents' experiences in schools and in families. *American Psychologist, 48,* 90-101.

24. Bierman, K. L., & McCauley, E. (1987). Children's descriptions of their peer interactions: Useful information for clinical child assessment. *Journal of Clinical Child Psychology, 16,* 9-18.

25. Hymel, S., & Frank, S. (1985). Children's peer relations: Assessing self-perceptions. In B. Schneider, K. Rubin, & J. Ledingham (Eds.), *Children's peer relations: Issues in assessment and intervention* (pp. 75-92), New York, NY: Springer.

26. Salley, C. G., Vannatta, K., Gerhardt, C. A., & Noll, R. B. (2010). Social self-perception accuracy: Variations as a function of child age and gender. *Self and Identity, 9,* 209-223.

27. Levine, J. M., Snyder, H. N., & Mendez-Caratini, G. (1982). Task performance and interpersonal attraction in children. *Child Development, 53,* 359-371.

28. Conger, J. C., & Keane, S. P. (1981). Social skills intervention in the treatment of isolated or withdrawn children. *Psychological Bulletin, 90,* 478-495.

29. Mathias, J. L., Biebl, S. J. W., & DiLalla, L. F. (2011). Self-esteem accuracy and externalizing problems in preschool-aged boys. *The Journal of Genetic Psychology: Research and Theory on Human Development, 172,* 285-292.

30. Dodge, K. A., & Feldman, E. (1990). Issues in social cognition and sociometric status. In S. R. Asher & J. D. Coie (Eds.), *Peer rejection in childhood* (pp. 119-155). New York, NY: Cambridge University Press.

31. Grunebaum, H., & Solomon, L. (1987). Peer relationships, self-esteem, and the self. *International Journal of Group Psychotherapy, 37,* 475-513.

32. Ausubel, D. P., Schiff, H. M., & Gasser, E. B. (1952). A preliminary study of developmental trends in sociempathy: Accuracy of perception of own and others' sociometric status. *Child Development, 23,* 111-128.

33. Hymel, S., Bowker, A., & Woody, E. (1993). Aggressive versus withdrawn unpopular children: Variations in peer and self-perceptions in multiple domains. *Child Development, 64,* 879-896.

34. Boivin, M., & Begin, G. (1989). Peer status and self-perceptions among early elementary school children: The case of rejected children. *Child Development, 60,* 591–596.

35. Egan, S. K., & Perry, D. G. (1998). Does low self-regard invite victimization? *Developmental Psychology, 34,* 299-309.

36. Parker, J. G., Rubin, K. H., Erath, S. A., Wojslawowicz, J. C., & Buskirk, A. A. (2006). Peer relationships, child development, and adjustment: A developmental psychopathological perspective. In D. Chicchetti & D. J. Cohen (Eds.), *Developmental psychopathology: Vol. 1. Theory and method* (pp. 421-493). Hoboken, NJ: John Wiley & Sons, Inc.

37. McHale, S. M., Dariotis, J. K., & Kauh, T. J. (2003). Social development and social relationships in middle childhood. In A. Easterbrooks & R. M. Lerner (Eds.), *Handbook of psychology: Vol. 6. Developmental psychology* (pp. 241–265). New York, NY: Wiley.

38. Parker, J. G., & Seal, J. (1966). Forming, losing, renewing, and replacing friendships: Applying temporal parameters to the assessment of children's friendship experiences. *Child Development, 67,* 2248-2268.

39. Parker, J. G., Saxon, J. L., Asher, S. R., & Kovacs, D. M. (1999). Dimensions of children's friendship adjustment: Implications for understanding loneliness. In K. J. Rotenberg & S. Hymel (Eds.), *Loneliness in childhood and adolescence* (pp. 201-224). New York, NY: Cambridge University Press.

40. Newcomb, A. F., & Bagwell, C. L. (1995). Children's friendship relations: A meta-analytic review. *Psychological Bulletin, 117,* 306-347.

41. Kupersmidt, J. B., DeRosier, M. E., & Patterson, C. J. (1995). Similarity as the basis for friendship: The role of sociometric status, aggressive and withdrawn behavior, academic achievement, and demographic characteristics. *Journal of Social and Personal Relationships, 12,* 439-452.

42. Bagwell, C. L., & Schmidt, M. E. (2011). *Friendships in childhood and adolescence.* New York, NY: Guilford Press.

43. Barbu, S. (2009). Similarity of behavioral profiles among friends in early childhood. *Child Health and Education, 1,* 5-18.

44. Haselager, G. J. T., Hartup, W. W., Van Lieshout, C. F. M., & Riksen-Walraven, M. A. (1998). Similarities between friends and nonfriends in middle childhood. *Child Development, 69,* 1198-1208.

45. Abrams, D., Rutland, A., & Cameron, L. (2003). The development of subjective group dynamics: Children's judgments of normative and deviant in-group and out-group individuals. *Child Development, 74,* 184–1856.

46. Tajfel, H. (1982). Social psychology of intergroup relations. *Annual Review of Psychology, 33,* 1-39.

47. Hogg, M. A. (2012). Social identity and the psychology of groups. In M. R. Leary & J. P. Tangney (Eds.), *Handbook of self and identity* (2nd ed., pp. 502-519). New York, NY: Guilford Press.

48. Harris, J. R. (2009). *The nurture assumption: Why children turn out the way they do.* New York, NY: Free Press.

49. Hogg, M. A., & Abrams, D. (Eds.). (2001). *Intergroup relations: Key readings in social psychology.* Philadelphia, PA: Psychology Press.

50. Sherif, M., Harvey, O. J., White, B. J., Hood, W. R., & Sherif, C. W. (1961). *Intergroup conflict and cooperation: The Robbers Cave experiment.* Norman, OK: University Book Exchange.

51. Dovidio, J. F., & Gaertner, S. L. (2010). Intergroup bias. In S. T. Fiske, D. T. Gilbert, & G. Lindzey (Eds.), *Handbook of social psychology* (5th ed., Vol. 2, pp. 1084-1121). Hoboken, NJ: John Wiley.

52. Hewstone, M., Rubin, M., & Willis, H. (2002). Intergroup bias. *Annual Review of Psychology, 53,* 575-604.

53. Deardorff, J., Hayward, C., Wilson, K. A., Bryson, S., Hammer, L. D., & Agras, S. (2007). Puberty and gender interact to predict social anxiety symptoms in early adolescence. *Journal of Adolescent Health, 41,* 102-104.

54. Poulin, F., & Pedersen, S. (2007). Developmental changes in gender composition of friendship networks in adolescent girls and boys. *Developmental Psychology, 43,* 1484-1496.

55. Hayward, C. (Ed.). (2003). *Gender differences at puberty.* New York, NY: Cambridge University Press.

56. Underwood, M. K., Beron, K. J., & Rosen, L. H. (2009). Continuity and change in social and physical aggression from middle childhood through early adolescence. *Aggressive Behavior, 35,* 357-375.

57. Crick, N. R., & Grotpeter, J. K. (1995). Relational aggression, gender, and social-psychological adjustment. *Child Development, 66,* 710-722.

58. Card, N. A., Stucky, B. D., Sawalani, G. M., & Little, T. D. (2008). Direct and indirect aggression during childhood and adolescence: A meta-analytic review of gender differences, intercorrelations, and relations to maladjustment. *Child Development, 79,* 1185-1229.

59. Ostrov, J. M., & Godleski, S. A. (2010). Toward an integrated gender-linked model of aggression subtypes in early and middle childhood. *Psychological Review, 117,* 233-242.

60. Brody, L. R. (1999). *Gender, emotion, and the family.* Cambridge, MA: Harvard University Press.

61. Chaplin, T. M., & Aldao, A. (2013). Gender differences in emotion expression in children: A meta-analytic review. *Psychological Bulletin, 139, 735-765.*

62. Garbarino, J. (1999). *Lost boys: Why our sons turn violent and how we can save them.* New York, NY: The Free Press.

63. Pollack, W. (1999). *Real boys: Rescuing our sons from the myths of boyhood.* New York, NY: Random House.

IMPACT OF SOCIAL SKILLS ON ADJUSTMENT

by: Melissa E. DeRosier, Ph.D. and Kevin Leary, Ph.D.

DESCRIPTION

Not only is a sense of belonging a basic human need,[1] but social support and connectedness are critically important for adjustment across a broad array of outcomes ranging from academic achievement to physical health to mental health.[2-4] Children who are able to establish and maintain positive social relationships are more likely to experience positive and successful outcomes. In contrast, children who have difficulty navigating the social environment are at substantially greater risk of poor adjustment across all areas of functioning, including academic failure, behavioral problems, and emotional difficulties.[5,6] In this chapter, we explore how social skill deficits translate into specific social problems with peers and we examine the various types of adjustment difficulties that are associated with these peer relationship problems.

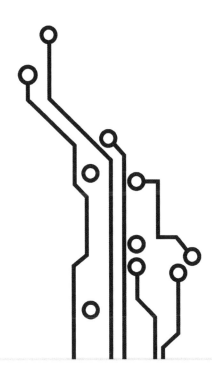

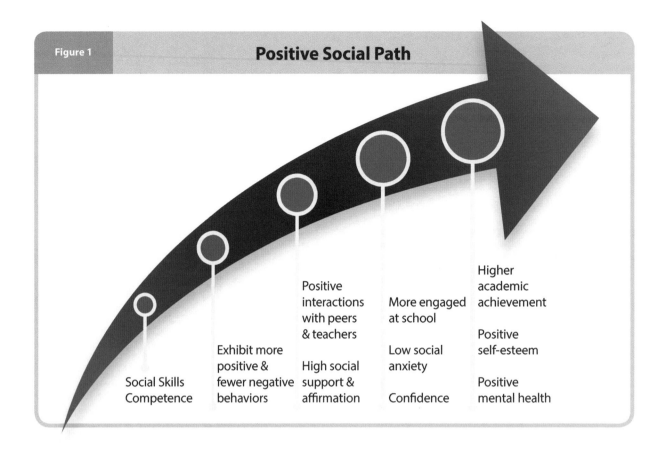

Figure 1

Positive Social Path

Social Skills Competence

Exhibit more positive & fewer negative behaviors

Positive interactions with peers & teachers

High social support & affirmation

More engaged at school

Low social anxiety

Confidence

Higher academic achievement

Positive self-esteem

Positive mental health

PATHS OF INFLUENCE

Social skills competence has a direct influence on social relationships which, in turn, directly impact adjustment.[5] However, the impact of social skills on adjustment is not simple or immediate; it's a process. Over time, social skills fuel your behavior and reactions in social situations which, in turn, determine others' responses to you. Over the course of this ongoing interchange, academic, behavioral, and emotional adjustment are impacted—negatively or positively, depending on the quality of the social interactions.

Figure 1 illustrates a positive social pathway. If you're socially skilled, you exhibit more prosocial behaviors and fewer antisocial behaviors. In effect, your social interactions with peers and teachers are more positive. You receive positive feedback—others like you and want to play with you—and you have access to social support. In the school environment, you feel accepted, so you want to go to school. You have friends to hang out with, so your social anxiety is low. Overall, you feel happy and confident at school, so you're able to concentrate on doing well academically. In the end, you feel good about yourself and you're more successful, academically as well as socially.

Negative Social Path

Lower academic achievement

Behavioral/ discipline problems

Negative self-esteem

Mental health problems

Low school engagement/ avoidance

High social anxiety

Negative emotions

Insecurity

Negative interactions with peers and teachers

Low social support and rejection

Exhibit more negative and fewer positive behaviors

Awkward and immature behaviors

Poor social skills

In contrast, **Figure 2** shows a negative pathway starting with poor social skills. As discussed in Chapter 1, children with low social competence may exhibit a number of negative, awkward, and antisocial behaviors, such as aggression, intrusiveness, withdrawal, or immaturity relative to their peers. They're also much less likely to display prosocial behaviors, such as cooperation and good communication. As poor social skills translate into negative social interactions, children often find themselves with few, if any, friends to turn to for help or companionship. For example, imagine others are playing a game and you jump right in, trying to take over and telling them how you're so much better at this game than they are. If this happens repeatedly, others may begin to purposely leave you out of games, telling you there are already enough players.

With more and more negative peer interactions, the school environment becomes a hostile place where children fear social failure and feel rejected by others. As would be expected, children with peer problems want to avoid this anxiety-producing place if possible, which results in greater absenteeism. In fact, 15% of all school absences are due to fears of being bullied at school.[7,8] And even when you're at school, it can be hard to concentrate on what the teacher is saying. You may be worrying about who you'll sit with at lunch or what names other kids might call you in the hallway next period. With these social threats all around you, academic goals seem much less pressing. In the end, your engagement in school suffers as does your academic performance.

With social failure come negative feelings about self and others.[11] When children don't have the requisite skills to successfully navigate social situations, whatever they try may not work well and may even make things worse. They may feel insecure, out of control, and unable to change things for the better. One reaction is to withdraw further and become increasingly socially isolated at school.[12] Social isolation and negative social experiences breed sadness and hopelessness, so that this reaction fosters significantly elevated risk for depression or other mental health problems over time.

Another reaction is directed outward—acting against others. As attempts to make friends or stop the teasing repeatedly fail, children often feel confused and frustrated. Not knowing how to more adaptively cope with these negative emotions, some children act them out on others through aggressive, domineering, and intrusive behaviors. When these behavior problems disrupt the classroom environment, teachers are likely to punish the disruptive child with disciplinary actions, such as office referrals for fighting.[13] These incidents further fuel negative reputational biases within the peer group, reinforcing the child's role as a 'troublemaker' or 'bad kid' and making it harder for him to break out of this negative pathway.

Children who are picked on, teased, or rejected by peers at school often develop somatic complaints, such as headaches, stomach pain, nausea.[9,10] While these types of non-specific symptoms can be an attempt—consciously or unconsciously—by the child to escape being at school, it's also the case that high anxiety, worry, and fear create these physical problems for children.

RISK FOR PROBLEMS WITH PEERS

Poor social skills place children at heightened risk for a range of peer problems from exclusion to verbal abuse to assault.[6, 14-15] Problems getting along with peers typically fall within three broad categories: rejection, victimization, and social isolation. These categories represent distinct types of peer problems that can occur alone, but often occur in combination for a given child.

Peer rejection involves the active dislike, avoidance, and exclusion of a child *by most other children* within the peer group. The rejected child is consistently left out of social activities because other children don't want to play with, hang out with, or be around the rejected child.

- **Robert** comes into the cafeteria for lunch. He asks a group of his classmates at a table whether he can join them and they say, *"Sure."* When he sits down, they all get up and go to another table.
- **Tonya** is always the last child to be picked for teams at school.
- **Carmen** has never been invited to a birthday party or other social event given by another child.
- When **Thomas** asks Todd if he will be his partner for the science fair, Todd says he already has his partners. Then later, Thomas sees Todd ask another kid to join his group.

The social experiences of rejected children differ from more socially accepted children in many ways. Their social approaches are more likely to be rejected by peers and they're more likely to be the victim of bullying and other forms of aggression by peers.[16] Some rejected children may maintain friendships with a small subset of children, but many are socially isolated within the peer group.[8, 17] With rejection, it's not simply that others ignore you or even passively forget to invite you to do things—the rejection is active and deliberate with the intent of avoiding interactions with you. Approximately 15% of children would be classified as rejected by the majority of their peers at school. As would be expected, the more highly rejected a child, the more negative that child's social experiences within the peer group.[18]

15% Rejected by majority of peers at school

Victimization involves being the victim of bullying behaviors, including assault, intimidation, humiliation, teasing, insults, and rumor spreading. Bullies may victimize directly—hurting the other child physically or verbally—or indirectly by organizing others to victimize a child. The victimization may be committed by one other child or many.

- **Allison's** teacher asks her to pass out worksheets to the class. As Beth takes the paper from Allison, she holds it at a distance and, with a disgusted look on her face, says, *"Yuck, cooties."* The class joins in laughing at Allison.
- When **Sam** is walking down the hall, Alex trips him. Sam and all his stuff falls to the floor, but Alex says, *"You retard! You better watch where you're going!"*
- Hal tells **TJ** that he'll be his friend if he picks the quarters out of the toilet for him. TJ does this while Hal and others look on and laugh.
- Laila tells **Kayla** that if she wants to be her friend, Kayla has to stop talking to Paula.

As you can see from these examples, bullying may take a variety of forms. Anything that's intended to frighten, coerce, threaten, intimidate, torment, or harass another person is bullying. Physical bullying consists of negative physical contact, such as hitting, kicking, pinching, shoving, slapping, biting, and choking as well as taking or destroying another person's belongings. Bullies can also physically intimidate and threaten others without actually touching them, by actions such as pantomiming shooting a gun or hitting with a fist. Perhaps due to movie and TV depictions, adults are most likely to associate the word 'bully' with an image of a physical bully—a bigger, stronger, meaner child who beats up on smaller, weaker victims. However, verbal bullying is actually the most frequent form of bullying.[19]

The verbal bully uses words to hurt, embarrass, or humiliate someone through teasing, taunting, name-calling, or insults. Any way that a child stands out or appears different from other children is a potential target for verbal abuse, particularly in the areas of looks ('fatso,' 'four eyes,' 'shorty'), intelligence ('geek,' 'retard'), and economic status ('bum'). Verbal harassment and slurs regarding a child's race or sexual orientation (real or fabricated) are also common. In recent years, cyber bullying has become a preferred method in which technology is used to communicate verbal abuse through e-mail, instant messages, texting, and social network postings.[20]

A third type of bullying is termed 'relational'. This kind of bullying directly targets a child's relationships or social status.[21] A relational bully may attempt to corrode someone's reputation by spreading false rumors about them or use malicious gossip to undermine a child's social status so others won't want to hang out with or be friends with her. Relational bullies are often socially skilled, so they can effectively use social pressure to persuade or coerce others to help them bully another child.

Bullying is an all too common problem among school age children. About 10-15% of children report being bullied on a regular basis of at least once a week[22] and over 45% of students fear harassment at school.[7] While bullying occurs throughout the school years, bullying typically escalates over the late elementary and middle school years, with middle school students reporting the highest frequency of bullying and interpersonal threats[7]. Bullying is problematic not only for those who are directly involved, but also for those who witness bullying among their peers. When bullying is allowed to occur within the school environment, fear, anxiety, and a perception of being unsafe tends to permeate the school climate.[15]

Social isolation refers to the absence of stable, positive friendships within the peer group. Socially isolated children have few, if any, close friends.

- When **Paul** first comes to school, other kids ask him to play, but he keeps turning them down. Now, nobody asks him to play.
- Almost every day, you'll see **Chloe** off to the side of the playground reading a book.
- **Chris** stands out as different. Other kids think he's weird or strange, so they just leave him alone.
- When the teacher asks the class to form small groups for a class project, **Jordan** remains seated at his desk. When the teacher asks why he isn't joining a group, Jordan asks if he can do the project by himself.

Social isolation may be imposed by others, as in the case of rejected children who are actively shunned and avoided by their peers, or it can be self-imposed. When children fear negative evaluations by others, are socially timid or shy, or feel high levels of social anxiety and self-consciousness, they may withdraw from social contact in an effort to avoid real or anticipated negative interactions with peers. Over time, children who avoid social contact can become overlooked or neglected within the peer group, so that other children simply forget about them and leave them alone.[23] Approximately

Bullying Statistics

15-20% of students regularly bully others

28% report being physically bullied

77% report being verbally bullied

Bullying peaks between 4th and 8th grades with 90% reporting being a victim of some kind of bullying

10% have no one to play with at school

56% have witnessed bullying at school

71% report bullying is an ongoing problem at school

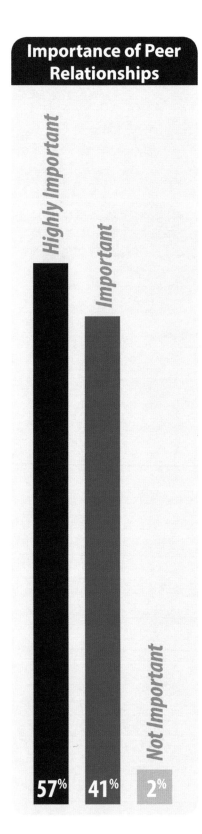

Importance of Peer Relationships

Highly Important

Important

Not Important

57%   41%   2%

10% of children report having no friends in their class and no one to play with at school.[24]

Regardless of the reason, the isolated child has few opportunities to engage in activities with same-aged peers. This limited access to social situations undermines the child's ability to develop those very social competencies he needs to integrate into the peer group more effectively. Fewer opportunities also mean the child is less likely to receive corrective feedback regarding his social behavior and he has fewer models for normative social behavior and practices. In effect, social isolation interferes with social skill development and the longer the child is socially isolated, the greater this developmental delay will become.

IMPACT OF PEER PROBLEMS

Decades of research underscores the insidious, damaging influence of peer problems. The quality of children's peer relationships has been repeatedly shown to directly and significantly influence academic, behavioral, and emotional adjustment. Further, peer problems place children at elevated risk for development of numerous negative outcomes.[6, 8, 25] In this section, we'll briefly summarize the following five sets of negative outcomes that have been linked to poor peer relationships in childhood and adolescence:

1. Negative self-concept
2. Internalizing problems
3. Externalizing problems
4. Academic failure
5. Future relationship problems

Negative Self-concept

Children's relationships with other children are critically important for their sense of well-being and adjustment.[26] Children are highly motivated to get along with and be accepted by their peers. For example, in a study of over 3,000 third through fifth graders, the majority—57%—of students reported that the quality of their social relationships with peers is highly important to them. Only 2% reported that peer relationships are unimportant.[27] When children experience social failure, their social self-concept—or social self-esteem—suffers. If your social interactions are negative, your social self-esteem will correspondingly be lower. As discussed in first two chapters of this book, the quality of your social interactions drives your social self-esteem, which to some extent drives how you feel about yourself more generally.

Children's perceptions of their abilities and behaviors relative to others are integral to the socialization process,[28] and those experiences influence children's views of themselves.[29-31] During the elementary and middle school years, as social cognitive processes mature, you gain clarity on where you stand relative to others socially and you're able to more objectively evaluate yourself compared to peers. With social comparative reasoning comes more accurate self-perceptions of your social abilities and popularity, and sometimes the news isn't good. If you experience peer problems during these formative years, the impact can be particularly long lasting as this social information becomes embedded in the foundation of your social self-esteem.

This early social sense of self is then carried into adolescence and adulthood, influencing children's social behavior and subsequent social relationships.[5] For example, if a child sees herself as socially incompetent or rejected by peers, she may elect to be alone rather than risk being left out. She may also feel hopeless and give up trying to improve her peer relationships. Over time, social experiences can either serve to reinforce or alter children's initial social self-esteem. Fortunately or unfortunately, self-esteem can fuel self-fulfilling prophesies: You act in ways based on expectations from earlier experiences that then produce the very outcomes you expected. Positive expectations, such as *Lots of people like me* or *People want to be friends with me,* lead to more confident, outgoing behaviors that actually make these expectations more likely to be true. Conversely, negative expectations, such as *No one really likes me* or *People don't want me around,* foster withdrawn, aggressive, or awkward social behaviors that then increase the likelihood of these very negative social outcomes.

It's easy to see how negative social self-esteem and poor peer relationships can reinforce one another in a vicious cycle over time. A key to breaking this cycle is identifying children with poor social skills and engaging them in social skills interventions that target social cognitive processes, so that the impact of negative social experiences on their social expectations and social self-esteem can be mitigated.

A key to breaking this cycle is identifying children with poor social skills and engaging them in social skills interventions.

Internalizing Problems

Internalizing problems are emotional and behavioral difficulties that are directed toward the self. As children experience peer problems and their social self-concept is undermined, they can blame themselves for their social problems. Along with negative feelings about self, they are also likely to feel negatively about the world—it's a terrible place that won't ever get better. As feelings of anxiety, sadness, and hopelessness become pervasive, a child's risk for anxiety and depressive disorders escalates tremendously.[32]

In an effort to manage these negative emotions, children naturally try to avoid potentially painful social situations, often keeping away from peers and social interactions as much as possible. Unfortunately, this avoidance results in the child becoming more and more socially isolated over time, and without one or more good friends for social support, the child's risk for internalizing problems escalates further.[17]

When children lack adaptive coping strategies, they may turn to maladaptive ways to try to diminish—or at least interrupt—these negative feelings about self and the world. They may try to numb the pain or lessen their anxiety through use of alcohol and other substances.[33] They may engage in behaviors that momentarily produce a sense of well-being through the release of endorphins, including risk-taking behaviors, such as reckless driving, or self-harming behaviors such as self-mutilation or cutting.[34] They may also seek acceptance and positive social contact by engaging in promiscuous sexual activities.[35] Each of these maladaptive coping strategies is an attempt to self-medicate in some way to alleviate negative emotions, at least in the short run. When these strategies are insufficient or ineffective, children may consider or attempt suicide. Suicide is the third leading cause of death among young people and for every suicide death, there are 100 other suicide attempts.[36] Children who experience bullying, victimization, social isolation, and rejection by peers are at significantly greater risk for contemplating, attempting, and committing suicide.[37]

Suicide is the third leading cause of death among young people.

Externalizing Problems

Externalizing problems are negative behaviors that are directed externally or outwards against others, including aggression, bullying, and delinquency. Whereas children who develop internalizing problems tend to blame themselves for their social difficulties, children who develop externalizing problems tend to see others as at fault. Social failure engenders not only sadness and confusion, but feelings of anger, frustration, and resentment which are then acted out on peers.

There are (at least) two distinct pathways interconnecting peer problems with externalizing behavior problems. The first pathway starts with the proactively aggressive child who enters social situations being mean and domineering with peers.[38] This child expects aggressive behavior by others, and therefore is preemptively aggressive in order to control the situation and gain the upper hand. Bullies are often proactive aggressors who see aggression as a successful means to their end. In some regards, they're correct in that others tend to do what they want and stay out of their way in order to avoid becoming the target. Proactive bullies are not well liked within the peer group, but they may not actually know this, since others tend to keep this information to themselves rather than confront the bullies.

The other pathway starts with a victim of bullying, a child who is not naturally aggressive, but rather is the object of bullying, teasing, and aggression by others. The anger and resentment that result from being bullied can promote what is called reactive aggression.[39] When first bullied, victims will often attempt to avoid the bully and places where the bully may be. The victimized child may seek out help from an adult, but more likely will not, since children typically see adults as ineffective for stopping a bully.[40] When avoidance of being bullied is unsuccessful, victims may seek revenge and retribution, taking matters into their own hands to escape or thwart further victimization.[40] In fact, reports indicate that over 50% of fights at school are initiated as retaliation against teasing or bullying.[41]

Without adaptive ways of coping with their anger and frustration, some victims react with emotionally-charged aggression towards others more generally. It's as if these negative emotions build up over time and then periodically explode outwards in an unplanned, impulsive manner. These children may also start engaging in proactive aggression towards other children in an attempt to gain a sense of control and power, and become bullies themselves. Of all aggressive types of children, the 'bully-victim' by far shows the most extreme level of externalizing behavior problems, both reactive and proactive.[39]

School Shootings

Between 1974 and 2000, targeted school violence occurred in 37 communities across the United States, including Columbine, CO, Pearl, MS, and Springfield, OR. As part of a task force brought together by the U.S. Department of Education and the U.S. Secret Service to create threat assessment guidelines for schools (www.secretservice.gov/ntac/ssi_guide.pdf), the editor of this book examined data related to these school shootings. While no universal reason for the violence was found across all these tragic events, there was clear evidence that peer problems fueled a large number of the school shootings. In 71% of cases, the attacker(s) felt bullied, threatened, persecuted, or injured by others at school prior to the incident. In one case, the shooter was identified as 'the kid everyone teased.' These shootings are termed 'targeted' because the school setting and people within it were explicitly targeted for violence. The school was where the bullying and perceived abuse of the shooter had occurred, and the attack was intended to stop the pain of these peer problems as well as to get revenge against those students and administrators who were seen as responsible for hurting the shooter or failing to protect him.

As might be expected, there's a strong and direct link between externalizing behavior problems in childhood and delinquency and criminality in adolescence and adulthood.[43-44] For example, 60% of children identified as bullies by age 8 have a criminal conviction by age 24.[45] Aggressive children are likely to engage in both violent forms of delinquent and criminal behavior and non-violent forms, such as lying, cheating, stealing, and vandalism. While the connection between early antisocial behavior and later delinquency and criminality is clear, the compounding impact of peer problems is also clear. Those children who are not only aggressive, but also rejected or victimized by their peers in childhood show the most severe and serious conduct problems later on.[46]

Academic Failure

A large body of research demonstrates that children's social skills and peer relationships have a direct impact on their school engagement, academic motivation, and academic performance. Children who are able to establish and maintain positive peer relationships are more successful in school, demonstrating greater engagement in the learning environment, higher levels of academic motivation, and higher academic achievement.[47-48] In contrast, children who experience social failure often disengage from school and are at substantially elevated risk for absenteeism, truancy, and dropping out.[7] Peer problems are also linked with poor academic performance, including lower math and reading GPA, lower standardized test scores, and negative academic self-esteem.[49-51] Though extreme negative academic outcomes, such as academic failure and drop-out, tend to manifest themselves in adolescence, the roots of these problems typically begin in childhood and develop over time[5].

Future Relationship Problems

Peer problems in childhood interfere with the development of positive social relationships, both in the near term and in the long term.[52] When children are rejected from the normative peer group, they tend to affiliate with other children who reinforce—rather than ameliorate—their own social skills problems. For example, children who can't find acceptance with peers their own age often turn to younger children, but these friendships only further delay their social skill development.[53] It's also the case that children rejected from the majority of their peers tend to seek out and form friendships with other children who experience similar types of social difficulties.[54-55] Socially shy and timid children tend to hang out with other shy, timid children. Aggressive, antisocial children tend to form social networks with other deviant peers. In particular, children who are victims of bullying by others may form alliances that then can work together to harass and bully others.

In effect, social isolation, rejection, and victimization set in motion a process called 'deviance training'.[13] When socially unskilled peers affiliate with one another more exclusively, negative behaviors and attitudes within this sub-group are compounded. Sub-group members reinforce one another's poor social skills as well as the particular deviant or maladaptive adjustment difficulties within the group.[5, 6, 39] Affiliating with depressed, anxious, self-abusing peers leads to more depression, anxiety, and self-abuse for you. Affiliating with antisocial, deviant peers leads to more antisocial and deviant behavior for you. This process not only worsens children's adjustment difficulties over time, but also further and further diminishes the likelihood that these children will be able to transition back into the normative peer group, thereby perpetuating their social isolation and deviant affiliations over time.

Deviance training compounds negative behavior and attitudes.

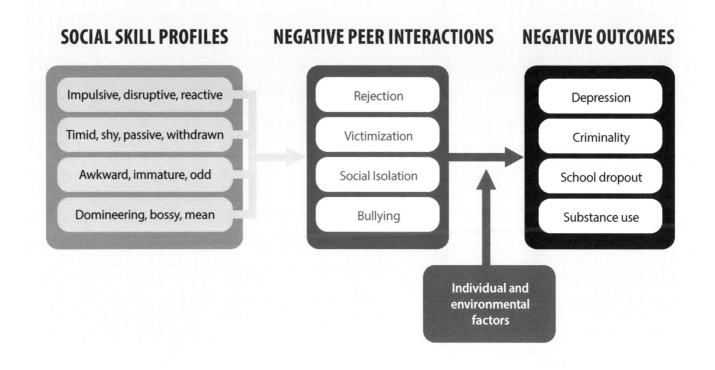

Unfortunately, without intervention, children's peer problems tend to be carried with them into adolescence and adulthood. Children with poor peer relationships tend to have more problematic romantic and work relationships later on.[56-57] As discussed earlier in this chapter, rejected youth tend to engage in promiscuous sexual activity and, as a result, are at elevated risk of becoming teen parents. In addition, social relationships in adulthood tend to be less stable, more conflictual, and less satisfying if the person had suffered peer problems during childhood and adolescence.

OVERLAP WITH PSYCHIATRIC DISORDERS

Peer problems often go along with psychiatric disorders, either as a feature of the disorder or as a side-effect of related symptoms. For example, children with **Attention-Deficit/Hyperactivity Disorder** (ADHD) are 5-10 times more likely to experience peer rejection. The behavioral symptoms of increased activity level and impulsivity that accompany ADHD are often seen as intrusive and disruptive by peers. Children with behavior disorders, such as **Oppositional Defiant Disorder** and **Conduct Disorder**, tend to be highly aggressive and mean with peers, and these antisocial behaviors substantially increase the likelihood that a child will be rejected by her peers.

Peer problems are much more likely for children with conditions that lead them to be seen as different from others in any way. Children with **learning disabilities** may be teased for being slow or academically different. **Physical disabilities**, such as being hearing impaired or in a wheelchair, also stand out as potential targets for teasing by peers. Children with pervasive developmental disorders, such as **Autism Spectrum Disorders** (ASD), are also at substantially greater risk for teasing and other peer problems.[58]

A primary component of ASDs is that the child exhibits socially immature, awkward, or inappropriate behavior. These behaviors are seen by peers as highly odd and strange, making children with ASDs easy targets for bullying. When children with ASDs have average or greater cognitive functioning (as is the case with high functioning ASDs and Asperger's syndrome), they are mainstreamed into the regular classroom for the majority of their school day. As a result, there are ample opportunities for these children to experience teasing, bullying, and victimization at the hands of their typically developing peers. In fact, over 60% of children and 46% of adolescents with ASD regularly experience peer victimization, compared to 10-15% for the general population.[59]

Over 60% of children and 46% of adolescents with ASD regularly experience peer victimization, compared to 10-15% for the general population.

MEDIATING AND MODERATING INFLUENCES

We know from the research literature that children's social skills directly impact the quality of their peer relationships and determine the likelihood they will experience negative peer interactions such as bullying and social isolation. In turn, the quality of children's peer relationships directly influences their adjustment. These pathways represent unique and independent prediction[5] that is not simply an artifact of other behavioral or psychiatric problems, such as aggressiveness or autism, nor solely due to other environmental factors, such as poverty. Rather, social skills directly impact the quality of children's peer relationships and peer problems directly contribute to the development of adjustment difficulties for children.

Thus, we know that children who experience poor peer relationships are at risk for a wide array of adjustment problems. However, the likelihood that a *specific child* will develop a particular negative outcome—or any significant problem at all—can be altered by other external factors in the child's life. The degree to which a given child is at risk for developing a specific negative outcome will vary depending on a number of individual and environmental factors. These factors can either exacerbate that child's risk, making him more likely to develop a negative outcome, or ameliorate the child's risk, making him less likely to develop a negative outcome.

Among the factors that have been found to mediate (or moderate) the impact of negative peer relationships on children's adjustment are individual characteristics of the child, chronicity of the peer problems, presence of other environmental stressors, and the quality of the teacher-child relationship.

Individual Characteristics

Some children develop depression in the face of negative peer interactions whereas others become delinquent or substance abusing. Some children drop out of school whereas others do not. While peer problems are detrimental at some level for all children, we know much less about the specific negative outcomes a given child will develop in response to peer problems. However, there is evidence that children's individual temperament and biological characteristics can predispose them to particular types of adjustment problems.[60-61] For example, a child with a low attention span or poor impulse control will be more likely to develop externalizing and acting out behavior problems whereas a temperamentally shy and timid child will be more likely to develop internalizing problems, such as anxiety and social withdrawal.

Much has been researched and speculated about how peer problems and risk for negative outcomes differ by the individual characteristics of *gender and race*.[62-63] Many of the presupposed differences have not been borne out through research. Overall, it appears that the connections between social skills, peer relations, and outcomes have more similarities than differences across boys and girls and across different racial sub-groups.[64] For example, both boys and girls exhibit bullying behaviors—of all types—and bullies are equally likely to come from any racial or ethnic group. However, there may be gender differences in the expression of negative outcomes. For example, if peer problems lead to depression, boys may be more likely to act out against others whereas girls appear to be more likely to hurt or abuse themselves.[65]

Chronicity

How often or how long a child experiences negative peer interactions can mediate their impact. As peer problems become more chronic and severe, the child's likelihood of developing serious negative outcomes significantly increases.[8, 43-44] Untreated peer problems tend to worsen over time, pushing children along the negative social pathway and making it increasingly difficult for them to improve their social skills and peer relationships. Intervening with peer problems before they become chronic and intractable has been repeatedly heralded as a key to preventing development of more serious maladjustment in adolescence and adulthood.

Intervening with peer problems before they become chronic and intractable has been repeatedly heralded as a key to preventing development of more serious maladjustment in adolescence and adulthood.

Environmental Stressors

Social support is particularly influential during difficult times.[66] When a child is faced with negative or stressful life events, a close social network bolsters her ability to cope with that event and helps prevent development of anxiety, depression, and other psychological disorders in response to stress. In effect, positive peer relationships operate as a protective factor, reducing the likelihood of negative outcomes in the face of stressful life events, such as poverty, loss of a loved one, or chronic illness.[6, 67-68]

However, the inverse is also true where lack of social support during times of stress places children at even greater risk for developing adjustment problems.[69-70] Regardless of the cause, social difficulties with peers are extremely stressful for children. In fact, children report that the stress of experiencing peer rejection is so high that only death of a parent exceeds it.[71] When peer problems are experienced alongside other stressful life events, this cumulative stress serves to substantially magnify the child's likelihood of developing academic, behavioral, and emotional adjustment problems.

Teacher-child Relationship

Given that much of our discussion centers on children's peer relationships within the school environment, it's relevant to consider the influence of other sources of social support within this environment—specifically the quality of the teacher-child relationship. Evidence suggests that teacher-child and peer social relationships are related; high teacher support tends to raise peer acceptance whereas low teacher support tends to exacerbate peer rejection.[72] Studies also show that teachers tend to prefer peer-accepted children over peer-rejected children, and that children who are rejected by their peers tend to also have problematic teacher-child relationships.[72-73] In effect, a positive teacher-child relationship can serve as a protective factor for children who experience peer problems whereas a poor teacher-child relationship serves to exacerbate the child's social problems. As with environmental stressors, this cumulative stress of low peer and teacher support compounds children's risk for negative outcomes, particularly low classroom engagement, poor academic achievement, and emotional adjustment difficulties at school.[74-75]

The stress of experiencing peer rejection is so high that only death of a parent exceeds it.

CHAPTER 3 NOTES

1. Baumeister, R. F., & Leary, M. R. (1995). The need to belong: Desire for interpersonal attachments as a fundamental human motivation. *Psychological Bulletin, 117,* 497-529.

2. Walton, G. M., & Cohen, G. L. (2011). A brief social-belonging intervention improves academic and health outcomes of minority students. *Science, 331,* 1447-1451.

3. Uchino, B. N. (2006). Social support and health: A review of physiological processes potentially underlying links to disease outcomes. *Journal of Behavioral Medicine, 29,* 377-387.

4. Hall-Lande, J. A., Eisenberg, M. E., Christenson, S. L., & Neumark-Sztainer, D. (2007). Social isolation, psychological health, and protective factors in adolescence. *Adolescence, 42,* 265-286.

5. Kupersmidt, J. B., & DeRosier, M. E. (2004). The role of peer relations in the development of negative outcomes: Explanatory processes. In K. A. Dodge & J. B. Kupersmidt (Eds.), *Children's peer relations: From development to intervention* (pp. 119-138). Washington, DC: American Psychological Association.

6. Parker, J. G., Rubin, K. H., Erath, S. A., Wojslawowicz, J. C., & Buskirk, A. A. (2006). Peer relationships, child development, and adjustment: A developmental psychopathology perspective. In D. Cicchetti & D. J. Cohen (Eds.), *Developmental Psychopathology, Vol. 1: Theory and method* (pp. 419-493). Hoboken, NJ: Wiley.

7. U.S. Bureau of Justice (2012). *Indicators of school crimes and safety: 2011.* Washington, DC: Bureau of Justice Statistics.

8. DeRosier, M. E., Kupersmidt, J. B., & Patterson, C. J. (1994). Children's academic and behavioral adjustment as a function of chronicity and proximity of peer rejection. *Child Development, 65,* 1799-1813.

9. Wolke, D., Woods, S., Bloomfield, L., & Karstadt, L. (2001). Bullying involvement in primary schools and common health problems. *Archives of Disease in Childhood, 85,* 197-201.

10. Fekkes, M., Pijpers, F. I. M., & Verloove-Vanhorick, S. P. (2004). Bullying behavior and associations with psychosomatic complaints and depression in victims. *The Journal of Pediatrics, 144,* 17-22.

11. Boivin, M., & Shelley, H. (1997). Peer experiences and social self-perceptions: A sequential model. *Developmental Psychology, 33,* 135-145.

12. Ladd, G. W. (2006). Peer rejection, aggressive or withdrawn behavior, and psychological maladjustment from ages 5 to 12: An examination of four predictive models. *Child Development, 77,* 822-846.

13. Dishion, T. J., Andrews, D. W., & Crosby, L. (1995). Antisocial boys and their friends in early adolescence: Relationship characteristics, quality, and interactional process. *Child Development, 66,* 131-151.

14. Asher, S. R., Parker, J. G., & Walker, D. L. (1996). Distinguishing friendship from acceptance: Implications for intervention and assessment. In W. M. Bukowski, A. F. Newcomb, & W. W. Hartup (Eds.), *The company they keep: Friendship during college and adolescence* (pp. 366-406). New York, NY: Cambridge University Press.

15. Olweus, D. (1993). *Bullying at school: What we know and what we can do.* Cambridge, MA: Blackwell.

16. Dodge, K. A., Coie, J. D., & Brakke, N. P. (1982). Behavior patterns of socially rejected and neglected preadolescents: The roles of social approach and aggression. *Journal of Abnormal Child Psychology, 10,* 389-410.

17. Rubin, K. H., & Mills, R. S. (1988). The many faces of social isolation in childhood. *Journal of Consulting and Clinical Psychology, 56,* 916-924.

18. DeRosier, M. E., & Thomas, J. M. (2003). Strengthening sociometric prediction: Scientific advances in the assessment of children's peer relations. *Child Development, 74,* 1372-1379.

19. Wang, J., Iannotti, R. J., & Nansel, T. R. (2009). School bullying among U.S. adolescents: Physical, verbal, relational, and cyber. *Journal of Adolescent Health, 45,* 368-375.

20. Kowalski, R. M., Limber, S. P., & Agatston, P. W. (2012). *Cyberbullying: Bullying in the digital age* (2nd ed.). Malden, MA: Blackwell Publishing.

21. Underwood, M. K. (2004). Sticks and stones and social exclusion: Aggression among girls and boys. In P. K. Smith & C. H. Hart (Eds.), *Blackwell handbook of child social development* (pp. 533-548). Malden, MA: Blackwell Publishing.

22. U.S. Department of Education. (2011). *Student victimization in U.S. schools: Results from the 2009 school crime supplement to the national crime victimization survey.* Washington, DC: National Center for Education Statistics.

23. Rubin, K. H., Coplan, R. J., & Bowker, J. C. (2009). Social withdrawal in childhood. *Annual Review of Psychology, 60,* 141-171.

24. Parker, J. G., & Asher, S. R. (1993). Beyond group acceptance: Friendship and friendship quality as distinct dimensions of peer adjustment. In W. H. Jones & D. Perlman (Eds.), *Advances In Personal Relationships* (Vol. 4). London: Kingley.

25. Woodward, L. J., & Fergusson, D. M. (2000). Childhood peer relationship problems and later risks of educational under-achievement and unemployment. *The Journal of Child Psychology and Psychiatry, 41,* 191-201.

26. Oberle, E., Schonert-Reichl, K. A., & Thomson, K. C. (2010). Understanding the link between social and emotional well-being and peer relations in early adolescence: Gender-specific predictors of peer acceptance. *Journal of Youth and Adolescence, 39,* 1330-1342.

27. 3-C Institute for Social Development. (2001). *Overview of Peer Connections through the 3-C Institute for Social Development.* Cary, NC: 3-C Institute for Social Development.

28. Ruble, D. N. (1983). The development of social comparison processes and their role in achievement-related self-socialization. In E. T. Higgins, D. N. Ruble, & W. W. Hartup (Eds.), *Social cognition and social development: A sociocultural perspective* (pp. 134-157). New York, NY: Cambridge University Press.

29. Dodge, K. A., & Feldman, E. (1990). Issues in social cognition and sociometric status. In S. R. Asher & J. D. Coie (Eds.), *Peer rejection in childhood* (pp. 119-155). New York, NY: Cambridge University Press.

30. Hymel, S., Bowker, A., & Woody, E. (1993). Aggressive versus withdrawn unpopular children: Variations in peer and self-perceptions in multiple domains. *Child Development, 64,* 879-896.

31. Boivin, M., & Begin, G. (1989). Peer status and self-perceptions among early elementary school children: The case of rejected children. *Child Development, 60,* 591–596.

32. Hymel, S., Rubin, K. H., Rowden, L., & LeMare, L. (2008). Children's peer relationships: Longitudinal prediction of internalizing and externalizing problems from middle to late childhood. *Child Development, 61,* 2004-2021.

33. Donnellan, M. B., Trzesniewski, K. H., Robins, R. W., Moffitt, T. E., & Caspi. A. (2005). Low self-esteem is related to aggression, antisocial behavior, and delinquency. *Psychological Science, 16,* 328-335.

34. Igra, V., & Irwin, Jr., C. E. (1996). Theories of adolescent risk-taking behavior. In R. J. DiClemente, W. B. Hansen, & L. E. Ponton (Eds.), *Handbook of adolescent health risk behavior* (pp. 35-54). New York, NY: Plenum Press.

35. Brown, L. K., Hadley, W., Stewart, A., Lescano, C., Whiteley, L., Donenberg, G., & DiClemente, R. (2010). Psychiatric disorders and sexual risk among adolescents in mental health treatment. *Journal of Consulting and Clinical Psychology, 78,* 590-597.

36. Centers for Disease Control and Prevention (2012). *Suicide: Facts at a glance.* Retrieved from http://www.cdc.gov/ViolencePrevention/pdf/Suicide_DataSheet-a.pdf.

37. Kim, Y. S., & Leventhal, B. (2008). Bullying and suicide: A review. *International Journal of Adolescent Medicine and Health, 20,* 133-154.

38. Hubbard, J. A., McAuliffe, M. D., Morrow, M. T., & Romano, L. J. (2010). Reactive and proactive aggression in childhood and adolescence: Precursors, outcomes, processes, experiences, and measurement. *Journal of Personality, 78,* 95-118.

39. Schwartz, D., Dodge, K. A., Pettit, G. S., & Bates, J. E. (1997). The early socialization of aggressive victims of bullying. *Child Development, 68,* 665-675.

40. Cintron, R. (2000). Listening to what the streets say: Vengeance as ideology. *Annals of the American Academy of Political and Social Science, 567,* 42-53.

41. Schwartz, D., Proctor, L. J., & Chien, D. H. (2001). The aggressive victim of bullying: Emotional and behavioral dysregulation as a pathway to victimization by peers. In N. Juvonen & S. Graham (Eds.), *Peer harassment in school: The plight of the vulnerable and victimized* (pp. 147-176). New York, NY: Guilford Press.

42. Boulton, M. J. (1993). Aggressive fighting in British middle school children. *Educational Studies, 19,* 19-39.

43. Nagin, D., & Tremblay, R. E. (1999). Trajectories of boys' physical aggression, opposition, and hyperactivity on the path to physically violent and nonviolent juvenile delinquency. *Child Development, 70,* 1181-1196.

44. Babinski, L., M., Hartsough, C. S., & Lambert, N. M. (1999). Childhood conduct problems, hyperactivity-impulsivity, and inattention as predictors of adult criminal activity. *The Journal of Child Psychology and Psychiatry, 40,* 347-355.

45. Olweus, D. (1991). Bully/victim problems among school children: Basic facts and effects of a school based intervention program. In I. Rubin & D. Pepler (Eds.), *The development and treatment of childhood aggression* (pp. 411-447). Hillsdale, NJ: Erlbaum.

46. Bierman, K. L., Smoot, D. L., & Aumiller, K. (1993). Characteristics of aggressive-rejected, aggressive (nonrejected), and rejected (nonaggressive) boys. *Child Development, 64,* 139-151.

47. Wentzel, K. R. (2005). Peer relationships, motivation, and academic performance at school. In A. J. Elliot & C. S. Dweck (Eds.), *Handbook of competence and motivation* (pp. 279-296). New York, NY: Guilford Press.

48. Wentzel, K. R. (2009). Peers and academic functioning at school. In K. H. Rubin, W. M. Bukowski, & B. Laursen (Eds.), *Handbook of peer interactions, relationships, and groups: Social, emotional, and personality development in context* (pp. 531-547). New York, NY: Guilford Press.

49. Guay, F., Boivin, M., & Hodges, E. V. E. (1999). Predicting change in academic achievement: A model of peer experiences and self-system processes. *Journal of Educational Psychology, 91,* 105-115.

50. DeRosier, M. E., & Lloyd, S. W. (2010). The impact of children's social adjustment on academic outcomes. *Reading and Writing Quarterly: Overcoming Learning Difficulties, 27,* 25-47.

51. Fleming, C. B., Haggerty, K. P., Catalano, R. F., Harachi, T. W., Mazza, J. J., & Gruman, D. H. (2005). Do social and behavioral characteristics targeted by preventive interventions predict standardized test scores and grades? *Journal of School Health, 75,* 342-349.

52. Kupersmidt, J. B., & Coie, J. D. (1990). Preadolescent peer status, aggression, and school adjustment as predictors of externalizing problems in adolescence. *Child Development, 61,* 1350-1361.

53. Ladd, G. W. (1983). Social networks of popular, average, and rejected children in school settings. *Merrill-Palmer Quarterly, 29,* 283-307.

54. Cairns, R. B., Cairns, B. D., Neckerman, H. J., Gest, S. D., & Gariépy, J. (1988). Social networks and aggressive behavior: Peer support or peer rejection? *Developmental Psychology, 24,* 815-823.

55. Pellegrini, A. D., Bartini, M., & Brooks, F. (1999). School bullies, victims, and aggressive victims: Factors relating to group affiliation and victimization in early adolescence. *Journal of Educational Psychology, 31,* 216-224.

56. Parker, J. G., & Asher, S. R. (1987). Peer relations and later personal adjustment: Are low-accepted children at risk? *Psychological Bulletin, 102,* 357-389.

57. Bagwell, C. L., Newcomb, A. F., & Bukowski, W. M. (1998). Preadolescent friendship and peer rejection as predictors of adult adjustment. *Child Development, 69,* 140-153.

58. DeRosier, M. E., & Mercer, S. H. (2009). Perceived behavioral atypicality as a predictor of social rejection and peer victimization: Implications for emotional adjustment and academic achievement. *Psychology in the Schools, 46,* 375-378.

59. Sterzing, P. R., Shattuck, P. T., Narendorf, S. C., Wagner, M., & Cooper, B. P. (2012). Bullying involvement and autism spectrum disorders: Prevalence and correlates of bullying involvement among adolescents with an autism spectrum disorder. *Archives of Pediatrics & Adolescent Medicine, 166,* 1058-1064.

60. Deater-Deckard, K. (2001). Annotation: Recent research examining the role of peer relationships in the development of psychopathology. *The Journal of Child Psychology and Psychiatry and Allied Disciplines, 42,* 565-579.

61. Fergusson, D. M., & Horwood, L. J. (1999). Prospective childhood predictors of deviant peer affiliations in adolescence. *Journal of Child Psychology and Psychiatry, 40,* 581-592.

62. Rose, A. J., & Rudolph, K. D. (2006). A review of sex differences in peer relationship processes: Potential trade-offs for the emotional and behavioral development of girls and boys. *Psychological Bulletin, 132,* 98-131.

63. Graham, S., Taylor, A. Z., & Ho, A. Y. (2009). Race and ethnicity in peer relations research. In K. H. Rubin, W. M. Bukowski, & B. Laursen (Eds.), *Handbook of peer interactions, relationships, and groups* (pp. 394-413). New York, NY: Guilford Press.

64. Spriggs, A. L., Iannotti, R. J., Nansel, T. R., & Haynie, D. L. (2007). Adolescent bullying involvement and perceived family, peer and school relations: Commonalities and differences across race/ethnicity. *Journal of Adolescent Health, 41,* 283-293.

65. Card, N. A., Stucky, B. D., Sawalani, G. M., & Little, T. D. (2010). Direct and indirect aggression during childhood and adolescence: A meta-analytic review of gender differences, intercorrelations, and relations to maladjustment. *Child Development, 79,* 1185-1129.

66. Furman, W., & Buhrmester, D. (1985). Children's perceptions of the personal relationships in their social networks. *Developmental Psychology, 21,* 1016-1024.

67. Criss, M. M., Pettit, G. S., Bates, J. E., Dodge, K. A., & Lapp, A. L. (2003). Family adversity, positive peer relationships, and children's externalizing behavior: A longitudinal perspective on risk and resilience. *Child Development, 73,* 1220-1237.

68. Sroufe, L. A., Duggal, S., Weinfield, N., & Carlson, E. (2000). Relationships, development, and psychopathology. In A. J. Sameroff, M. Lewis, & S. M. Miller (Eds.), *Handbook of developmental psychopathology* (Vol. 2, pp. 75-91). New York, NY: Kluwer Academic/Plenum Publishers.

69. DuBois, D. L., Felner, R. D., Brand, S., Adan, A. M., & Evans, G. E. (1992). A prospective study of life stress, social support, and adaptation in early adolescence. *Child Development, 63,* 542-57.

70. Cohen, S., & McKay, G. (1984). Social support, stress, and the buffering hypothesis: A theoretical analysis. In A. Baum, S. E. Taylor, & J. E. Singer (Eds.), *Handbook of psychology and health* (pp. 253-267). Hillsdale, NJ: Lawrence Erlbaum.

71. Johnson, J. H. (1988). *Life events as stressors in childhood and adolescence.* Newbury Park, CA: Sage.

72. Hughes, J. N., Cavell, T. A., & Willson, V. (2001). Further support for the developmental significance of the quality of the teacher-student relationship. *Journal of School Psychology, 39,* 289-301.

73. Hughes, J. N., Zhang, D., & Hill, C. R. (2006). Peer assessments of normative and individual teacher-student support predict social acceptance and engagement among low-achieving children. *Journal of School Psychology, 43,* 447-463.

74. Furrer, C., & Skinner, E. (2003). Sense of relatedness as a factor in children's academic engagement and performance. *Journal of Educational Psychology, 95,* 148–162.

75. Hughes, J. N., & Kwok, O. (2006). Classroom engagement mediates the effect of teacher-student support on elementary students' peer acceptance: A prospective analysis. *Journal of School Psychology, 43,* 465–480.

PART II

TRADITIONAL SOCIAL SKILLS ASSESSMENT

TRADITIONAL SOCIAL SKILLS ASSESSMENT

OVERVIEW

Before moving on to talk about game-based social-emotional learning platforms and their value for social skills assessment (SSA), it's important to first have an understanding of how SSA has historically been conducted. In this section of the book, we explore the four most common methods that have traditionally been used for SSA in schools and healthcare settings: (1) Behavioral rating scales, (2) Behavioral observations, (3) Peer nominations, and (4) Interviewing.

Unfortunately, there's no "one size fits all" SSA strategy. The choice of whether and when to employ a given SSA method depends on a number of situation-specific factors. What's the purpose of this assessment? How will the information be used? Are there adequate resources, such as time and personnel, to conduct the assessment? Is there evidence to support the validity and reliability of the information that will be generated through this assessment? Is the assessment method appropriate for this child given his age, developmental stage, or special needs? The answers to these questions will inform which SSA method or methods best fit your particular situation.

In the first chapter of this section, we examine various common goals for SSA, such as screening to identify children with social skill deficits, monitoring a child's progress during the course of an intervention, and evaluating the impact of an intervention for helping a child achieve particular outcomes. The next four chapters explore each traditional SSA method in turn, highlighting the benefits and limitations of its use. The final chapter of this section summarizes the relative strengths, weaknesses, costs, and benefits of these traditional SSA approaches. This chapter serves as a springboard for the next section of the book in which we explore the ways that game-based assessment can move SSA beyond the limitations of these traditional methods.

Goals of Social Skills Assessment (SSA)

by: Melissa E. DeRosier, Ph.D.

DESCRIPTION

When selecting a social skills assessment (SSA) approach, it's important to consider what the data is going to be used for. What information do you need? How do you want the data to inform your decisions? How will you use the data?

While researchers may have their own reasons to conduct SSA, we're going to focus our discussion on the practical uses of this data within schools and in healthcare settings where the core purpose of SSA is to inform intervention planning.[1] **Figure 1** summarizes three ways that data collected through SSA can be used to guide the intervention planning process: (1) to help you identify children who have particular social skill deficits and would benefit from intervention (**Screening**); (2) to monitor whether a child's social skills or social behavior change—positively or negatively—during the course of an intervention (**Progress Monitoring**); and (3) to evaluate whether a child who participates in a social intervention actually shows improvement in targeted social, behavioral, or emotional outcomes (**Evaluation**).

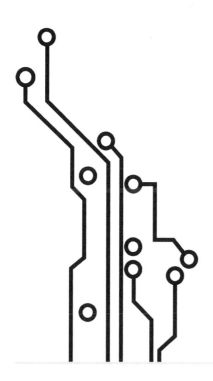

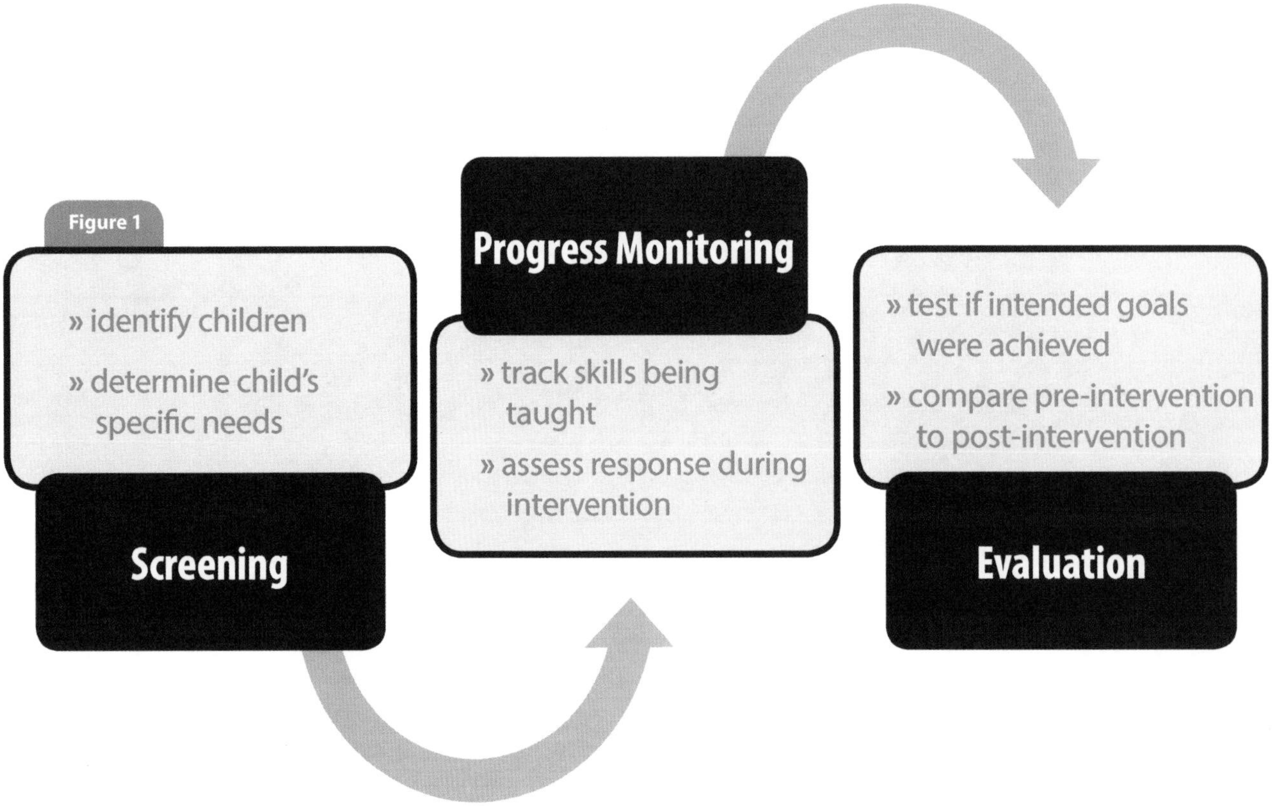

Figure 1

Screening
» identify children
» determine child's specific needs

Progress Monitoring
» track skills being taught
» assess response during intervention

Evaluation
» test if intended goals were achieved
» compare pre-intervention to post-intervention

In addition, whether you're screening, monitoring, or evaluating, you need to consider what type of data you want to collect. In SSA, you can focus your data collection in three distinct, but related, areas: social literacy, social performance, or social adjustment. This decision will help guide your selection of SSA methods in order to employ those that are best suited to your data collection needs. In this chapter, we first review the differences in these types of data and then discuss when and how to collect data to achieve specific screening, progress monitoring, and evaluation goals. In subsequent chapters of this section, we refer back to this chapter when discussing the pros and cons of each SSA approach for meeting specific assessment goals.

TYPES OF DATA

A variety of data types can be collected through an assessment—whether it be an assessment for screening, progress monitoring, or evaluation. The first step in the assessment process is to select the type of data to be collected. **Table 1** displays various types that are relevant to social, emotional, and behavioral assessment.

Table 1

Data type	What's measured?	What's your goal?	Criterion for success?
Social literacy	Knowledge and comprehension	Increase understanding of subject matter	Demonstrate acquired learning in subject area
Social performance	Capacity to act prosocially	Increase social skills and self-efficacy	Demonstrate improved skills and confidence
Social adjustment	Social, emotional and behavioral outcomes	Increase prosocial behavior; decrease emotional and behavioral problems	Demonstrate improved social, emotional and behavioral functioning in real world

Social Literacy

Social literacy refers to the child's knowledge and understanding of particular social skills, such as impulse control or communication. In other words, does the child understand what these terms mean, why they're important, when you need to use them, how they impact social relations, and other dimensions of social skills comprehension? A social literacy assessment is similar to an academic assessment in which the child responds to questions in order to demonstrate he understands the subject matter being taught.

So, literacy assessments are cognitive in nature, reflecting the child's level of intellectual understanding of social skills or social relationships, regardless of whether she can actually demonstrate these social skills. For example, on a questionnaire or in an interview, a child may be able to correctly define what impulse control is and how to use it, but then may impulsively react when put into a difficult social situation, such as being teased. Similarly, a child may understand cognitively what it means to communicate and what he's supposed to do to communicate clearly, but when put into an anxiety-provoking situation, he freezes and can't speak. Understanding is essential, but not sufficient, for performance.

Social Performance

If you want to measure social performance, you'll need to assess whether a child can actually perform social skills. There are two interrelated components to social performance: your ability to use social skills effectively and appropriately in social situations AND your self-efficacy or confidence in your ability to perform the social skill or behavior. If you know what to do in a social situation, but you don't believe in yourself, you're not likely to actually implement those social skills. Conversely, if you believe you can handle any social situation, but you don't have the requisite social skills, you won't be very successful. Both of these components are vital for social performance.

Interventions that provide children with opportunities to practice applying social skills in different situations improve not only social literacy, but also social performance. As the child gains experience applying a social skill and receives feedback on her performance, her ability to perform that skill increases, along with her belief that she can be successful. As with academic subjects, repeated practice improves and refines social skills. It also decreases performance anxiety, which can prevent children from demonstrating the skills they know.

To assess social performance, you could ask those who routinely interact with the child to report on her social abilities or use of particular social skills. For example, a teacher could rate the frequency with which the child 'says please and thank you,' on a scale from almost never to almost always. Alternatively, you could present the child with particular social situations—say, joining a group of peers, dealing with teasing, cooperating on a project— and assess her ability to engage in social problem solving to apply social skills successfully. These social situations can be presented as hypothetical scenarios, structured role plays, or virtual simulations. The child could also be observed within unstructured real-life settings, such as playing on the playground or working with peers in the classroom. To collect information regarding the child's self-efficacy for performing social tasks, you can ask the child directly or ask the opinion of adults who observe the child on a regular basis.

Social Adjustment

Just as academic literacy and performance foster real-life consequences, there are real-life consequences of social literacy and performance. If a child is knowledgeable in academic subjects and able to demonstrate these skills in class, he's more likely to be engaged in school, be promoted to the next grade level, and graduate from high school. Similarly, if a child is knowledgeable in social skills and able to apply those skills in everyday life, he's more likely to have high quality relationships with others, experience fewer negative social interactions, and exhibit more positive emotional and behavioral adjustment.

Therefore, you may wish to collect data that measure the child's social, emotional, and behavioral adjustment in areas that we know are directly related to social skills. As discussed in Chapter 3, poor social skills interfere with adjustment across a wide array of areas, including increased risk for: (1) problematic behaviors, such as classroom disruptiveness, getting into fights, and immaturity; (2) peer relationship problems, including peer rejection, social isolation, and being a bully or being victimized by a bully; and (3) emotional difficulties, such as social anxiety, low self-esteem, and depression.

We would expect that children who exhibit these adjustment problems would also demonstrate significant deficits in their social skills, and vice versa. We would also expect that, as children gain in their understanding and application of social skills through participation in a social intervention, their social, emotional, and behavioral adjustment would also improve. In order to assess children's adjustment in these areas, you first need to select the specific outcome or outcomes of interest and then select one or more measures with documented validity and reliability. While there are a wide array of assessment methods, they typically include reports by those who regularly observe the child as well as child self-report measures. These measures often assess the frequency with which the child exhibits specific behaviors—such as the number of times the child has been in an argument over the past month—or the degree to which the child experiences specific problems—such as 'gets left out of games or activities by other kids' on a scale from *not true for this child to very true for this child*. As a general rule of thumb, child self-report is typically more reliable and valid for assessing internalizing or emotional difficulties, whereas outside reports, such as those from parents or teachers, are generally more reliable and valid for assessing externalizing behavior problems.[2-4] This is because externalizing behaviors are usually overt and easily observable compared to internal feelings and thoughts that the child may or may not confide to others. Self-, parent-, and teacher-report of peer relationship problems vary in their usefulness—children may under-report their social difficulties and often teachers and parents are unaware of peer problems. Collecting data directly from the child's peers has been found to be the most reliable and valid assessment tool for social problems with peers, particularly peer rejection and victimization.[5-6]

> **Child self-report** is typically more reliable and valid for assessing **internalizing** problems whereas **outside reports**, such as those from parents or teachers, are generally more reliable and valid for assessing **externalizing** problems.

THREE TYPES OF ASSESSMENT

The primary purpose of SSA is to guide the intervention planning process. SSA data drive decisions about who receives social intervention, when the intervention has achieved specified goals, and when the intervention strategy needs to be revised for a given child. Data collected through SSA can serve three distinct intervention planning purposes. **Table 2** summarizes key similarities and differences across these three different types of assessment. While each type has a specific purpose, they should not be viewed as isolated from one another, but rather interdependent and essential components of solid, data-informed, social, emotional, and behavioral intervention planning.

Table 2

	Screening	Progress Monitoring	Evaluation
Goal	Identify children in need of social, emotional, or behavioral intervention	Ensure progress is being made as a function of participating in the intervention	Ensure outcomes are being achieved as a function of participating in the intervention
Comparison	To external norm	Within intervention group or individual child	Within individual child
Target	Specific skill(s) or outcome(s)	Specific skill(s) or behavioral target(s)	Specific outcome(s)
Timepoints	Infrequent, periodic	1 or more times during intervention	Pre → post → follow-up
Times	Prior to invention	During intervention	Before and after intervention
Use of data	As a first step in intervention planning	To continue or revise intervention plan	To inform future intervention planning

Screening

The primary purpose of a screening assessment is to identify children for intervention. You may have a particular intervention for which you want to select children for participation. This would be a **targeted screening**. For example, if you want to implement a friendship group, you'd target your screening to identify those children who have few friends; if you want to implement an anger management group, you'd target your screening to identify those children with poor emotion regulation skills, and so on.

On the other hand, you may want to conduct a **general screening** where your intent is to assess the relative strengths and weaknesses among children in a large group, such as across a grade or school, for the purpose of determining which intervention or interventions are needed. For example, if you assessed the social skills of 4th graders and discovered many of the children struggled with communication skills, you could then select a classroom level intervention that specifically addressed this need.

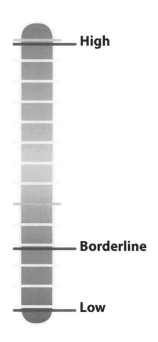

For either of these types of screening assessments, what you're looking for are children who exhibit particular skill or performance weaknesses compared to their peers. In order to identify children with particular weaknesses, you must be able to compare how well a given child scores relative to how well his peers score. In other words, your screening tool must be able to estimate the position of each child compared to some norm-reference group. This comparison group could be a **local norm**. An example of this would be administering a measure to all students in a grade, rank ordering their scores from lowest to highest, and then selecting the students who scored in the lowest 15th percentile.

Alternatively, you can use a screening instrument that compares an individual's score to a **national or population-based norm**. These norms are established by the assessment developer who administers the instrument to a large representative sample of children—say 500 12-year old boys and girls across the country—and conducts a series of psychometric tests to determine cut-offs for high, medium, and low performance across this sample.[7] Then, once established, these cut-offs can be used to compare a given child's score with those of children in this independent, population-based group.

The advantage of using a screening tool with population-based norms is that you can establish one child's intervention needs without having to assess all children across a local comparison group. The advantage of using a screening tool with local norms is that you can see how the child performs compared to peers in his immediate social context. The parallel in the academic assessment world would be looking at a child's grades in a class vs. scores on a standardized assessment. Each approach has its own strengths and weaknesses for providing information about a given child.

For example, imagine a child demonstrates poor impulse control compared to a national sample of same-aged children, but also scores at an average level compared to peers in his grade at school. What would this mean for intervention planning? The population-based score suggests he should participate in an intervention to improve his impulse control. However, his immediate peers are also struggling with impulse control, many even more so. So, wouldn't it be better for the school to implement a universal intervention to increase impulse control across the entire grade? When selecting a screening instrument, it's helpful to consider which will provide the most relevant information for intervention planning and to then select the one with norms that will be most informative for your particular situation.

Screening is the starting point for intervention. Therefore, it occurs before intervention begins and is typically administered only as needed. In the school setting, you may want to screen all children at the beginning of a new school year to help you plan what interventions you'll administer that year. Or, you may administer a screening when a particular problem arises for a child or for a group of children. For example, if bullying behaviors escalate, you may want to administer a screening to identify those children who are behaving like bullies so you can intervene with them.

Progress Monitoring

The goal of progress monitoring is to ensure that a child is benefiting from intervention at an appropriate rate over the course of intervention. Progress monitoring tracks a child's progress as she participates in the intervention. If a child is benefiting, we would expect to see incremental improvement in the areas targeted by the intervention over time. If, however, the child is not benefiting or even getting worse, we would see a neutral or negative trend over time. For example, in **Figure 2**, TJ and Sally each show positive growth in their ability to perform social skills as they participate in the intervention. In contrast, Johnny really isn't improving significantly and Vonnie actually

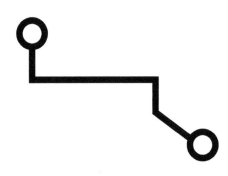

seems to be performing more poorly over time. Rather than wait until the end of an intervention to see whether or not it worked, progress monitoring enables you to revise your intervention plan mid-course if it looks like a child is not benefiting. This way, you can be more responsive to the child's needs and more likely to achieve targeted social goals for that child. In the Figure 2 example, the goal may be for each child to achieve a score of 4 by intervention

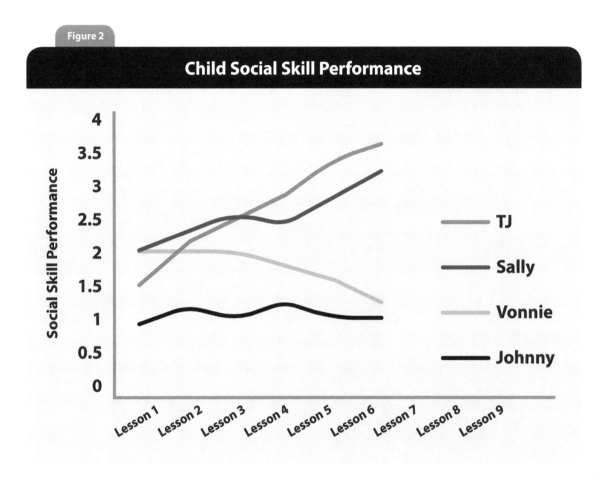

end, so it's clear that Sally and TJ are likely to achieve this benchmark with continued intervention. However, Vonnie and Johnny are not progressing well, and may need another kind of intervention to be successful. Given that data must be collected repeatedly over the course of an intervention, it's important that progress monitoring assessments be brief. We suggest no more than 10 questions. For example, if a child participates in an intervention on a weekly basis, then progress monitoring data will be collected on a weekly basis as well. If these assessments are too long, it will not be feasible for an intervention provider to routinely complete them, especially if that provider must report on multiple children in an intervention.

Because data for progress monitoring is collected frequently and over short periods of time, the assessment instrument must be sensitive to small increments of growth and directly related to what the child is learning and practicing in the intervention. Further, because these assessments need to be targeted to a particular intervention, they are typically customized to that intervention, rather than being general-use questionnaires. Appropriate data for progress monitoring include targeted social literacy and social performance assessments. Assessment of broad or major social milestones—such as significantly improved social self-esteem, lower peer victimization, or greater social maturity—should be the focus of evaluation, not progress monitoring.

Monitoring of children's progress as a function of social intervention can include the following two types of assessment, **Social Literacy Probes** and **Social Performance Checks**.

<u>Social literacy probes</u> are curriculum-based assessment items that evaluate a child's understanding of the subject matter taught during a specific lesson. These probes will therefore be different for each lesson. For example, if Lesson 3 of Intervention 'X' teaches impulse control, then progress monitoring questions of social literacy for that lesson should focus specifically on the child's understanding of impulse control. These questions are typically asked directly to the child, either in written or verbal form. Here are examples of social literacy probes for impulse control:

> Though self-efficacy is an integral part of social performance, you would not expect self-efficacy to change substantially from week to week. Therefore, it's appropriate to measure pre- and post-intervention self-efficacy as part of an evaluation assessment, rather than as part of progress monitoring.

- **Multiple-choice example**: If you stop and think before you do or say something, you are being… (a) smart, (b) responsible, (c) concerned, (d) scared.
- **Interview example**: Alec was explaining to a friend how he had done so well on a test. He told his friend that he read each question twice so he was sure he understood the question before he tried to answer it. Is this a good example of impulse control? (Answer—yes, because he took time to think about what the question was really asking before responding.)

<u>Social performance checks</u> are application-focused items that determine the degree to which the child can effectively and appropriately use the social skills being taught through the intervention. So, if the intervention is designed to increase communication, cooperation, and impulse control, these checks would assess the frequency with which the child exhibits good social skills in these areas. Unlike social literacy probes, social performance checks will

be the same questions completed repeatedly throughout the intervention. They could be completed immediately following each lesson, for instance. Social performance checks are commonly completed by the intervention provider, so it's important that questions target specific high-frequency social behaviors that the provider has the opportunity to witness during intervention lessons or in real-life situations with the child. For example, the teacher could report on the frequency with which the child used appropriate tone of voice (communication skill), shared things and was helpful in a group (cooperation), and had difficulty waiting for her turn (impulse control) over the past week.

It's important that the data produced through progress monitoring be easily summarized, so the intervention provider can quickly see whether progress is being made. Data from probes and checks can be summarized as percentages, so that findings for a child are comparable across weeks as well as across students. For example, if a child responds correctly to 3 out of 5 social literacy probes, then his percent correct is 60%. Similarly, if a child is able to demonstrate appropriate social skills most of the time for 3 out of 5 social performance checks, then his demonstrated level of social performance is 60%. Employing comparable statistics like these also enables intervention providers to set targeted social goals for individual children, such as *"Sally is expected to demonstrate appropriate social skills 80% of the time by intervention end."*

In summary, progress monitoring is conducted to provide data that can answer two questions:

1. Is the child making progress towards mastery of targeted social skills? and
2. Is the child making progress as a function of social intervention as expected?

Evaluation

The goal of an evaluation assessment is to establish the extent to which targeted outcomes change in response to the implementation of an intervention. Often, there are specific areas of concern that drive the decision to implement an intervention. For example, if bullying is a particular problem in your school, you're going to select an intervention which, based on past research on that intervention, you expect will result in lower incidents of

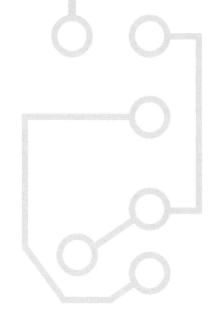

bullying among children who receive it. Similarly, if you want to decrease classroom disruptiveness and improve school engagement, you'll select an intervention that has documented evidence of positive results in these areas.

Published research studies can show that an intervention produces significant improvement for particular outcomes, yet because these studies look at aggregate differences across groups of children, the results do not tell us anything about how an individual child will be affected by an intervention. We know that there are individual differences in children's responsiveness to any intervention; some children respond as expected and others do not, for various reasons. So we can't assume that a given child will react favorably to an intervention—we have to actually collect data to evaluate its effectiveness. This is why evaluation assessments are essential. You need to document whether significant change in your targeted outcome(s) occurs with an individual child over time as a function of his participating in the intervention.

Setting-up an evaluation. You've identified children who exhibit particular social skill deficits or problematic behaviors or who are at risk for serious problems like depression, peer victimization, or academic failure. Then, you've selected an intervention that is intended to ameliorate or improve these targeted outcomes of concern. Now, it's time to set up your evaluation.

You need to first define your specific outcomes of concern by answering the following set of questions:

- What specific outcomes do I expect to change?
- When do I expect these changes to be noticeable?
- How will I know that significant change has occurred?

Table 3 displays some possible outcomes that could be targeted through social intervention. Of course, when you select an intervention, you typically have a particular outcome or outcomes in mind. However, social interventions often impact more than one outcome, so you might wish to include assessment of several related outcomes in the same evaluation. For example, a bully prevention program would be expected to lower bullying behavior among children, but given the negative impact of bullying on school engagement, you may also expect to observe improvements in classroom disruptiveness and absenteeism.

Table 3

Proximal		Outcomes		Distal
Social Skills	**Social Behaviors**	**Peer Relations**	**Emotional Difficulties**	**Academic Performance**
• Cooperation	• Disruptiveness	• Peer rejection	• Low self-esteem	• Absenteeism
• Communication (verbal & non-verbal)	• Fighting	• Social isolation	• Social anxiety	• Low school engagement
• Emotion regulation	• Immaturity	• Bullying	• Depression	• Low academic motivation
• Empathy	• Oddness, awkwardness	• Victimization	• Suicidality	• Low grades
• Impulse control	• Risky behaviors	• Friendship quality	• Substance use	• Low test scores
• Initiation	• Delinquency		• Low anger control	
• Social self-efficacy	• Withdrawal			

In order to determine whether significant benefits of intervention are present for a child, you would collect the *same* outcome measure both before and after he participates in the intervention. By using the same measure across two timepoints—pre- to post-intervention—you can examine the difference between these two scores to determine the direction and magnitude of change in that outcome. (If you use different measures at the different timepoints, the scores will not be comparable.) For example, if a child scored in the 25th percentile on a questionnaire assessing communication at pre-intervention, and then scored at the 65th percentile on this same measure following intervention, he clearly showed significant improvement in his communication skills in response to intervention.

When choosing outcomes to evaluate, it's also important to consider the timing of your assessments. Specifically, when should the post-intervention data be collected? In Table 3, outcomes are listed on a continuum from proximal to distal, indicating how quickly you would be likely to notice change in these outcomes for children in response to intervention. On the proximal end of the scale are social skills and social behaviors that are often directly targeted during social intervention, so you would expect to see changes in these outcomes relatively quickly. On the other end of the scale are more distal or long-term outcomes; changes in these will be slower to emerge because of their more complex, multi-faceted nature.

Take, for example, a child who participates in a social skills intervention. She learns and practices new prosocial skills, so that when the program is completed she possesses better social literacy, social behaviors, and social self-efficacy. Now, it's time for her to put these newly acquired social skills into practice within real-life settings with peers. Unfortunately, however, group dynamics are more resistant to change. When a child has previously demonstrated socially unacceptable behaviors, her peers come to expect negative behavior from her. When she behaves positively, her efforts are likely to be rebuffed by peers—at least at first.[8-11] The child must keep at it, continuing her prosocial attempts until this negative reputational bias within the peer group is worn down. Thus, an effective social intervention may not immediately show significant benefits for more distal outcomes. It takes time—sometimes months or even longer—for positive changes in children's social skills and social behavior to transform into improvements in peer relations as well as emotional and academic benefits.[12-14] This is exactly what was found in a study by the book's editor. Children showed better social skills, higher self-efficacy, and more prosocial behavior immediately following intervention, but it took a year for a significant reduction in peer victimization to emerge.

Therefore, you should schedule your evaluation assessments at intervals that provide a reasonable amount of time for change to be evident. For proximal outcomes, an immediate post-intervention assessment should be appropriate. For more distal outcomes, there should be a longer interval before the follow-up assessment.

Once you've decided on your outcomes of interest and the timepoints for assessment, you next need to determine how you're going to assess these outcomes. The following set of questions will help guide your selection of assessment methods:

- What are the most *reliable* and *valid* ways to collect these data?
- What assessment methods are *feasible* and *doable*?
- *Who* will provide these data?
- *How* will I collect these data?

Helping you answer these questions is the focus of the next several chapters.

SUMMARY

In summary, an effective assessment accomplishes three main objectives which guide the intervention planning process to best meet the needs of individual children:

1. To identify children who are at risk for or are experiencing difficulties and who may need extra instruction or intervention in order to progress.

2. To monitor progress during intervention to determine whether children are making adequate improvement in critical social skills and to identify any children who may be falling behind or are not benefiting from intervention.

3. To evaluate whether the intervention provided is effective for achieving targeted outcomes of concern.

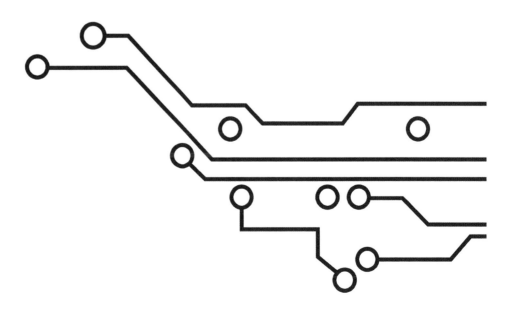

CHAPTER 4 NOTES

1. Erdley, C. A., Nangle, D. W., Burns, A. M., Holleb, L. J., & Kaye, A. J. (2010). Assessing children and adolescents. In D. W. Nangle, D. J. Hansen, C. A. Erdley, & P. J. Norton (Eds.), *Practitioner's guide to empirically-based measures of social skills* (pp. 69-86). New York, NY: Springer.

2. Achenbach, T. M., McConaughy, S. H., & Howell, C. T. (1987). Child/adolescent behavioral and emotional problems: Implications of cross-informant correlation for situational specificity. *Psychological Bulletin, 101,* 213-232.

3. March, J. S., Parker, J. D. A., Sullivan, K., & Stallings, P. (1997). The Multidimensional Anxiety Scale for Children (MASC): Factor structure, reliability, and validity. *Journal of the American Academy of Child and Adolescent Psychiatry, 36,* 554-565.

4. Rey, J. M., Schrader, E., & Morris-Yates, A. (1992). Parent-child agreement on children's behaviours reported by the Child Behavior Checklist (CBCL). *Journal of Adolescence, 15,* 219-230.

5. Cillessen, A. H. N., & Marks, P. E. L. (2011). Conceptualizing and measuring popularity. In A. H. N. Cillessen, D. Schwartz, & L. Mayeux (Eds.), *Popularity in the peer system* (pp. 25-56). New York, NY: Guilford Press.

6. Cillessen, A. H. N., & Mayeux, L. (2004). From censure to reinforcement: Developmental changes in the association between aggression and social status. *Child Development, 75,* 147-163.

7. DeVellis, R. F. (2003). *Scale development: Theory and applications* (2nd ed.). Thousand Oaks, CA: Sage Publications.

8. Hymel. S., Wagner, E., & Butler, L. J. (1990). Reputational bias: View from the peer group. In S. R. Asher & J. D. Coie (Eds.), *Peer rejection in childhood* (pp. 156-188). New York, NY: Cambridge University Press.

9. Mikami, A. Y., Lerner, M. D., & Lun, J. (2010). Social context influences on children's rejection by their peers. *Child Development Perspectives, 4,* 123-130.

10. Dodge, K. A., Coie, J. D., & Brakke, N. P. (1982). Behavior patterns of socially rejected and neglected preadolescents: The roles of social approach and aggression. *Journal of Abnormal Child Psychology, 10,* 389-410.

11. Crick, N. R., & Dodge, K. A. (1994). A review and reformulation of social information-processing mechanisms in children's social adjustment. *Psychological Bulletin, 115,* 74-101.

12. DeRosier, M. E. (2004). Building relationships and combating bullying: Effectiveness of a school-based social skills group intervention. *Journal of Clinical Child and Adolescent Psychology, 33,* 125-130.

13. DeRosier, M. E., & Marcus, S. R. (2005). Building friendships and combating bullying: Effectiveness of S.S.GRIN at one-year follow-up. *Journal of Clinical Child and Adolescent Psychology, 34,* 140-150.

14. Harrell, A., Mercer, S., & DeRosier, M. E. (2009). Improving the social-behavioral adjustment of adolescents: The effectiveness of a social skills group intervention. *Journal of Child and Family Studies, 18,* 378-387.

5

Guidelines for Evaluating SSA Options

by: Melissa E. DeRosier, Ph.D.

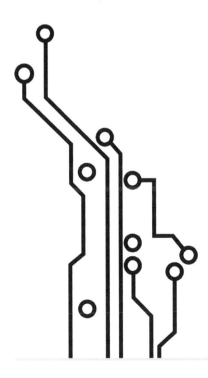

DESCRIPTION

Once you've decided on your goals for social skills assessment (SSA) and your timepoints for collecting data, you need to determine what method or methods you're going to use to collect these data. Traditional options for social skills assessment (SSA) include: (1) behavioral rating scale questionnaires, (2) behavioral observations of the child, (3) peer nominations, and (4) an interview with the child.[1-4] Unfortunately, there's no clear winner among these options—each offers its own set of strengths and weaknesses. What you must do is weigh these options to determine which will best meet your SSA needs. In this chapter, we provide some structure for weighing these options. We define a set of four areas that are relevant to SSA selection and then introduce the rating scale that we apply in the coming chapters to each SSA approach.

CRITERIA FOR SELECTION

To help you in the evaluation process, the next several chapters review traditional SSA options in terms of both practical considerations and factors influencing data quality. For each SSA method, we'll help you answer the following questions:

- **Feasibility to administer**—How feasible and doable is it for me to administer this SSA method within my time, financial, and staffing constraints?

  » **Training/expertise needed**—How much training or expertise is required to administer this SSA method with children? Who provides the data about the child?

  » **Time efficiency**—How much time does it take to collect data?

  » **Cost effectiveness**—What is the cost of data collection for each child?

- **Utility of data**—How useful and meaningful will the collected data be for informing my intervention planning?

  » **Psychometrically sound**—Is there documented evidence of this SSA method's validity and reliability?

  » **Norm-based cut-offs**—Will the results be easy to interpret? Will the data tell me how well the child performs relative to her peers?

  » **Contextually relevant**—Will the results correspond to specific real world social situations?

- **Accuracy of data**—Is this SSA method likely to provide unbiased and accurate data about this child?

  » **Measurement**—Is the SSA method administered in a standardized, consistent way across children? Are scores generated according to clearly and consistently defined parameters?

  » **Respondent bias**—To what degree can a child's scores be influenced by biases on the part of the respondent (the reporter of information about the child)?

  » **Accuracy checks**—Is there a way to estimate how valid and accurate the results are for a child?

An additional factor to weigh is the degree to which an SSA method is **engaging for children**. If the child is the respondent, both the feasibility of administration and the quality of data generated can be impacted by his engagement in the assessment process.[5-7] For example, it may be difficult to elicit responses from an uninterested, unmotivated child, so you may get only limited data and the validity of those data may be questionable. In contrast, an engaged child will be more willing to respond and to provide more accurate and truthful data.

In the following chapters we examine the ways that different SSA options address each of the above areas. In addition to discussing an SSA method's relative pros and cons, we provide ratings for each area using the scale presented here.

Chapter 16 provides a summary table so you can easily compare ratings in each area across traditional and game-based SSA methods.

Selecting an assessment method can be difficult because none of the traditional SSA options offer both high feasibility and high-quality data. Often, getting the best data involves time-consuming, sophisticated methods that may not be possible in everyday practice in schools or healthcare settings. You'll need to find the optimal balance for your situation. You'll want to select the SSA method(s) that will result in the most meaningful and useful data for your intervention planning purposes and that will fit within your staffing, time, and financial constraints.

Rating Legend

- = Very good in this area
- = Generally good
- = Generally fair
- = Generally poor
- = Very poor in this area

CHAPTER 5 NOTES

1. Christ, T. J., Riley-Tillman, T. C., Chafouleas, S., & Jaffery, R. (2011). Direct behavior rating: An evaluation of alternative definitions to assess classroom behaviors. *School Psychology Review, 40,* 181-199.

2. Crowe, L. M., Beauchamp, M. H., Catroppa, C., & Anderson, V. (2011). Social function assessment tools for children and adolescents: A systematic review from 1988 to 2010. *Clinical Psychology Review, 31,* 767-785.

3. Jiang, X. L., & Cillessen, A. H. N. (2005). Stability of continuous measures of sociometric status: a meta-analysis. *Developmental Review, 25,* 1-25.

4. Matson, J. L., & Wilkins, J. (2009). Psychometric testing methods for children's social skills. *Research in Developmental Disabilities, 30,* 249-274.

5. Enzmann, D. (2013). The impact of questionnaire design on prevalence and incidence rates of self-reported delinquency: Results of an experiment modifying the ISRD-2 questionnaire. *Journal of Contemporary Criminal Justice, 29,* 147-177.

6. Casas, F., González, M., Navarro, D., & Aligué , M. (2013). Children as advisors of their researchers: Assuming a different status for children. *Child Indicators Research, 6 (2),* 193-212.

7. Christian, B. J., Pearce, P. F., Roberson, A. J., & Rothwell, E. (2010). It's a small, small world: Data collection strategies for research with children and adolescents. *Journal of Pediatric Nursing, 25,* 202-214.

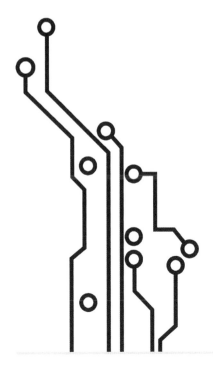

USING BEHAVIORAL RATING SCALES FOR SSA

by: Melissa E. DeRosier, Ph.D.

DESCRIPTION

The most common approach to assessing children's social skills is the behavioral rating scale. These questionnaires present a series of statements designed to assess the child's social functioning in one or more areas. Whoever is completing the questionnaire (the 'respondent'), rates each statement on a defined scale to indicate the degree to which that statement is true for the child of interest.

Responses are made on what is called an 'ordinal' scale because the choices reflect increasing or decreasing order. The number of response choices can vary from just two (a dichotomous scale) to several (typically no more than seven choices). Here are some examples:

- 0=false, 1=true
- 1=never true, 2=sometimes true, 3=very often true
- 1=every day, 2=several times per week, 3=a couple times per week, 4=no more than once per week, 5=never

The areas assessed through these questionnaires can include specific **social behaviors** (hits others, says please

Please think about your relationship with your child and their social and emotional behavior. After reading each item below, please circle the number that corresponds to the scale below. Circle "0" if the item is not at all true of your child. Circle "3" if the item is very true of your child. Be sure to answer all items.

0	1	2	3
Not at all true	A little bit true	Somewhat true	Very true

1. Gets angry easily.	0 1 2 3		26. Plays well with others.	0 1 2 3
2. Often feels sad.	0 1 2 3		27. Threatens or bullies others.	0 1 2 3
3. Has difficulty expressing emotion.	0 1 2 3		28. Expresses positive emotion appropriately.	0 1 2 3
4. Has difficulty regulating emotion.	0 1 2 3		29. Behaves impulsively or irrationally.	0 1 2 3
5. Is generally a happy child.	0 1 2 3		30. Interrupts others.	0 1 2 3
6. Expresses positive emotion often.	0 1 2 3		31. Inappropriately express negative emotion.	0 1 2 3
7. Expresses negative emotion often.	0 1 2 3		32. Tries to get revenge when feels wronged.	0 1 2 3
8. Cries a lot.	0 1 2 3		33. Has feelings hurt easily.	0 1 2 3
9. Understands others' emotions.	0 1 2 3		34. Has mood swings.	0 1 2 3
10. Expresses sympathy for others.	0 1 2 3		35. Is comfortable interacting with others in groups.	0 1 2 3
11. Has difficulty getting along with other children.	0 1 2 3		36. Has difficulty maintaining attention.	0 1 2 3
12. Gets in fights with others.	0 1 2 3		37. Is easily excitable.	0 1 2 3
13. Is well-liked by peers.	0 1 2 3		38. Assumes the worst of others.	0 1 2 3
14. Gets in trouble at school.	0 1 2 3		39. Is easily embarrassed.	0 1 2 3
15. Makes friends easily.	0 1 2 3		40. Feels depressed.	0 1 2 3
16. Loses temper during conflict.	0 1 2 3		41. Expresses empathy.	0 1 2 3
17. Teases others.	0 1 2 3		42. Gets easily upset.	0 1 2 3
18. Remains calm during disagreements.	0 1 2 3		43. Behaves aggressively during disagreements or arguments.	0 1 2 3
19. Is lonely.	0 1 2 3		44. Easily frustrated.	0 1 2 3
20. Appears anxious in groups.	0 1 2 3		45. Invites friends to play.	0 1 2 3
21. Is easily frustrated.	0 1 2 3		46. Hits or hurts others.	0 1 2 3
22. Does not express emotion.	0 1 2 3		47. Is disruptive at school.	0 1 2 3
23. Can talk clearly about emotions.	0 1 2 3		48. Has difficulty fitting in with peers.	0 1 2 3
24. Responds positively to criticism.	0 1 2 3		49. Does not maintain friendships.	0 1 2 3
25. Cares about others' feelings.	0 1 2 3		50. Laughs often.	0 1 2 3

Please describe any other concerns you may have about your child's social or emotional behavior.

_____

_____

_____

or thank you, talks with his mouth full), specific **social tasks** (cooperates with other kids, communicates clearly, helps others who look upset), or more general areas of **social adjustment** (gets along well with same-age peers, is often left out of play by peers, gets picked on or teased by peers). Typically, rating scales include groups of items intended to assess the child's functioning for a particular social behavior, task, or adjustment area. For example, if a questionnaire includes a scale designed to assess impulse control, the respondent may be asked to rate the degree to which the child is restless in class, speaks out of turn, gets into arguments, and other items that, together, are expected to measure impulse control. The scores for these individual items would be combined into one composite impulse control scale score. By not relying on just one or two questions, the resulting scale score should be a more reliable reflection of the child's social functioning in that target area. These scale scores can be simple sums or averages across items or standardized scores—such as t-scores, percentile ranks, stanines—that reflect how the child's score compares to the set of scores obtained from an independent reference group, say a national sample of 500 12-year old boys.[1]

Respondents

Rating scales can be completed by anyone who regularly observes the child's social behavior and interactions, including parents, teachers, or the child himself. Many well-established rating scale measures include parallel forms for these different respondents. In general, you want to collect data from someone who is close to the child and has many opportunities to observe and interact with him in a variety of settings. The closer the relationship, the more likely that scores will reflect a true picture of the child's social functioning. However, as discussed below, each respondent carries a set of possible biases that can skew their scores. For this reason, if you're relying on a behavioral rating scale for your SSA, it's advisable to have more than one respondent complete the questionnaire so you can compare and contrast different views of the child. Unfortunately though, no clear guidelines are available to help you combine this information in a meaningful way or to guide you when discrepancies across respondents are evident. At that point, you just need to make your best judgment.

Developmental Considerations

It's essential that the rating scale questionnaire be specifically designed for children in your target age group. As discussed in earlier chapters, social behavior and social relationships change dramatically throughout the elementary, middle, and high school years. The questions included in the measure need to ask about social interactions relevant to the target age group—asking about romantic relationships for a kindergartner is premature, hopefully—and the resulting data needs to be interpretable relative to other children of the same age. For example, physical aggression, crying, help-seeking, and many other behaviors fluctuate greatly with development. The data resulting from your questionnaire needs to take into account the typical level or frequency of these behaviors for children of the same age, so you can judge whether the child you're assessing scores outside a normative developmental range (lower or higher than expected).

In addition to developmentally relevant content, the way the questionnaire is designed must be developmentally appropriate when children serve as respondents.[2-4] The format, structure, and presentation of information—how questions are worded, how items are laid out on the page, and how children indicate their response choice, for instance—must take development into account. For example, literacy and reading comprehension levels can vary widely even among children of the same age. Reading difficulties are common across many areas, including vocabulary, fluency, and comprehension, particularly for children with learning disabilities.[5-8] A child's ability to respond to questions, and the quality of those responses, will be negatively impacted if the literacy demands of a questionnaire are too high. Children also tend to have more limited attention spans and lower motivation to answer questions compared to older respondents.[4] Say, for example, you want to administer a rating scale that presents multiple questions one after the other down the page—a typical format for many questionnaires. Adolescents and adults are likely to be able to easily complete this questionnaire, but younger children may find the format visually distracting and overwhelming. They may struggle to stay focused and on task, which undermines their ability and motivation to complete the questionnaire. To get high quality data with children—high response rates, thoughtful responses, accurate information—developmental considerations must be embedded into the layout and design of the questionnaire.[5-7] Therefore, when selecting your rating scale measure, make sure it's been shown—through research—to be appropriate and usable for children in your target age group.

Rating Legend

 = Very good in this area

 = Generally good

○ = Generally fair

◑ = Generally poor

● = Very poor in this area

STRENGTHS AND WEAKNESSES

In the following review of the relative strengths and weaknesses of using behavioral rating scales for SSA, we discuss how feasible this approach is to administer, the quality of the resulting data (its usefulness and accuracy), and how engaged child respondents are likely to be. To help guide our discussion, we provide summary ratings in each area and then present our reasons behind these ratings. At the end of this discussion, we also provide overall ratings to summarize how effective we believe behavioral rating scales are for accomplishing intervention screening, progress monitoring, and evaluation functions (see Chapter 4). These ratings are purely our best judgments based on available evidence.

Feasibility of Administration

Of all possible SSA methods, behavioral rating scales are the most commonly used.[9] In large part, this popularity reflects their relative low cost, the low training requirements for administrators, and their time-efficient administration. Typically, no particular training or expertise is needed to administer or complete a questionnaire. There are some exceptions to this rule, such as the Child Behavior Checklist[10] (CBCL), which can only be purchased (and thereby used) by a trained professional with a relevant Master's or doctoral degree. Directions for administering, scoring, and interpreting data from behavioral rating scales are generally provided to administrators in a written manual of some type. At the beginning of each questionnaire, written instructions are provided that guide the respondent. Because this SSA method presents text-based questions, there is a literacy demand on respondents, but it's typically acceptable for the person conducting the SSA to read questions aloud if needed, so literacy is not necessarily a barrier to collecting data.

Ratings of Behavioral Rating Scale SSA

Feasible to administer

Training/expertise needed

Time efficiency

Cost effectiveness

Behavioral rating scales are very time efficient. You can collect a great deal of data quickly. It takes approximately 1-2 minutes per question for children to complete items, with less time needed for older respondents. The number of items for a given questionnaire can vary greatly, with the more reliable and valid measures often including 30 or more questions. For example, the Social Skills Improvement System[11] (SSIS) includes 79 items to assess 10 social skill and social behavior scales within one questionnaire. Behavioral rating scales are also an efficient way to collect data about many children at once, particularly if they can complete the questionnaire independently.

The cost per child to collect rating scale data also tends to be quite low. Some well-established measures, such as the Loneliness and Social Dissatisfaction Questionnaire,[12] can be used free of charge. However, free measures don't typically include software to assist in data collection or interpretation, so they need to be administered and scored by hand, which increases time costs to the administrator. Even the more expensive instruments, such as the CBCL or SSIS, are cost effective. An initial $500 or so would be needed to purchase all necessary professional materials and scoring software. The data collection forms then cost about $2 per respondent plus the cost of the time needed for data entry and printing the report of results.

Utility of Data

The utility of the data from behavioral rating scales can vary widely. Some yield very useful data that can definitely be used to inform intervention planning, while others have no evidence supporting their use. Because questionnaires are so easy to find and use, it's very important to make sure your questionnaire(s) have strong scientific backing. The measure needs to have documented **evidence** supporting its validity and reliability ("psychometrics"). Validity means that you can trust that the questionnaire actually measures what it claims to measure. Reliability means that it measures something consistently so findings are comparable over time and across people. If a rating scale has not been tested with children in the target age group, it's impossible to know how valid or reliable the collected data will be. Currently, a number of psychometrically sound rating scale questionnaires can be used to inform intervention planning for children (see examples below).

Ratings of Behavioral Rating Scale SSA

- Utility of data
- Psychometrically sound
- Norm-based cut-offs
- Contextually relevant

Another dimension of utility is whether the data resulting from the rating scale can tell you anything about how this child ranks compared to similar peers. Many psychometrically sound questionnaires provide useful information on how a child is functioning in a given area. For example, on a loneliness questionnaire where items are rated from 1=*never true for this child* to 5=*always true for this child*, a scale score of 4 would tell us clearly that this child is experiencing a high level of loneliness at school. However, few rating scales enable you to also gauge how this score compares to what we would expect to find for other children the same age. Being able to easily see if a child's score is similar, worse, or better than his peers is very useful for intervention planning purposes. In order to do this, the rating scale must provide cut-offs based on norm-referenced estimates that clearly indicate where a child ranks relative to his peers (see Chapter 4).

A third aspect of utility is contextual relevance; that is, the degree to which data from a rating scale measure is likely to correspond to a child's real-world social experiences. Social behaviors are not discrete, isolated actions that can be assessed independently of the context within which they occur.[13] In fact, the 'correctness' of a given social response is largely dependent on its context. For example, your activity level, formality of speech, and how you're supposed to engage with others will all vary depending on whether you're on the playground, in the classroom, or at the dinner table. Similarly, the degree to which a social act is adaptive or appropriate will vary based on the situation.[14-15] What are the particular social demands of a situation—is this an achievement situation or a play situation? What behavior, emotions, and reactions are others bringing to the situation—is someone teasing you or are they crying? And what are the relationships among these individuals—are they peers or is there an authority figure?

Rating scale items typically present simple, static descriptions with little, if any, contextual information. How often does the child use an appropriate tone of voice? How well does the child interact with other children? Does the child play or work alone? For most children, the most accurate response is probably 'it depends.' But when faced with a questionnaire where you must pick a response, respondents tend to consider whatever set of circumstances in which they've observed the child. So, the child's score represents an aggregate across an unknown set of different social situations. In effect, questionnaire data has limited specificity, so what it tells us about this child's ability to demonstrate any particular social skill in any particular situation is very limited.[16-17]

>> **WARNING**

As with all rating scales, the ratings in this book reflect the authors' own subjective opinions—based on our experience and understanding of the literature. Proceed with caution.

Accuracy of Data

The more accurate the data gathered through SSA, the more useful that information will be for intervention planning. SSA approaches using consistent measurement methods will result in more objective data and therefore conclusions that better reflect reality. Consistency is a strength of behavioral rating scales. A questionnaire includes a pre-determined set of questions and response choices and clear instructions for completion that do not vary across situations. The same unambiguous algorithms are used to generate scores regardless of respondent or administrator. However, user error can still introduce inconsistencies. Some administrators may add, delete, or alter items on a questionnaire so that it's no longer standardized across respondents. It's also possible for administrators to inadvertently influence children's attention or responses through their intonation or non-

Ratings of Behavioral Rating Scale SSA

Objectivity of data

Standardized measurement

Respondent bias

Accuracy checks

scripted comments during administration.[18] Paper-and-pencil questionnaires are more prone to these inconsistencies than are computerized ones, but unfortunately data collection software is still a rarity.

Where behavioral rating scales really fall short is in the area of respondent biases. By definition, ratings are subjective opinions that will be biased in some way. Expectations for how children 'should' act, reputational biases about the child, the respondent's past history with the child, and the respondent's own social skills can each drastically alter scores.[9, 19] Where possible, select a behavioral rating scale measure that includes very specific and behavioral questions. The more specific the question, the less subjectivity will impact scores. For example, the question "How many times has the child interrupted class in the past week?" leaves less room for interpretation than the question, "How well does this child get along with others?"

When children are responding about themselves, social desirability biases will also influence scores.[20] Children may want to make themselves look good in the eyes of the administrator, so they may respond in ways that reflect favorably on them, regardless of the truth. Questions with an obvious 'correct' response will result in less accurate data. For example, if the questionnaire asks about socially undesirable behaviors, such as 'setting fires' or 'bullying others,' the child may be reluctant to admit to these clearly 'wrong' behaviors, so his scores will underestimate reality.

Several approaches can help alleviate the impact of respondent biases on rating scale scores. Some rating scales embed accuracy checks into the questionnaire itself. For example, the Multidimensional Anxiety Scale for Children (MASC1) includes several questions that pull for the social desirability bias, such as 'I always tell the truth.' These items form an Inconsistency Scale score which lets administrators know the degree to which the other scale scores may be skewed by the child's desire to appear in a positive light. Unfortunately, very few rating scale measures include these types of accuracy checks.

Computerized administration may also be helpful for lowering the impact of respondent biases on scores. For example, for questions in which social desirability effects are likely to be large, such as antisocial behaviors, respondents are more likely to admit engaging in these behaviors via computerized surveys.[22] Research suggests that computer administration of rating scales may result in more accurate data, but again, very few questionnaires currently provide computerized administration with children.

We also advise you to gather data from multiple respondents, in order to collect different opinions of the same child from different perspectives. Data from multiple sources can help guide your intervention planning for this child. However, there is little understanding of how to combine information across respondents in a meaningful or useful way,[23-24] so your personal judgment will be needed to make decisions at this point.

Engaging for Children

In our experience, children tend to enjoy sharing information about themselves. But rating scales can be perceived as being like schoolwork, especially lengthy, repetitive questionnaires, so the likelihood that a behavioral rating scale will engage children is relatively low. Children's tolerance for completing questionnaires increases with age, even if they are still not particularly interested. With younger children, low engagement means low motivation to provide thoughtful, honest responses—or to respond at all. In effect, low engagement can undermine the quality and accuracy of the data you collect. You should try to at least select a rating scale that has proven to be usable with children in your target age, so it's clear that they can complete the measure easily and accurately. Then, you can encourage children's engagement in the process by emphasizing the value of the information they're providing and by positively reinforcing their attention and completion of the questionnaire. "You're doing great. Just five more to go!"

Ratings of Behavioral Rating Scale SSA

Engaging for children

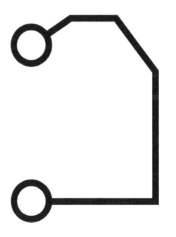

Use of Behavioral Rating Scales for Intervention Planning Purposes

Useful for screening ◑

Useful for progress monitoring ◑

Useful for intervention evaluation ◑

Overall Ratings

Given these various strengths and weaknesses, behavioral rating scales can be a highly feasible, useful, and effective approach to SSA. Just remember that the quality of your data will be directly related to the quality of the rating scale you use. Carefully select measures that have documented evidence supporting their use for children. If you use psychometrically strong, easy-to-use rating scales, the resulting data can be very informative. This SSA approach is recommended for all intervention planning purposes, particularly if it's included as one piece of a multi-faceted approach combining several different SSA methods.

Behavioral Rating Scale Examples

A wide variety of rating scale measures are currently available, with many providing standardized scores allowing comparison across children of a same-aged norm group. Below are several examples of potentially useful rating scales for SSA.

- *Social Skills Improvement System*[25] (SSIS; For Purchase) - The SSIS is a multi-rater instrument that assesses children's social skills (Communication, Cooperation, Assertion, Responsibility, Empathy, Engagement, Self-Control), Problem Behaviors (Externalizing, Bullying, Hyperactivity/ Inattention, Internalizing, Autism Spectrum), and Academic Competence (Reading Achievement, Math Achievement, Motivation to Learn) via parent (79 items), teacher (67 items), and student forms (75 items).

- *Social Skills and Behavior Inventory*[26] (SSBI; For Purchase) - The SSBI is a 75-item questionnaire measuring children's social skills and related behaviors in the school context. While the SSBI was originally developed for use by teachers, it has been successfully adapted for use by parents and as a child self-report. The SSBI measures six key social skills areas, including Impulse Control, Communication, Cooperation, Social Initiation, Empathy, and Emotion Regulation, as well as five behavioral scales: Internalizing, Externalizing (bullying, relational bullying, aggressiveness, disruptiveness, and hyperactivity), Assertion, Social Acceptance, and Academic Performance.

• *Behavior Assessment System for Children*[27] (BASC-2; For Purchase) - The BASC is an extensive set of rating scales and forms that consists of five behavioral assessments covering behavior patterns, emotions and feelings, and the developmental history of the child. Children complete the Self-Report of Personality in which they respond to 139 items with yes or no responses. The Teacher Rating Scales include 100-139 items, depending on the age of the child, and assess adaptive and problem behaviors in the school setting. The Parent Rating Scales measure adaptive and problem behaviors in the community or at home and contains 134-160 items, depending on the age of the child.

• *Matson Evaluation of Social Skills with Youngsters*[28] (MESSY; For Purchase) - The MESSY is an assessment of children and adolescents' social skills and identifies potential problem behaviors. Additionally, the measure can be used to assess progress in programs designed to develop children's social skills. The MESSY includes both verbal and nonverbal behavior with items that refer to discrete, observable behaviors rather than global personality traits. Children complete a self-rating checklist comprised of 62 items and teachers respond to a 64 item scale assessing children's social skills.

• *The Multidimensional Anxiety Scale for Children (2nd Edition)*[21] (MASC-2; For Purchase) - The MASC-2 is a comprehensive, multi-rater assessment of children's anxiety-related symptoms. It measures a range of physical, cognitive, emotional, and behavioral symptoms and consists of scales assessing Separation Anxiety/Phobias, Generalized Anxiety Disorder, Social Anxiety, Obsessions and Compulsions, Physical Symptoms, Harm Avoidance, and Response Style Inconsistency. The self-rated child form and the parent rating form are both comprised of 50 items

• *Achenbach System of Empirically Based Assessment*[29] (ASEBA; For Purchase) - The ASEBA is an evidence-based assessment system that measures competencies, adaptive functioning, and behavioral, emotional, and social problems. The school-age assessments include the Child Behavior Checklist (CBCL; completed by parents), the Teacher's Report Form (TRF; completed by teachers), and the Youth Self Report (YSR; completed by children). With regard to the assessment of social behavior, these scales include measures of empirically based syndromes such as children's aggressive behavior, social problems, anxiety, and withdrawal. Additionally, these scales consist of items that are consistent with DSM classifications such as Oppositional Defiant Problems, Conduct Problems, and Attention Deficit/Hyperactivity Problems. Moreover, this battery of assessments includes a number of observational measures including the Semi-structured Clinical Interview for Children and Adolescents (SCICA), Teacher Observation Form (TOF), Direct Observation Form (DOF), and Brief Problem Monitor (BPM).

• *Loneliness and Social Dissatisfaction Questionnaire*[30] (LSDQ; Free) - This measure assesses children's self-reported feelings of loneliness and dissatisfaction with their social relationships. Children respond to 24 items and are asked to rate the degree to which each statement is true on a 3-point scale (0=no, 2=sometimes, 2=yes).

• *Social Self-Efficacy and Outcome Expectancy Questionnaire*[31] (Free) - This assessment measures children's perceptions of how confident they are that they would be able to perform a given social behavior, and how likely they believe it to be that their behavior will result in a desired social outcome. Children respond to 20 items across two subscales (self-efficacy, outcome expectancy) on a 5-point Likert scale.

• *Social Anxiety Scale for Children-Revised*[32] (SASC-R; Free) - The SASC-R assesses children's anxiety in social situations via 22 items distributed among three subscales. Items from these subscales measure children's fear of negative evaluations by peers, social avoidance and distress in novel situations, and generalized social anxiety and distress.

• *Piers-Harris Children's Self-Concept Scale, Second Edition*[33] (Piers-Harris 2; For Purchase) - This measure of children's self-concept assesses children's self-perceptions via 60 items across six subscales including their own physical appearance, intellectual status, happiness and satisfaction, anxiety, behavioral adjustment, and popularity. Children's self-ratings can be combined to assess overall self-concept and can be separated by subscale to determine self-concept in various domains. For social skills assessment, the behavioral adjustment subscale measures children's problematic behaviors in both home and school settings. Low scores on this subscale are associated with behavioral disorders such as conduct disorder, oppositional defiant disorder, and attention-deficit/hyperactivity disorder.

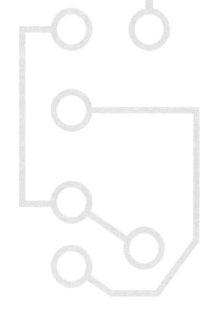

CHAPTER 6 NOTES

1. Gravetter, F. J., & Wallnau, L. B. (2011). *Essentials of statistics for the behavioral sciences (7th ed.)* Belmont, CA: Wadsworth.

2. Enzmann, D. (2013). The impact of questionnaire design on prevalence and incidence rates of self-reported delinquency: Results of an experiment modifying the ISRD-2 questionnaire. *Journal of Contemporary Criminal Justice, 29,* 147-177.

3. Casas, F., González, M., Navarro, D., & Aligué, M. (2013). Children as advisors of their researchers: Assuming a different status for children. *Child Indicators Research, 6*(2), 193-212.

4. Christian, B. J., Pearce, P. F., Roberson, A. J., & Rothwell, E. (2010). It's a small, small world: Data collection strategies for research with children and adolescents. *Journal of Pediatric Nursing, 25,* 202-214.

5. Ehri, L.C. (1994). Development of the ability to read words: Update. In R.M. Ruddell & H. Singer (Eds.), *Theoretical models and processes of reading* (pp. 323-358, 4th ed.). Newark, DE: International Reading Association.

6. Harris, K. R., & Graham, S. (1996). *Making the writing process work: Strategies for composition and self-regulation.* Cambridge, MA: Brookline Books.

7. Helwig, R., Rozek-Tedesco, M. A., Tindal, G., Heath, B., & Almond, P. J. (1999). Reading as an access to mathematics problem solving on multiple-choice tests for sixth-grade students. *The Journal of Educational Research, 93*(2), 113-125.

8. Swanson, H. L. (1999). Reading research for students with LD: A meta-analysis of intervention outcomes. *Journal of Learning Disabilities, 32,* 504-532.

9. Gresham, F. M. (2011). Social behavioral assessment and intervention: Observations and impressions. *School Psychology Review, 40,* 275-283.

10. Achenbach, T. M., & Edelbrock, C. S. (1991). *Manual for the Child Behavior Checklist and Profile.* Burlington: University of Vermont.

11. Gresham, F. M., & Elliott, S. N. (2008). *Social Skills Improvement System—Rating Scales manual.* Minneapolis, MN: Pearson Assessments.

12. Asher, S. R., Hymel, S., & Renshaw, R. D. (1984). Loneliness in children. *Child Development, 55,* 1456-1464.

13. Warnes, E. D., Sheridan, S. M., Geske, J., & Warnes, W. A. (2005). A contextual approach to the assessment of social skills: Identifying meaningful behaviors for social competence. *Educational Psychology Papers and Publications, 42,* 173-187.

14. Parker, J., Rubin, K., Erath, S., Wojslawowicz, J., & Buskirk, A. (2006). Peer relationships, child development, and adjustment: *Developmental psychopathology* perspective. In D. Cicchetti & D. J. Cohen (Eds.), Developmental psychopathology (pp. 419-493). New York, NY: Wiley.

15. Asher, S. R., & Coie, J. D. (1990). *Peer rejection in childhood.* New York, NY: Cambridge University Press.

16. Crowe, L. M., Beauchamp, M. H., Catroppa, C., & Anderson, V. (2011). Social function assessment tools for children and adolescents: A systematic review from 1988 to 2010. *Clinical Psychology Review, 31,* 767-785.

17. Matson, J. L., & Wilkins, J. (2009). Psychometric testing methods for children's social skills. *Research in Developmental Disabilities, 30,* 249-274.

18. Landau, S., Russell, M., Gourgey, K., Erin, J., & Cowan, J. (2003). Use of the Talking Tactile Tablet in mathematics testing. *Journal of Visual Impairment and Blindness, 97,* 85-96.

19. Christ, T. J., Riley-Tillman, T. C., Chafouleas, S., & Jaffery, R. (2011). Direct Behavior Rating: An evaluation of alternate definitions to assess classroom behaviors. *School Psychology Review, 40,* 181-199.

20. Paulhus, D. L. (1991). Measurement and control of response bias. In Robinson, J. P., Shaver, P. R., & Wrightsman, L. S. (Eds.), *Measures of social psychological attitudes* (Vol. 1, pp. 17-59). San Diego, CA: Academic Press.

21. March, J. S., Parker, J. D. A., Sullivan, K., Stallings, P., & Conners, C. K. (1997). The Multidimensional Anxiety Scale for Children (MASC): Factor structure, reliability, and validity. *Journal of the American Academy of Child & Adolescent Psychiatry, 36,* 554-565. More information: http://www.mhs.com/product.aspx?gr=cli&id=overview&prod=masc2

22. Comley, P. (2005). *Understanding the online panelist.* In Annual ESO MAR World Research Conference.

23. Achenbach, M. T. (2011). Definitely more than measurement error: But how should we understand and deal with informant discrepancies? *Journal of Clinical Child & Adolescent Psychology, 40,* 80-86.

24. Kraemer, H. C., Measelle, J. R., Ablow, J. C., Essex, M. J., Boyce, W., & Kupfer, D. J. (2003). A new approach to integrating data from multiple informants in psychiatric assessment and research: Mixing and matching contexts and perspectives. *The American Journal of Psychiatry, 160,* 1566-1577.

25. Gresham, F. M., & Elliott, S. N. (2008). *Social Skills Improvement System: Rating Scales.* Bloomington, MN: Pearson Assessments. More information: http://psychcorp.pearsonassessments.com/haiweb/cultures/en-us/productdetail.htm?pid=PAa3400&Community=CA_Psych_AI_Behavior

26. DeRosier, M. E., Craig, A. B., & Sanchez, R. P. (2012). Zoo U: A stealth approach to social skills assessment in schools. *Advances in Human-Computer Interaction.*For more information, email: info@centervention.org

27. Reynolds, C. R., & Kamphaus, R. W. (2004). *Behavior assessment system for children (2nd ed.).* Circle Pines, MN: American Guidance Service. More information: http://psychcorp.pearsonassessments.com/pai/ca/productlisting.htm?Community=CA_Psych_AI_Behavior

28. Matson, J. L., Neal, D., Fodstad, J. C., Hess, J. A., Mahan, S., & Rivet, T. T. (2010). Reliability and validity of the Matson Evaluation of Social Skills with Youngsters. *Behavior Modification, 34,* 539-558.

29. Achenbach, T. M. (2009). *The Achenbach System of Empirically Based Assessment (ASEBA): Development, findings, theory, and applications.* Burlington, VT: University of Vermont Research Center for Children, Youth and Families. More information: http://www.aseba.org/

30. Cassidy, J., & Asher, S. (1992). Loneliness and peer relations in young children. *Child Development, 63,* 350-365. To download for research purposes: http://www.excellenceforchildandyouth.ca/sites/default/files/meas_attach/Loneliness_and_Social_Dissatisfaction_Questionnaire_(LSDQ)_i.pdf

31. Ollendick, T. H., & Schmidt, C. R. (1987). Social learning constructs in the prediction of peer interaction. *Journal of Clinical Child Psychology, 16,* 80-87.

32. La Greca, A.M., & Stone, W. L. (1993). Social Anxiety Scale for Children-Revised: Factor structure and concurrent validity. *Journal of Clinical Child Psychology, 22,* 17-27. Measure can be obtained by contacting the author: alagreca@miami.edu.

33. Piers, E. V., & Herzberg, D. S. (2002). *Piers-Harris Children's Self-Concept Scale-Second Edition Manual.* Los Angeles, CA: Western Psychological Services. More information: http://portal.wpspublish.com/portal/page?_pageid=53,112628&_dad=portal&_schema=PORTAL

7

Using Behavioral Observations for SSA

by: Chelsea Bartel, Ph.D. and Melissa E. DeRosier, Ph.D.

DESCRIPTION

Direct observation of the child's social behavior is a common approach to social skills assessment (SSA).[1-3] Our discussion in this chapter focuses on **naturalistic observations**, in which the child's behavior is observed in his natural environment. In other words, the observer simply watches the child as he goes through a typical everyday social situation, such as playing on the playground at recess or working with other children on a class project. This natural or real-world method is the type of observation most often used in the assessment of social skills.[3-4] There are other observational SSA approaches, but compared to naturalistic observation, their uses are limited. For example, in **analogue observation**, a social situation is artificially created to elicit specific behaviors. Say you want to see how a child will deal with conflict, so you set up a role play in which other children antagonize or irritate that child. Unfortunately, analogue observation data are of limited use for SSA because the contrived nature of the situation makes the results very difficult to generalize to real life.[5] Another observation method is called **self-monitoring**, in which the child monitors his own behavior in social situations. This approach is also of limited utility for SSA since it's susceptible to reporter biases that undermine the reliability and validity of the data.[4,6,7]

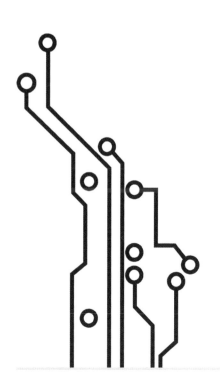

Types of Naturalistic Observation

Naturalistic—also known as ecological—behavioral observation is best when it incorporates three core components: (1) observation and recording of behaviors as they occur in the natural environment; (2) use of a coding system that clearly and specifically describes the behaviors to be recorded; and (3) use of trained, objective observers.[8-9] Two naturalistic observation methods that include these components are narrative recording and structured coding systems.

Narrative recording. With narrative recording—also known as anecdotal observation—the observer creates a detailed picture or story describing the behavior of the child and his peers in his environment. Typically, narrative recording is an early step in the assessment process; it can help the observer get to know the child and generate hypotheses that then can be tested through other, more structured assessment methods.[9] These observations can be conducted in the home, within peer groups, in the classroom, or anywhere the child may exhibit the behaviors in question. Narrative recording does not require the use of any specific instruments or tests.[4] It can be as straightforward as observing a child in a given setting and writing down any observable behaviors in the environment, or it can incorporate a more structured guide to assist the observer in documenting important events.[9] Narrative recording is best conducted while children are interacting during unstructured times such as recess or lunch.[4] Due to the free-flowing nature of this type of observation, there are few published tools to assist observers in conducting narrative recordings.[4] However, Walker and Severson developed a useful guide—the Systematic Screening for Behavior Disorders (SSBD)—which provides a tool to structure narrative recording for one of its social subscales, the Peer Social Behavior Code (PSBC).[10] Using this guide, the observer watches the child during unstructured activities and notes the child's behaviors at 10-second intervals. The PSBC specifies five recording categories: Social Engagement, Participation, Parallel Play, Alone, and No Codable Response. Peer interactions are simply coded as either positive or negative, and the observer can compare the child's frequency of behaviors to normative tables. Research supporting the strong validity and technical properties of the PSBC make it a useful tool for structuring naturalistic observations.[11]

Structured coding systems. Structured coding systems enable observers to collect quantitative data—not just qualitative comments on observations. The observer records the occurrence of specific behaviors during the course of the observation. Structured systems typically fall into five common types: (1) event recording, (2) interval recording, (3) time sample recording, (4) duration recording, and (5) latency recording.[4] Each type is summarized in **Table 1** and then discussed in greater detail below.

Five Types of Structured Coding

Coding Procedure	Definition
Event Recording	Observer records the number of times specific behaviors occur over the course of the observation period
Interval Recording	Observer records whether or not specific behaviors occur within a given period, which can be specific, short time intervals or the entire observation period
Time Sample Recording	Observer records whether or not a specific behavior is present at a specified time point
Duration Recording	Observer measures the amount of time the child engages in a specific behavior or activity
Latency Recording	Observer measures the amount of time that passes between a given cue event and the onset of a behavior

Event recording—also called event sampling or frequency sampling—is the most frequently used structured observation method.[3] It's useful for observing low-rate behaviors that have a discrete beginning and end, that are roughly equivalent in duration, and that do not occur so frequently that they are difficult to distinguish from one another.[4,9] Examples of social behaviors that can be measured with event recording include saying "hello," initiating a conversation, responding to direct questions from peers or adults, and engaging in aggressive behaviors such as hitting.

Interval recording—also called time sampling, interval sampling, and interval time sampling—is another commonly used structured observation method.[3,9] It's similar to event recording in that the observer records whether or not target behaviors occur over the observation period; however, specificity of measurement is increased because the whole observation period is divided into short intervals. For example, a 10-minute observation session may be broken into one minute time intervals or even 10 second time intervals, and the observer indicates whether or not the target behavior occurred

during each of these pre-specified intervals. In partial-interval recording, the observer counts the target behavior as occurring if it's observed at any point during the specified interval. In whole-interval recording, the behavior is counted only if it occurs throughout the entire interval. This observation method is well-suited for observing social behaviors that do not have a clear beginning and end, such as roughhousing, sharing, watching an activity, or being on-task.[9] It's also useful for recording behaviors that occur at such a high rate that it's difficult to count each and every instance.

Time sample recording is similar to interval recording, in which the observation period is first divided into intervals. However, in time sampling, the observer notes target behaviors occurring only at the exact start of each interval rather than behaviors occurring during the entire interval.[4] With time sampling, the observer looks at the child and records whether the target behavior is present at that point in time. Observers may use alarm clocks or timers to indicate when they need to look at the child and make a recording. An advantage of time sampling over other observational methods is that the observer does not need to spend all her time and attention on the observed child. She can engage in other activities and only record observations at discrete time points, making it easier to conduct this type of observation during the course of a busy school day. In addition, the length of each interval can vary, unlike the identical time schedule used in interval recording, so there's more flexibility regarding when the observer can conduct the specific observations. Time sample recording is useful for observing the same types of social behaviors that are best observed with interval recording and it has the advantage of requiring only one observation per interval.[4] However, time sampling can only provide an estimate of how frequently a child engages in a given behavior. It does not document each and every occurrence of that behavior during an observation period.

Duration recording measures the amount of time a child spends engaged in a specific social behavior. Essentially, the observer records how long a target behavior lasts. This observational system is particularly useful for recording behaviors and activities that have a clear beginning and end, such as an argument, a conversation, or a cooperative project with a peer.[4,9] Duration recording is also good for recording high-frequency behaviors that are difficult to accurately record by counting the number of occurrences, such as yelling, running, or talking.

Latency recording also measures time, but rather than duration, the observer records the amount of time it takes for the child to exhibit a particular behavior following an event that is intended to prompt or cue the child for that behavior.[4,9] For example, how much time does it take the child to comply with a request made by the teacher? Or, how long does it take the child to respond to a question from a peer? It's important that the behavior being observed has a clear beginning so it's easy to tell when that behavior starts. It's also important that the prompt for that behavior—verbal, visual, or other cue—be easily and clearly identified.

Respondents

Naturalistic observations can be completed by anyone who can observe the child's social behavior, including parents, teachers, or the child himself. However, observations are most informative when they are conducted by adults who have been trained in how to systematically record specific types of behavior over a period of time. Additionally, use of independent observers who have little knowledge of or prior experience with the child yields less biased data. Reports by teachers, parents, or others who know the child are likely to be influenced by preconceived notions they may have regarding how this child behaves. This issue of observer bias will be revisited in greater detail when we discuss the weaknesses of the observation method for assessing social skills.

STRENGTHS AND WEAKNESSES

In the following review of the relative strengths and weaknesses of using naturalistic observation for SSA, we discuss how feasible it is to administer, the quality of the resulting data—in terms of how useful and accurate those data are likely to be—and how engaged children are likely to be as respondents. To help guide our discussion, we provide summary ratings in each area and then present our reasons behind these ratings. At the end of this discussion, we also provide overall ratings to summarize how effective we believe behavioral observational methods are for accomplishing intervention screening, progress monitoring, and evaluation functions (see Chapter 4). These ratings are purely our best judgment based on available evidence.

Rating Legend

- ● = **Very good in this area**
- ◐ = **Generally good**
- ○ = **Generally fair**
- ◑ = **Generally poor**
- ● = **Very poor in this area**

Feasibility of Administration

Ratings of Observation-Based SSA

Feasible to administer ◐

Training/expertise needed ◑

Time efficiency ◐

Cost effectiveness ◐

Observation is one of the primary tools used to assess behaviors and social interactions,[4] and it's often a preferred method for most SSA purposes.[3] The popularity of this method is likely due to the seeming simplicity of conducting observations. Indeed, untrained observers can observe children in social situations and note behaviors. But for data to be useful, observers should have training in appropriate observation methods and data recording techniques. This training often includes didactic instruction and supervised practice, in which the observer-in-training is paired with a skilled observer watching the same social situation. The two observers compare their data following the observation to determine whether they agree on what behaviors the child engaged in during that observation period. This is called 'inter-rater reliability' and the higher this reliability, the more accurate and useful the data are likely to be.

The time needed to conduct the observations themselves is often reasonable, typically ranging from 5-60 minutes. There are, however, substantial 'hidden' time costs involved in observational methods. For example, it takes time by the observer to identify target behaviors and then select and refine the coding system to measure those behaviors.[3] Additionally, depending on the type of social behavior you're hoping to observe, you may have to observe the child multiple times in different situations before the behavior of interest is displayed.

The extensive time required to adequately train observers and conduct a sufficient number of observations across situations and settings adds up to real financial costs. Although the data gained through observation may be useful as a starting point for further assessment of behavior, this method is more expensive in terms of time and money than it may at first appear. Data collected via observation are generally combined with data gathered through other assessment methods, such as rating scales and interview methods, to provide an overall understanding of the child's social skills. Though beneficial, combining these multiple assessment methods increases the total time and training necessary to analyze and understand the data collected. These combined expenses should be considered when determining whether to include an observational method for SSA.

Utility of Data

The utility of data gathered from observing behaviors in natural settings depends on the nature of the observations and the training level of the observer. Because observations can vary so widely in their quality—ranging from anecdotal notes on a five-minute observation to carefully recorded and charted data over time—it's essential to establish clear goals for the observation at the outset in order to gather relevant and usable data. Data obtained from direct observations of behavior can suffer from threats to reliability and validity ('psychometrics').[4] Reliability means that the observational data measures something consistently so findings are comparable across time, situations, and people. Validity means you can trust that the observations are actually measuring what you intend to measure. **Table 2** outlines these various threats for observational approaches.

Inter-rater reliability (the agreement between two observers), test-retest reliability (the consistency of behavior over time and situations), and internal consistency reliability (how consistent the parts of an assessment tool are for measuring the same characteristics) are often difficult to establish with direct behavioral observation methods.[9] Reliability can suffer for any number of reasons. For example, the child could discover that she's being observed and change her behavior, so the frequency counts or duration measures do not reflect naturally occurring social behavior by the child. Further, the specific setting used for the observation or the specific scales chosen to record behavior could hamper generalizability of findings.[9] Reliability can be improved by conducting multiple observations, but research indicates that as many as six separate observations may be needed to reliably measure social behavior for young children—requiring additional time and resources.[12]

There are also several threats to validity when using direct observation to measure children's social skills. Personal qualities of the observer, such as his beliefs or values, can influence which behaviors are noticed and coded. The observer may hold personal biases about which behaviors are socially acceptable, and these beliefs can influence which behaviors they record. For example, if the observer strongly believes that aggression by girls is wrong, the same behavior may be recorded as aggressive if the child is female, but not if

Ratings of Observation-Based SSA

Utility of data

Psychometrically sound

Norm-based cut-offs

Contextually relevant

Table 2

Threats to Validity of Direct Behavioral Observation for the Assessment of Social Skills

Threat	Potential Consequences
Poorly defined observational domains	Observational recording system is either too cumbersome or too vague
Unreliability of observers	Observers drift from original definitions of behaviors; inter-rater reliability decreases
Lack of social comparison data	Interpretations of behavior are not based on a normative perspective; deviancy may be under- or over-estimated
Observer reactivity	Child behavior is influenced by the presence of the observer
Situational specificity of behavior	Interpretations of observational data may not represent the larger picture
Inappropriate recording techniques	Behaviors are not adequately depicted; inappropriate conclusions are reached
Biased expectations of observer	Borderline behaviors may be systematically coded in a biased manner

the child is male. Observers may also struggle with the observation system—perhaps they have difficulty consistently recording behaviors in a particular area—so they may fail to note important behaviors or inaccurately record them.

Another part of utility to consider is if the data from observation methods can tell you how the child's behavior compares to similar peers. In order to do this in an objective way, the observation system must provide scores and cut-offs based on norm-referenced estimates that clearly indicate where this child's score ranks relative to his peers (see Chapter 4). For example, if a school psychologist observed a child in his classroom to assess attention, the psychologist might list a series of observable behaviors indicating attention—sitting in his seat, eyes focused on teacher, hands engaged with only necessary materials—and track the frequency of each behavior over time. If the psychologist wanted to determine whether the student's score of *"in seat for 70% of observed intervals"* was typical for a child his age, she would need access to norm-referenced estimates for that specific task in that specific setting. Most observation methods do not facilitate such comparisons.[4] Thus, although the observer can gather myriad data about a child's behaviors, it is often difficult to determine whether those behaviors are truly out of the ordinary.

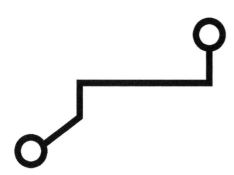

A third element of the utility of data collected from observation-based SSA is the degree to which the data reflect the child's real-world social behavior. In this domain, observations excel. In fact, *"analyzing children's behavior in natural settings … is the most ecologically valid method of assessing children's social skills."*[12] Conducting observations of social skills in the natural setting also facilitates functional assessment, allowing the observer to identify factors that lead to the social behavior and the consequences of that behavior in the child's everyday life.[4,9] That is, trained observers can notice the situations or events that trigger certain behaviors and the objective characteristics of those behaviors, as well as subsequent events that can influence the likelihood of these behaviors occurring again. When these causal and reinforcing relationships are understood, targeted intervention plans can be created.

Accuracy of Data

It's essential for the data gathered through SSA to be accurate. Without accurate data, it's impossible to implement successful interventions to improve appropriate social skills and remediate those needing development. A drawback of observational methods is that they often lack consistency. Observers will always differ in exactly what behaviors they see, children will differ in how they behave depending on various external factors, and observational coding systems themselves come in many forms, each with their own strengths and weaknesses.

Ratings of Observation-Based SSA

Objectivity of data	○
Standardized measurement	◐
Respondent bias	○
Accuracy checks	◐

Respondent biases also interfere with the accuracy of observational data. As noted in the previous section, the observer's personal beliefs and experiences can hamper the reliability and validity of the data obtained through observations. If the observer is already familiar with the child, as is often the case in the school setting, objectivity is also an issue. For example, if a teacher is aware that her student was 'aggressive' during the previous academic year, that teacher may be more inclined to be on the lookout for aggressive behaviors—and even to interpret age-appropriate behaviors as more aggressive than they actually are. Observer bias is an issue that can plague observational data, and another reason for using well-trained, independent observers whenever possible.

One way to ensure that data are valid is to include checks on the accuracy of data for that child. Other SSA methods, such as rating scales, sometimes incorporate accuracy checks by including items designed to measure whether the respondent is trying to present the child in an overly favorable or overly unfavorable light. With behavioral observations, accuracy checks can be included by having two people observe the same behavior and then comparing those observations. This method, however, is time-consuming, and is typically limited to the research setting due to its impracticality. Behavioral observations as they typically occur do not include accuracy checks.

Ratings of Observation-Based SSA

Engaging for children	n/a

Engaging for Children

Most naturalistic behavioral observation is designed to allow for observation of behavior without the child knowing that he is being observed. If children are aware that they are being observed, they often change their behavior. These behavioral changes—which can occur consciously or unconsciously—are called 'reactivity.' If the goal is to gather information about how the child behaves in a typical, naturalistic setting, it's essential to mitigate reactivity as much as possible. Thus, observation-based SSA should not actually engage the child directly.

Use of Observation-Based SSA for Intervention Planning Purposes

Useful for screening	
Useful for progress monitoring	
Useful for intervention evaluation	

Overall Ratings

If administered by objective, trained observers using a structured coding system, observational methods can offer more objective and contextually relevant data compared to other SSA methods. However, structured behavioral observations are time-intensive and require highly trained personnel to gather and interpret the data, which makes regular use of this methodology infeasible for most educational settings.[1,13] In addition, research has found that problems identified through observations often don't align with the teacher's report of students' social behavior,[14] which can complicate identification of children for intervention. Overall, this SSA approach is recommended for the early stages of identifying problem behaviors, and possibly for intervention evaluation purposes. It should always be augmented with other forms of SSA in order to obtain the most accurate information.

Observation Coding System Examples

Observers can access numerous published structured coding systems for conducting event recording, interval recording, time sample recording, and duration/latency recording. Using established observation systems is beneficial because such systems provide structure and reminders to the observers, ideally increasing their accuracy in recording their observations. Five commonly used systems designed for assessing social behavior via behavioral observational methods are outlined in **Table 3**.

Table 3

Structured Coding Systems for Assessing Child Social Behavior

Structured Coding System	Publisher	Designed to Assess...
School Social Behavior Scales, Second Edition (SSBS-2)	Brookes Publishing[15]	social competence and antisocial behavior
Social Skills Improvement System (SSIS)	Pearson[16]	social skills, academic competence, problem behaviors
Walker-McConnell Scales of Social Competence and School Adjustment	Singular Publishing[17]	teacher- and peer-preferred social competencies
Behavior Observation Record (BOR)	Iverson & Segal[18]	social behaviors and the quality or effectiveness of these behaviors on a playground
PROCORDER	Tapp & Walden[19]	Computer-based system for observing social interactions

CHAPTER 7 NOTES

1. Christ, T. J., Riley-Tillman, T. C., Chafouleas, S., & Jaffery, R. (2011). Direct behavior rating: An evaluation of alternate definitions to assess classroom behaviors. *School Psychology Review, 40*(2), 181-199.

2. Sheridan, S. M., & Walker, D. (1999). Social skills in context: Considerations for assessment, intervention, and generalization. In C. R. Reynolds & T. B. Gutkin (Eds.), *The handbook of school psychology* (pp. 686-708). Hoboken, NJ: Wiley & Sons.

3. Merrell, K. W. (2001). Assessment of children's social skills: Recent developments, best practices, and new directions. *Exceptionality, 9*(1 & 2), 3-18.

4. Merrell, K. W. (2008). *Behavioral, social, and emotional assessment of children and adolescents* (3rd ed.). New York, NY: Routledge.

5. Hintze, J. M. (2005). Psychometrics of direct observation. *School Psychology Review, 34,* 507-519.

6. Keller, H. R. (1986). Behavioral observation approaches to assessment. In H. Knoff (Ed.), *The assessment of child and adolescent personality* (pp. 353-397). New York, NY: Guilford.

7. Nelson, R. O., & Hayes, S. C. (Eds.). (1986). *Conceptual foundations of behavioral assessment.* New York, NY: Guilford.

8. Jones, R. R., Reid, J. B., & Patterson, G. R. (1979). Naturalistic observation in clinical assessment. In P. McReynolds (Ed.), *Advances in psychological assessment* (Vol. 3, pp. 42-95). San Francisco, CA: Jossey-Bass.

9. Sattler, J. M., & Hoge, R. D. (2006). *Assessment of children: Behavioral, social, and clinical foundations* (5th ed.). San Diego, CA: Jerome M. Sattler.

10. Walker, H. M., & Severson, H. (1992). *Systematic screening for behavior disorders.* Longmont, CO: Sopris West.

11. Indeed, according to Merrell[4], "The PSBC is an exemplary interval-based coding procedure for direct observation of child social behavior and may serve as a model for constructing similar coding systems for more specific purposes." (p. 389).

12. Elliott, S. N., & Gresham, F. M. (1987). Children's social skills: Assessment and classification practices. *Journal of Counseling and Development, 66,* 96-99.

13. Merrell, K. W., & Gimpel, G. A. (1998). *Social skills of children and adolescents: Conceptualization, assessment, treatment.* Mahwah, NJ: Lawrence Erlbaum Associates.

14. Tversky, B., & Marsh, E. J. (2000). Biased retellings of events yield biased memories. *Cognitive Psychology, 40,* 1-38.

15. Merrell, K. W. (1993). Using behavior rating scales to assess social skills and antisocial behavior in school settings: Development of the School Social Behavior Scales. *School Psychology Review, 22,* 115-119. For more information on the SSBS-2, visit: http://www.brookespublishing.com/resource-center/screening-and-assessment/ssbs-2-hcsbs/

16. Gresham, F. M., & Elliott, S. N. (2008). *Social Skills Improvement Rating System Rating Scales.* Minneapolis, MN: NCS Pearson.

17. Walker, H. M., & McConnell, S. R. (1995). *Walker-McConnell Scale of Social Competence and School Adjustment.* San Diego, CA: Singular Publishing Group.

18. Segal, M., Montie, J., & Iverson, T. (2000). Observing for individual differences in the social interaction styles of preschool children. In K. Gitlin-Weiner, A. Sandgrund, & C. Schaefer (Eds.), *Play diagnosis and assessment,* 544-562.

19. Tapp, J., & Walden, T. (2000). Procorder: A system for collection and analysis of observational data from videotape. *Behavioral observation: Technology and applications in developmental disabilities,* 61-70.

USING INTERVIEW METHODS FOR SSA

by: Chelsea Bartel, Ph.D. and Melissa E. DeRosier, Ph.D.

DESCRIPTION

An interview is simply what it sounds like—a professional has a private one-on-one conversation with a child during which he asks a series of questions and records the responses. The primary goal of an interview is to gather information both through verbal feedback—the child's answers to specific interview questions—and through the child's nonverbal behaviors during the interview.[1] For example, how much does the child fidget or appear to be uncomfortable when discussing certain topics? Does the child get agitated or upset when asked about his behavior? Is the child closed and hostile with the interviewer or open and pleasant?

You should combine interview data with other SSA approaches, rather than relying on an interview as the only source of information. When interviewing a child, you can ask about behaviors you observed from other SSA methods, and you can begin to put data into a more contextual framework. Our discussion in this chapter includes a brief description of the various types of interviews that can be conducted for SSA, followed by an analysis of the strengths and limitations of this assessment approach.

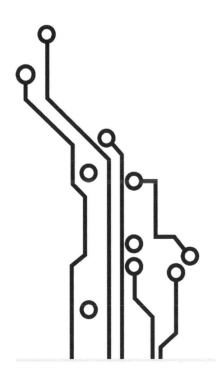

Interviewers

> The quality of the data resulting from an interview will be directly proportional to the skill of the interviewer.

Interview methods are most often used by trained psychologists, psychiatrists, counselors, social workers, and other mental health professionals.[2,3] In the school setting, interviews are most likely to be conducted by the school psychologist or counselor, but teachers and other school professionals can also use the interview approach. These clinical interviews are intended to provide a better understanding of the child's behavior in particular situations, as well as any underlying motivations, perspectives, emotions, and beliefs that are driving that behavior.

While on the surface the interview method sounds easy and simple, of all the assessment methods, this one likely requires the highest level of professional training. The quality of the data resulting from an interview will be directly proportional to the skill of the interviewer. **Table 1** provides just a sampling of the skills that are essential for an interviewer to have in order to collect full, accurate, and informative data during an interview with a child. These skills come with years of training, supervision, and practice. The more open-ended the questions and unstructured the interview process, the more critical these skills will be for determining the quality and usefulness of the gathered data.

Table 1

Essential Skills for Interviewers and Their Impact on the Interview Process

Essential Interviewer Skills	Impact on the Interview
Understands normative development	Able to accurately judge whether reported and observed behavior lies within normal limits
Can speak at the child's level	Able to establish rapport easily, put the child at ease, build trust, and engage the child in conversation so he speaks more freely
Is comfortable with children	Is at ease, friendly, and open when interacting with the child, so the child feels at ease and comfortable
Has high self-control	Does not overreact to statements by the child, able to keep a calm, cool demeanor regardless of what the child says or does, which provides a safe environment for the child to share his thoughts and feelings
Knows how to ask questions	Does not ask leading questions that let the child know what answer is wanted, knows how to use follow-up questions to pull out more information (without spooking the child)
Uses reflective listening	Able to take the child's perspective and accurately reflect back to the child what is heard, which helps the child feel understood and be more likely to share
Can read non-verbal cues	Able to discern when the child is being truthful or not, can sense when the child is becoming anxious, can pick up on when *what* is said does not match *how* it's said

Respondents

Interviewers most commonly engage directly with the child during the interview process. However, you can also interview others who are knowledgeable of the child's behaviors and social interactions, such as parents, siblings, teachers, and other key figures in the child's life.[4]

Interview Types

Typically, trained interviewers enter into the child interview process with a goal in mind. In the case of social skills assessment, the goal of the interview is to gather information from the child about interactions with peers as well as internal thoughts and feelings affecting social interactions. Even with this common goal of assessing social skills, the interview itself can unfold differently depending to a large extent on the approach to the interview.[1] Interviews typically fall into one of three categories: (1) **unstructured**, in which the interview proceeds in an open-ended, free-flowing manner with very few guidelines; (2) **semi-structured**, in which the interviewer follows set guidelines, but has some flexibility in the phrasing of questions and the format of the interview, and; (3) **structured**, in which the interviewer follows a strictly prescribed, scripted sequence of questions.

Behavioral Interviewing for SSA

A subset of interviewing methods that is especially relevant to the assessment of social skills is called **behavioral interviewing**. *"The primary objective of behavioral assessment is to obtain descriptive information about problem behavior and the conditions maintaining it".*[5] These interviews are usually semi-structured, and they focus on identifying problem behaviors and the things that happen before ('antecedents') and after ('consequences') behaviors that might be encouraging the child's poor social skills. Haynes and Wilson provide eight reasons to conduct a behavioral interview,[6] which are summarized in **Table 2**.

For school-aged children, behavioral interviewing most often occurs within the context of behavioral consultation. The behavioral consultation technique is structured to include four stages: (1) problem identification; (2) problem analysis; (3) plan implementation; and (4) problem evaluation.

Table 2

Purposes of Behavioral Interviews

1. Gather more information about a child's concerns and goals

2. Determine the antecedents and consequences maintaining problem behaviors

3. Gather background information on the child and his current situation

4. Identify the things that are encouraging the child's behavior ('reinforcers')

5. See how much insight the child has into his own behavior

6. Educate the child about his behaviors and their effects

7. Obtain permission from the child and parent to conduct SSA

8. Discuss the goals and plan for SSA

Usually, behavioral consultation includes two adults. One person leads the interview ('consultant') and one person works directly with the child on a regular basis ('consultee'). In schools, the consultant is often a school psychologist or other professional with training in behavioral problem solving, and the consultee is often a teacher who is concerned about her student's behavior. The consultant interviews the consultee with two goals in mind: (1) to improve the child's mental health and educational development, and (2) to change specific, measurable, observable behaviors.[7,8] Consultants encourage consultees to be active participants and problem solvers during the interview process. In this way, classroom teachers can apply what they learn through the guided interviews and develop skills for solving similar problems in the future.

We highlighted behavioral interviewing as an important tool for SSA because it is often used in schools, and there are data to support its effectiveness. However, a major criticism of behavioral interviewing—and behavioral consultation specifically—is the accuracy of the information. We generally trust that adults can give reliable and valid information in an interview, but children may not be consistent or accurate when they are interviewed. As a result, when we rely on behavioral interviewing because we trust its reliability and validity, we often neglect to consider the child's first-hand perspective. This issue is analyzed in greater detail below, with a review of the strengths and weaknesses of the interview approach more generally.

STRENGTHS AND WEAKNESSES

In the following review of the relative strengths and weaknesses of using interviews for SSA, we discuss how feasible they are to administer, the quality of the resulting data, and how engaged children are likely to be as respondents. To help guide our discussion, we provide summary ratings in each area and then present our reasons behind these ratings. At the end of the discussion, we also provide overall ratings to summarize how effective we believe interviews are for accomplishing intervention screening, progress monitoring, and evaluation functions (see Chapter 4). These ratings are purely our best judgment based on available evidence.

Feasibility of Administration

In order to conduct effective assessment interviews with children, interviewers should be trained in general interviewing skills, such as reflective listening and ways to establish rapport. They will also need to learn and practice the specific requirements of the interview protocol, if one is being used.[1] If interviewers are not trained in these skills, the interviews will not be objective and will not provide useful data. And the training is not fast or easy. Seemingly simple interviewing techniques, such as asking open questions and reflecting interviewees' feelings in a neutral way, are actually quite difficult to master.[10]

Interviews can also take more time than many other forms of assessment.[4] There is the time for the interview itself, which can range from just a few minutes with a child to multiple longer sessions that include parents or teachers. It also takes time to conduct interviews with multiple sources to get the best and most well-rounded picture of a child. For example, during an evaluation, the school psychologist might interview the child, his parents, and multiple teachers. Gathering the perspectives of these different sources and comparing the data is quite informative for SSA and intervention planning, but is certainly time-intensive.

Rating Legend

◑ = Very good in this area

◐ = Generally good

○ = Generally fair

◐ = Generally poor

◑ = Very poor in this area

Ratings of Interviews for SSA

Feasible to administer	○
Training/expertise needed	◐
Time efficiency	○
Cost effectiveness	◐

The cost of interviews for SSA is generally low, as there are many semi-structured interview protocols available at no cost.[1] These questionnaires are often included in textbooks that trained interviewers would be familiar with, such as *Assessment of Children: Behavioral, Social, and Clinical Foundations.*[1] If you're using a published interview protocol, however, you'll need to purchase the protocol from the publisher (and demonstrate the specified level of training, licensure, or certification required to access the interview tool). In sum, although the interviews themselves do not involve special equipment or materials beyond a set of interview questions, the cost of interviews often lies within the amount of time required to prepare for the interview, to conduct the interview, and then to analyze and interpret the information you gather.

Utility of Data

Arguably the most important limitation of using interviews to gather any information from children is that reliability and validity are difficult to establish. Researchers vary in their warnings in this area, noting that interviews should only be used for assessment purposes with children over age five[11] or over age nine,[12] or simply noting that reliability and validity are difficult to establish with 'young children.'[1] Merrell summarizes the issue by cautioning *"as a general rule, the younger the child, the more difficult it is to obtain useful behavioral data in an interview, and the more important other behavioral assessment sources will be."*[4]

Ratings of Interviews for SSA

Utility of data	○
Psychometrically sound	◐
Norm-based cut-offs	◑
Contextually relevant	●

The reason for these psychometric problems is two-pronged. First, children (like adults) could intentionally provide inaccurate information in an interview setting.[1,2,4] As such, you don't want to rely only on the child's reporting of events, relationships with peers, or typical behavior in various social situations when conducting SSA. Second, children's cognitive and language skills may be lower than is needed within a verbally-demanding interview setting.[1] Children may not have the verbal skills to adequately understand or answer interviewers' questions, which could lead them to unintentionally provide limited or inaccurate information. Taken together, these issues mean that the data gathered through interviews are likely to be unreliable,[12,13] show poor agreement between parent- and child-reports of events,[2] and not be comparable across time.[1]

Another measure of data utility is whether you can use the data to compare the child to peers his age. You can make these kinds of comparisons if the assessment tool is norm-referenced, which means that data are available about how children typically perform on this assessment measure. Norm-based cut-offs are usually associated with assessment tools, such as behavior rating scales, in which it is easier to determine whether the child's pattern of answers is similar to responses given by his peers. The flexibility and less-structured nature of interviews makes establishing such cut-offs exceedingly difficult. The bottom line is that it's usually not practical to try to compare one child's interview responses to those of other children his age as a means of SSA.

When determining the contextual relevance of interview data, the question is whether the results of an interview correspond to specific real-world situations. One of the key advantages of interviewing children directly for SSA is that you can ask the child for his perspective on his friendships, family relationships, and behavior.[2] We often overlook the child's understanding of his social skills, which is an important part of the evaluation. A strength of interviews is that you can use them to understand the child's viewpoint, as well as his understanding of what sorts of things encourage or discourage his social behaviors.[2,14,15] However, you should keep in mind the limitations of interview data and remember to include other forms of SSA.

Accuracy of Data

Interviews are more flexible than many other forms of assessment,[1,2,4] because as an interviewer you can set the pacing and tone of the interview, you can follow up on unclear responses, and you can decide which questions to ask in the moment, based on the child's comfort level. This flexibility comes at a cost, though. The cost is that the data you gather through interviews can be highly biased and inaccurate.[4] Bias is much less problematic when using a structured interview that is administered in a standardized, consistent way across children. However, interviewers rarely use highly structured interview tools because the tools are rigid and don't allow you to talk with the child as you normally would. You can use a semi-structured interview for more freedom in how you interact with the child, but the information you get from these interviews is still more qualitative than quantitative. That is, you might have more insight into child's social skills after an interview, but you usually can't get consistent and clear scores from an interview.

Ratings of Interviews for SSA

Objectivity of data   ◑

Standardized measurement   ◐

Respondent bias   ●

Accuracy checks   ●

As discussed with respect to the validity and reliability of interview data, it's easy for interviewers, parents, teachers, or children to cause bias in interview data. Children can intentionally or unwittingly provide false information, and all interviewees are of course reporting their own interpretation of events which is influenced by their own experiences and beliefs.[1,4] Response biases are also a problem. For example, if the interviewer is asking about antisocial, clearly negative behavior such as fighting or teasing, the child might not be completely honest due to something called 'social desirability bias.' He may deny engaging in these behaviors or under-report these behaviors because he wants to please the interviewer or he doesn't want the interviewer to think negatively about him.

In sum, it's often not feasible to estimate how valid and accurate interview results are for a child. The problem is that interviews are subjective—they are your interpretation of what someone is asking you or telling you. Sometimes objective, unbiased data are available to confirm the accuracy of what children or adults report in interviews, which can help. Checking for accuracy when using interviews to assess social skills usually consists of corroborating the collected information with data gathered through other forms of SSA.[2]

Ratings of Interviews for SSA

Engaging for children

Engaging for Children

A notable strength of using interviews to assess social skills is that the interview format can directly engage children in the assessment process.[1,4] The face-to-face nature of the interview allows children to meet and interact with the interviewer. During interviews, you can establish rapport with the child and actively engage her in conversation about social issues.[1,4] You can also observe children's nonverbal behaviors and incorporate this broader knowledge of the child into the assessment process.[1,2,4] Some children very much enjoy the interview process because they receive direct attention from an adult and it takes them out of their everyday classroom environment. Others, however, may not like the question-and-answer format and may become anxious in such a setting. In the end, whether or not interviews are engaging for children depends on the child himself combined with the interviewer's skills for conducting a good interview.[10]

Overall Ratings

Interviews with children can take a variety of forms, from completely unstructured to highly-prescribed. The goals of these interviews vary, ranging from simply establishing rapport with the interviewer to arriving at a specific diagnosis. When you're using interviews to understand a child's social skills, you should consider using behavioral interviewing. You can overcome some of the problems with interviews by using behavioral interviewing, because it focuses on detailing the objective aspects of behaviors and social interactions. However, behavioral interviewing is often conducted with adults in the child's life rather than the child himself, which detracts from some of the noteworthy strengths of this interview assessment method.

The overview provided here of the strengths and limitations of using child interviews for SSA suggests that although this traditional assessment method has merits, its limitations can be quite significant. In particular, structured interviews—which yield the most accurate and usable data of the various intervention methods—are often impractical for everyday use because they require highly trained interviewers and significant time to conduct and interpret the interview.[4] The research literature stresses that child interviews cannot be relied upon as the sole source of information in any assessment.[2] You should always supplement interviews with other assessment methods, such as behavioral observations and rating scales. However, you'll add considerable time and resource costs to the assessment by incorporating data from multiple sources.

Use of Interviews for Intervention Planning Purposes

Useful for screening	○
Useful for progress monitoring	○
Useful for intervention evaluation	◐

Interview Examples

A number of published, empirically-tested options are available for both semi-structured and structured interviews with children. Examples are provided in **Table 3**.

Table 3

Examples of Published Interview Protocols for Use with Children

Type of Interview	Examples
Semi-structured	• Semi-structured Clinical Interview for Children and Adolescents (SCICA)[2] » Developed with attention to children's cognitive levels and interaction styles to yield scores which can be combined with observation and self-report scores • Schedule for Affective Disorders and Schizophrenia for School-Age Children (K-SADS)[16] » Designed to assess current and past episodes of psychopathology, including severity of psychiatric symptoms • Child and Adolescent Functional Assessment Scale (CAFAS)[17] » Assesses the degree of impairment in youth with emotional, behavioral, psychiatric, or substance use problems
Structured	• NIMH Diagnostic Interview Schedule for Children (NIMH-DISC-IV)[18] » Diagnostic interview designed to assess more than 30 psychiatric disorders occurring in children and adolescents • Diagnostic Interview for Children and Adolescents (DICA-IV)[19] » Screening tool for a broad range of behavioral problems, including a list of critical items highlighting responses that reflect a potential for dangerous behavior

CHAPTER 8 NOTES

1. Sattler, J. M., & Hoge, R. D. (2006). *Assessment of children: Behavioral, social, and clinical foundations* (5th ed.). San Diego, CA: Jermone M. Sattler.

2. McConaughy, S. H., & Achenbach, T. M. (2001). *Manual for the Semistructured Clinical Interview for Children and Adolescents* (2nd ed.). Burlington, VT: University of Vermont, Research Center for Children, Youth, & Families.

3. Watkins, C. E., Campbell, V. L., Nieberding, R., & Hallmark, R. (1995). Contemporary practice of psychological assessment by clinical psychologists. *Professional Psychology Research and Practice, 26,* 54-60.

4. Merrell, K. W. (2008). *Behavioral, social, and emotional assessment of children and adolescents* (3rd ed.). New York, NY: Routledge.

5. Gross, A. M. (1984). Behavioral Interviewing. In T. H. Ollendick & M. Herson (Eds.), *Child behavior assessment: Principles and practices* (pp. 61-79). New York, NY: Pergamon.

6. Haynes, S. N., & Wilson, C. C. (1979). *Behavioral assessment.* San Francisco, CA: Jossey Bass.

7. Bergan, J. R. (1977). *Behavioral consultation.* Colombus, OH: Charles E. Merrill.

8. Bergan, J. R., & Kratochwill, T. R. (1990). *Behavioral consultation and therapy.* New York, NY: Plenum Press.

9. Gutkin, T. B., & Curtis, M. (1999). School based consultation theory and practice: The art and science of indirect service delivery. In C. R. Reynolds & T. B. Gutkin (Eds.), *Handbook of school psychology* (3rd ed., pp. 598-637). New York, NY: Wiley.

10. Ivey, A. E., & Ivey, M. B. (2006). *Intentional interviewing and counseling: Facilitating client development in a multicultural society* (6th ed.). Belmont, CA: Brooks/Cole.

11. McMahon, R. J., & Forehand, R. (1988). Conduct disorders. In E. J. Mash & L. G. Terdal (Eds.), *Parent training: Foundations of research and practice* (pp. 298-328). New York, NY: Guilford.

12. Edelbrock, C. S., Costello, A. J., Dulcan, M. K., Conover, N. C., & Kalas, R. (1986). Parent-child agreement on child psychiatric symptoms assessed via structured interview. *Journal of Child Psychology and Psychiatry, 27,* 181-190.

13. Boyle, M. H., Offord, D. R., Racine, Y., & Sanford, M. (1993). Evaluation of the Diagnostic Interview for Children and Adolescents for use in general population samples. *Journal of Abnormal Child Psychology, 21,* 663-681.

14. La Greca, A. M. (1990). *Through the eyes of the child.* Boston, MA: Allyn & Bacon.

15. Hughes, J. N., & Baker, D. B. (1990). *The clinical child interview.* New York, NY: Guilford.

16. Puig-Antich, J., & Chambers, W. (1978). *The Schedule for Affective Disorders and Schizophrenia for School-Age Children.* New York, NY: New York State Psychiatric Association. For more information on the K-SADS, please visit: http://www.psychiatry.pitt.edu/research/tools-research/ksads-pl

17. Hodges, K. (1987). Assessing children with a clinical research interview: The child assessment schedule. In R. J. Prinz (Ed.), *Advances in behavioral assessment of children and families* (Vol. 3, pp. 203-233). Greenwich, CT: JAI. For more information on the CAFAS, please visit: http://www2.fasoutcomes.com/Content.aspx?ContentID=12

18. Shaffer, D., Fisher, P., Lucas, C. P., Dulcan, M., & Schwab-Stone, M. E. (2000). NIMH Diagnostic Interview Schedule for Children, Version IV (NIMH DISC-IV): Description, differences from previous versions, and reliability of some common diagnoses. *Journal of the American Academy of Child and Adolescent Psychiatry, 29,* 28-38.

19. Reich, W., Welner, Z., Herjanic, B., & MHS Staff. (1997). *Diagnostic Interview for Children and Adolescents – IV (DICA – IV).* North Tonawanda, NY: Multi-Health Systems. For more information on the DICA-IV, please visit: http://www.mhs.com/product.aspx?gr=edu&prod=dicaiv&id=overview

9

USING PEER NOMINATIONS FOR SSA

by: Melissa E. DeRosier, Ph.D., Jim Thomas, Ph.D., and Chelsea Bartel, Ph.D.

DESCRIPTION

The assessment approaches we've discussed so far each rely on the judgment of one or at most a handful of people who determine a child's social skills level or the degree to which a child is experiencing social problems. Each of these SSA methods—behavioral rating scales, behavioral observations, and interviewing—are plagued by potential respondent biases that can substantially alter the data. As a result, it can be very difficult to know how much the data gathered through these SSA methods actually reflects reality.

We know that the judgment of a single individual yields less accurate information than the combined judgments of multiple people with different experiences and perspectives on the child.[1] In this chapter, we discuss **peer nominations**—also called sociometrics—which capitalize on this phenomenon to yield highly reliable and valid information about the child. In essence, the peer nomination SSA method gathers the opinions of a wide array of respondents—typically, all children within a classroom or grade—and generates consensus data across these informants.

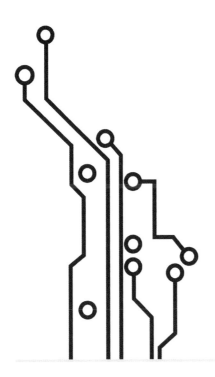

The Sociometric Method

Use of sociometrics dates back to the 1930s[2] when Jacob Moreno defined sociometry as *"the inquiry into the evolution and organization of groups and the position of individuals within them."* His goal was to uncover the hidden sub-groups—or what we now call cliques—within a larger group and understand the pecking order of individuals with that group. One of the results of his work was the creation of sociograms, or social maps. **Figure 1** shows what a sociogram may look like for a given group of people. Moreno's work was seminal in helping us think beyond dyadic relationships to consider group dynamics and broader systems that impact and drive social relationships and behavior within a particular group. Moreno's original purpose for using sociometry was to figure out how roommates should be paired within a residential facility for delinquent girls. He found that pairing roommates on the basis of their sociometric affiliations—placing together girls who were at a similar level on the pecking order—significantly reduced incidents of running away from the facility.[2] If girls who were too dissimilar

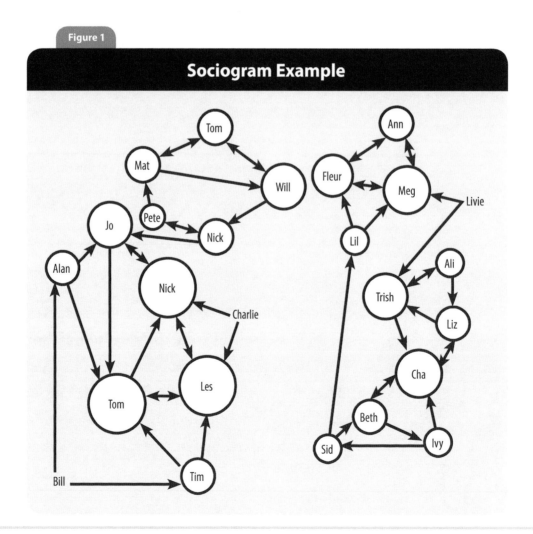

Figure 1

Sociogram Example

in terms of their social power or social influence were placed together, the pair was more likely to experience disharmony, such that one of the girls was more likely to run away. In contrast, roommates at a similar social level bonded more easily; this social support helped each girl cope better with her life circumstances and resulted in fewer runaways.

Assessing Social Affiliations

While Moreno's work has since contributed significantly to a number of fields—sociology in particular—it also led to a new approach to SSA commonly referred to as **peer nominations**. Researchers started administering the peer nomination technique to ask children to nominate peers—in their classroom, grade, or other peer group—who fit specific descriptions. Aligning with Moreno's original intent, this early use of peer nominations tended to focus on questions about affiliation—who do you sit next to at lunch, who do you play with on the playground, who do you talk to? This information was helpful for determining more or less strong social connections among children and sub-groups within a broader peer group.

However, in the 1960s, researchers realized that by collecting only positive nominations, they were not capturing critical information about the negative side of social relationships. When you ask about positive connections among peers, you're only able to say children have fewer or greater positive affiliations relative to other children in their peer group. This is certainly useful information, but researchers found that the absence of positive affiliations is not the same thing as the presence of negative affiliations. These are actually distinct social experiences that have very different antecedents and consequences for the child.[3]

So, researchers started combining positive and negative nominations to help them distinguish between children who were actively disliked and socially excluded from those who simply did not have a lot of positive affiliations.[4] For example, children were asked to nominate—on separate forms—peers they like and peers they don't like, peers they want to play with and peers they don't want to play with, etc. And when the researchers combined these two sets of nominations, they were able to flesh out a much more detailed map of the social structure of the peer group.

By asking for both positive and negative nominations, researchers found they could calculate two critical dimensions of social affiliations: Social Impact and Social Preference.[4]

> *Social Impact = # of positive nominations + # of negative nominations*
> *Social Preference = # of positive nominations - # of negative nominations*

Social impact essentially represents a given child's 'social valence' or prominence within the peer group—how often is this child noticed by other children, positively or negatively? Social preference, on the other hand, reflects the ratio of positive to negative nominations received by the child. Higher social preference scores indicate the child is more liked than disliked among his peers; lower scores indicate the child is more disliked than liked.

Assessing Social Status. In the 1980s, Coie, Dodge, and Coppotelli moved this system further to assign children to what are called 'sociometric status groups' based on patterns of positive and negative nominations (see **Figure 2** illustrating these groups).[5] They asked children the very direct questions of *"who do you like the very most"* and *"who do you like the very least."* By

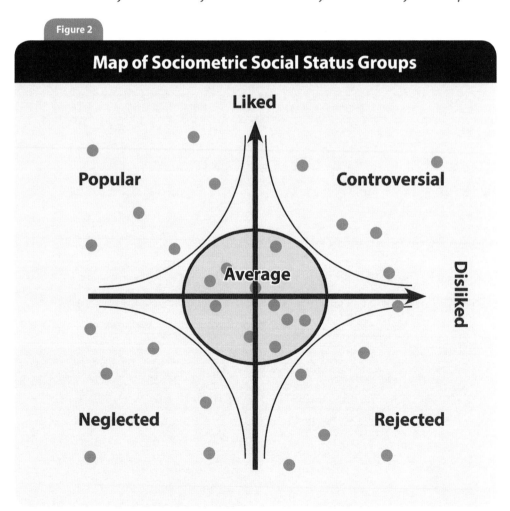

Figure 2

Map of Sociometric Social Status Groups

summing and standardizing these nominations across the entire nominating group, these researchers were able to plot children according to how well liked and disliked they were within this particular peer group, and thereby assign children to one of five social status groups:[6]

- **Popular**—a child with many positive and few negative nominations;
- **Controversial**—a child with many positive and many negative nominations;
- **Neglected**—a child with few positive and few negative nominations;
- **Rejected**—a child with few positive and many negative nominations; and
- **Average**—a child who receives some of each type of nomination, but neither to an extreme level compared to other children in the peer group.

Assessing Social Skills & Behavior. Peer nominations are also useful for determining the degree to which a child demonstrates a particular social behavior or social skill relative to other children within her peer group.[5, 6] Instead of being used to assess how much children like or dislike their peers, sociometrics can be used to ask children to identify those who fit specific behavioral descriptors. **Table 1** displays a number of behavioral nominations

Table 1

Sample Peer Nomination Questions for Specific Social Areas

Social Area Assessed	Nominate children who:
Aggressive behavior	• Start fights with peers • Call other children mean names • Act like bullies
Relational aggression	• Tell others not to be friends with someone • Ignore or exclude others from the group • Talk about other kids behind their backs
Victimization by peers	• Get teased or called names a lot • Get picked on, beat up, or bullied a lot
Immaturity	• Say or do weird or strange things a lot • Act younger than other kids in your grade
Social isolation	• Play or work alone a lot • Act or seem shy with other kids
Prosocial behavior (social skills)	• Are really good at talking with other kids (communication) • Are really good at cooperating, sharing, and working with other kids (cooperation) • Are really good at understanding other kids' feelings and helping kids feel better when they're upset (empathy) • Are really good at joining in activities and conversations with other kids (initiation) • Are really good at controlling what they do or say, can wait their turn, and follow directions (impulse control) • Are really good at controlling how they feel, even when upset (emotion regulation)

that could be included as part of a social skill assessment, but essentially this same methodology could be applied to any specific behavioral descriptor you want to assess.

Over the past several decades, a huge number of studies have examined the interrelationships among behavioral sociometric items, social status groups, and child outcomes.[7, 8, 9] For example, sociometrically popular children tend to be highly skilled socially and seen as friendly and caring by their peers. In contrast, sociometrically rejected children tend to have poor social skills across many areas and are seen by their peers as aggressive, intrusive, or unpleasant. These social status groups have also been found to be highly stable across time and across situations.[8] For example, a child who is rejected at school tends to also be rejected in her other peer groups. Furthermore, rejected social status has been repeatedly shown to place children at elevated risk for a myriad of future negative outcomes, including academic failure and dropping out of school, depression and suicide, substance abuse, and delinquent and criminal behavior.[9, 10] (see Chapter 3)

While a detailed discussion of this literature is well beyond the scope of this book, it's important to underscore that research has consistently supported the validity—construct, predictive, discriminant—and utility of the peer nomination assessment approach with children from pre-school through high school and with children from diverse ethnic, racial, and economic backgrounds.[7, 8, 11] Of most relevance for SSA, peer nominations provide you with a way to establish local norms (see Chapter 4) and then clearly understand where a given child stands in a particular social area—social acceptance, social behavior, social skills—relative to others within this local peer group.

Administration & Scoring. In peer nominations, a set of children (often a class or grade) nominates peers in that set who match specific descriptors of interest—plays or works alone, is helpful and kind, is my friend, etc. Each descriptor is presented to children on a separate form listing the names of all the children within the nominating group, such as all children in the 4th grade at school. Similar to group administration of standardized academic tests, a trained professional—teacher, counselor, or researcher—typically collects peer nomination data with children in a classroom setting. The professional sets up the room so children have privacy—such as folders to shield their responses—reads aloud each item from a standardized script, and ensures quiet and privacy while children complete their nominations.

Classroom Administration Script

LEADER:
1. write your name(s) on the board, e.g. Mr. Jones, Ms. Clark
2. pass out the packets to children;
3. **CONTINUALLY** walk around room and monitor their progress as non-intrusively as possible. If it looks like a a child doesn't understand a question or questionnaire, stop and help him/her-- **DON'T WAIT FOR THE CHILD TO ASK FOR HELP.**
4. ensure quiet and privacy—use glances, stand behind or near a disruptive child, separate children, or quietly ask them to get back on task, as needed.

LEADER:

Hello. My name is Ms.___ and this is Mr.___. We're going to hand out packets and ask you to answer some questions about you and your friendships with other kids here at "XX". Everyone will be getting their own packet and every packet is just the same. Today, you're going to be answering lots of questions, so it's very important that you be as quiet as possible, pay attention, and keep working so we can finish up. But, if you have any questions as we go along, raise your hand and one of us will come to you.

OK. Pull out your pages in your packet, but keep them in order. Please use the folder to keep your answers more private, like this (DEMONSTRATE). We want you to know that everything you answer on these pages is confidential. Who knows what that means? (get responses—reinforce correct ones) Right, it means everything you say on these pages is private. So, you're NOT to talk with any other students about what you say on these pages; you need to keep your answers private from other kids just like we're going to keep them private. What we're asking about today is very important and we need to know it, but it's also important to keep your answers to yourself so no one's feelings get hurt. You can tell your parents about what you did today and what you answered, but remember to keep it private with other kids. OK? (wait for assent)

If you feel uncomfortable or upset about any question, you can skip it, but try to answer as many of the questions as you can. If you feel uncomfortable or upset by a question, just raise your hand and we'll come talk with you. We really appreciate your filling these pages out, but, if you chose to, you can stop at any time without anything bad happening to you. OK? (wait for assent) OK, let's get started. Remember to raise your hand if you have a question.

SOCIOMETRIC Items:

We've given you a list of the names of all the kids in your grade here at "XX". Find your teacher's name and then look for your own name on the list for your class. If your name is not on the list, raise your hand. If there is somebody whose name is not on the list, write their name on the board and ask the class to add this person to the bottom of the correct teacher's list, so they can nominate this child if they want. I will read the questions aloud as you read silently. If there are any questions as we go along, please raise your hand and one of us will come to you. Feel free to stop me any time if I'm going too fast.

Page 1: Like Most.

*Here's the first one. **Everybody likes some people more than they like others. Are there some boys or girls in your grade who you like more than others? Look at the names on this page and circle the names of ALL the kids who you like the very most.** Demonstrate on board. Look up at me when you're done, so I'll know when we're ready to go on. Make sure that everyone is filling this question out correctly before moving on!*

Page 2: Like Least.

*Now, let's all turn the page. At the upper lefthand corner, you should see a '2'. **Just like there are some kids who you like the most, there are probably some boys or girls who you like less than other kids. Circle the names of ALL the kids who you like the very least.** This doesn't mean you hate them; it just means you like them less than other kids. Remember, children are free to not to answer this or any other question, as they choose.*

Page 3: Fights.

*Let's turn the page again. You should see a '3' by the question at the top of the page. I'm going to read you some descriptions of kids we know at other schools. Then, I'll ask you if these descriptions sound like anybody in your grade. Listen carefully. **This person fights a lot. They may say mean things to other kids or they push them or hit them. Who is most like this in your grade? Circle the names of ALL the kids in your grade who fight a lot.** Look up at me when you're done. Make sure kids are quiet and do **not** share their nominations with others.*

In the early iterations of sociometrics, children were asked to indicate just three other children who fit a description. However, researchers found that the nominations were more reliable and did not take substantially longer to administer if children were allowed to nominate as many peers as they wanted—from zero to all.[3] Therefore, in recent years, unlimited peer nominations are commonly used. Plus, allowing children to nominate themselves can provide useful information into their social self-perceptions which can be helpful for intervention planning. For example, a child who is rejected by his peers and knows (and admits) that he's rejected by his peers would be more motivated to engage in social skills training than a rejected child who doesn't know (or denies) being rejected.

Traditionally, children make their nominations by circling names on a paper form. For each descriptor, there's a separate page containing the list of names of all children who can be nominated. Children's names are typically alphabetized by first name—because that is how children know one another—in a column under their teacher's name. These pages are typed up by the professional and compiled into a packet for each child.

Sample

Sample Sociometric Question

PAGE 1: CIRCLE THE NUMBERS NEXT TO THE NAMES OF **ALL** THE KIDS IN YOUR GRADE WHO **FIGHT A LOT**.

Teacher 1	Teacher 2	Teacher 3
Adam Ant	Alisha Purple	Alec Park
Bill Dinosaur	Sam Yellow	Marvin Beach
Peggy Lizard	Taylor Green	Misha Camp
TJ Pigeon	Zach Aquamarine	Sharri Mall

Several attempts to computerize the peer nomination assessment method have been made over the years. For example, Drs. DeRosier and Thomas developed the SCAN (Sociometric Collection and Analysis) software which streamlines the collection, analysis, and interpretation process for administrators.[12] SCAN and other computerized applications can greatly decrease—but not eliminate—the considerable training, statistical expertise, and time needed to use this SSA approach.

STRENGTHS AND WEAKNESSES

In the following review of the relative strengths and weaknesses of using peer nominations for SSA, we discuss how feasible this approach is to administer, the quality of the resulting data, and how engaged children are likely to be as respondents. To help guide our discussion, we provide summary ratings in each area and then present our reasons behind these ratings. At the end of this discussion, we also provide overall ratings to summarize how effective we believe peer nominations are for accomplishing intervention screening, progress monitoring, and evaluation functions (see Chapter 4). These ratings are purely our best judgment based on available evidence.

Rating Legend

- = Very good in this area
- = Generally good
- = Generally fair
- = Generally poor
- = Very poor in this area

Feasibility of Administration

The primary weakness of the peer nomination method is its infeasibility for everyday—or even periodic—use by schools. Because computerized software can significantly improve feasibility, we've separated out our ratings according to whether you administer peer nominations by hand in the traditional fashion or use one of the newer software packages, such as SCAN.

Substantial training and expertise is needed to administer peer nominations, calculate scores, and interpret results. It's critical that the professionals administering the data collection script do so in a standardized way, so they do not bias or influence children's responses. For example, when asking children who they like the very least, if the administrator uses a disapproving tone of voice, hovers over children as they make their selections, or makes side comments such as *"this doesn't happen in our school much"* or *"everyone should like everyone else, but . . . ,"* then children are not going to be open and honest when completing this item. Training, including a good deal of practice and corrective feedback by a supervisor, is needed to ensure administrators can collect unbiased, reliable data with children.

Ratings of Peer Nominations for SSA

	By hand	Software
Feasible to administer	Very poor	Generally poor
Training/expertise needed	Very poor	Generally poor
Time efficiency	Generally poor	Generally fair
Cost effectiveness	Generally poor	Generally fair

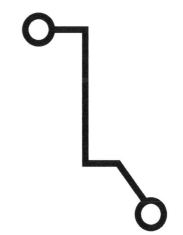

A huge amount of data are generated through this assessment method, making it impossible to calculate scores without aid of a computer. It takes considerable time to enter the data into the computer, and it also takes considerable expertise to run the statistical program needed to calculate scores. A few software products—such as SCAN—are available to automate the scoring process once the data are entered, but interpreting the data can still be difficult. What exactly does a standardized score of 1.28 for bullying mean? Or a standardized score of -.36 for social preference? Or a borderline rejected status categorization? To interpret these results, the professional must understand probability theory and a normal bell curve distribution of means and standard deviations, as displayed in **Figure 3**.

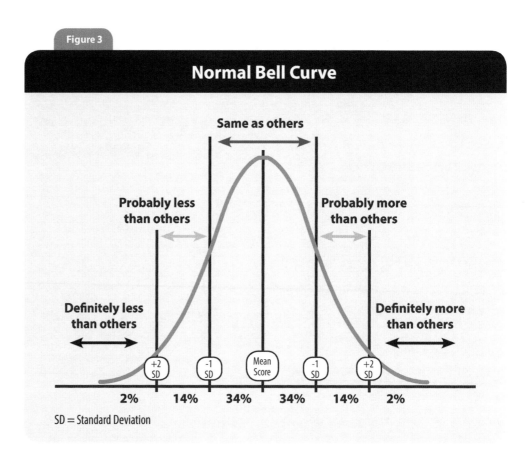

In addition, the professional must understand that sociometrics generate a 'snapshot' of the social map that specifies where a child is relative to others in **that peer group at that time**. These scores are highly dependent on who is included in the sample of nominating and nominated children and are not necessarily comparable across time or across different peer groups. The statistics that are generated are based on the specific set of children in the nominating group at the time of data collection. If you removed data for, say the six most aggressive children in the group, and re-ran the scoring program, the remaining children's scores on aggression would change because now you're asking how a given child compares to the other children included in this smaller set. Those children who were only moderately aggressive when the six highly aggressive children were included in the sample will now appear to be much more aggressive within this smaller set. Similarly, if you wish to assess change in scores over time, it's important to make sure you include essentially the same children in the nominating set at each time point. It's not necessary to ensure the exact same set of children—which is impossible with absences from school and children moving in and out of a school—but you want to have at least 80% overlap across assessment time points. In addition, you need to make sure that children have not been systematically left out of the sample, as in the case of removing all highly aggressive children on purpose.[3, 13, 14] Scores resulting from sociometric methods will be impacted by differences in nominating groups, but the impact will be negligible as long as these differences are due to normally occurring events within the school environment and most of the same children are included at both time points. As is evident from this discussion, considerable training is needed to understand these types of parameters since they may impact scores.

Because sociometrics were created primarily as a research tool, the methodology is not really user friendly and the results make more sense in the research world—where you're interested in examining correlations across different groups of children, for example—than in real-life practice where you are most interested in the needs of individual children. On the positive side, the administrator can gather a great deal of information about a large group of children within a relatively brief administration period (typically 2-5 minutes per sociometric item). While the overall time cost to administer, score, and interpret sociometrics is high, the time cost per child is relatively low. Also, the financial cost of administering sociometrics with children is very low or even free if the administrator types up the nomination lists and enters and scores the data himself. In general, sociometric software programs for scoring are quite affordable (for example, SCAN is $75 per year for unlimited usage).

Ethical Considerations in the Use of Sociometrics. The nature of peer-report measures raises ethical issues that are important to consider. The approach requires children to think about both negative and positive characteristics of their peers and then report these opinions. This task clearly has the potential to create distress, both from the perspective of having to report sometimes undesirable behaviors in others and from the perspective of knowing others are rating you on these same characteristics. These ethical considerations have led some to abandon sociometrics and instead rely on teacher- or parent-report measures.[15] Unfortunately, peer nomination is one of the only ways we have to gather the unique perspective of peers on the social environment which will be different—and potentially more accurate—than the perspective of adults.

In fact, children who experience peer problems tend to keep that information to themselves. Telling an adult is often viewed by children as probably ineffective for helping them solve the problem and potentially likely to make things worse.[16, 17] Further, children who engage in negative social behaviors are quite adept at keeping their acts of bullying and rejection away from the eyes of adults.[16] So, adults may actually be unaware of negative social interactions among children and, as a result, teachers and parents tend to fail to identify children who actually do experience significant peer problems—leading to what are called 'false negatives.'[18] For example, in a study of 3rd through 5th graders, teachers identified only 17% of the children who peers identified as significantly rejected.[19] (see **Figure 4**)

Figure 4

Teacher-Report of Peer Rejected Children

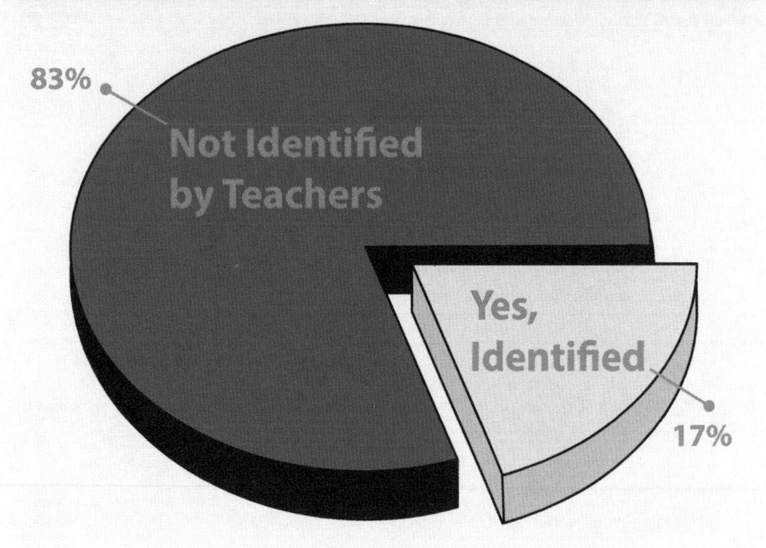

83%

Not Identified by Teachers

Yes, Identified

17%

Self-report measures of peer problems are similarly inaccurate. Biases in both directions occur. For example, aggressive children tend to report better peer relations and popular children tend to report worse peer relations than is actually the case.[20] Similarly, only about 50% of rejected children accurately report their social status.[21] These biases may be self-defensive or reflect greater inaccuracy when interpreting social cues.[22]

The value of peer-report data has led researchers to directly examine the ethical questions surrounding the use of sociometrics. One of the most important studies was conducted by Lara Mayeux[13] and her colleagues. These researchers administered a traditional social-status sociometric measure to third grade students and they also developed the Classroom Testing Survey to measure the children's and teacher's memory and perceptions of the testing process. During a one-hour interview with each child, the researchers assessed the children's reactions to the peer nomination process. Results revealed promising information about the ethics of using sociometrics. First, children rarely talked with one another about their responses following participation, which suggests that potentially harmful discussions may not be a substantial risk after all. Second, and most importantly, *"most children and their teachers reported no negative emotional reactions to the sociometric testing, nor did they report that children were treated differently by peers following the procedure."* Thus, the major concern that participation leads to negative emotions and/or changes in how participants are treated was shown to be a much smaller risk than assumed.

Though a great deal of evidence by these and other researchers has shown that the negative impact of peer nominations is very low,[13, 14, 22] it's nevertheless important to minimize any potential harm when using this SSA method. A number of suggestions and safeguards can help in this regard, including ensuring privacy of all participants during administration, ending the session by having children complete a positive survey or structured activity, and carefully monitoring for negative reactions during and after administration.[15, 23] These safeguards—combined with the demonstrated low risks of harm—suggest peer nominations can be used in a responsible and ethical manner.

Ratings of Peer Nominations for SSA

Utility of data	◑
Psychometrically sound	◕
Norm-based cut-offs	◑
Contextually relevant	◑

Utility of Data

A primary strength of peer nominations is the utility of the data it generates. Since Coie's seminal work in 1982, over 20,000 research studies have included sociometric methods, so there is a wealth of scientific evidence guiding their use and interpretation.[3, 7, 8, 9] As discussed earlier in this chapter, when administered correctly, peer nominations are unparalleled in their psychometric soundness, in terms of validity and reliability of results.

The ability to generate a sociogram—or social map—across all children within the peer group is a key advantage of peer nominations. In essence, sociometrics allow professionals to determine the local norms for a given social behavior or skill and then map exactly where each child falls relative to

the other children in his peer group. This information is extremely helpful for intervention planning. For example, you can clearly identify which children are least socially skilled or who has the fewest friends in class, so you can implement appropriate interventions to help these children achieve social functioning more in line with that of their peers. However, this strength is also a weakness in that sociometrics can *only* generate local norms—they say nothing about national or population-based norms (see Chapter 4). In other words, while a score may indicate a child is much more socially immature than other children in 4th grade at his school, this does not necessarily mean he is immature compared to 4th graders more generally.

By their very nature, sociometrics are contextually relevant because it's the child's standing within a particular social context that is being measured. Peer nominations reflect the peer group's consensus opinion about a child's social behavior based on their past experiences together. Thus, a child's real-world behavior with these peers would be expected to closely match his sociometric scores. In fact, research studies do support this correspondence.[23, 24] For example, if a child scores two standard deviations above the mean for the social withdrawal peer nomination, she would definitely be more likely to play or work alone at school.

Of course, the data generated through peer nominations don't necessarily tell us anything about how a child would behave or be seen by peers within a different social context, such as his peer group at church or in his neighborhood. So there's a limit to its contextual relevance for other social situations. However, research indicates that sociometric results for a given child are highly consistent across different settings.[8, 25] For example, if a child is seen as a bully in his school peer group, he's likely to be seen as a bully in other non-school peer groups.

Ratings of Peer Nominations for SSA

Objectivity of data	○
Standardized measurement	○
Respondent bias	◑
Accuracy checks	◑

Accuracy of Data

If administered properly, peer nominations provide a more reliable picture of the social structure than all other traditional SSA methods. Sociometric measurement is more reliable because it integrates the views of multiple informants, such as all children across an entire grade. By assessing the consensus across informants—rather than relying on the perspective of just one or two individuals—the impact of respondent bias on resulting scores is greatly decreased.

However, there's an important caveat regarding the accuracy of peer nomination data. If the administrator is poorly trained, inaccuracies in the data are likely to occur. These are sensitive questions and children will look to the administrator for clues as to how open and honest they can truly be. If it's clear the administrator disapproves of a question, children will pick up on his tone of voice and inadvertent comments, so fewer nominations are made. Or if the administrator fails to maintain proper behavior management of the class, children may fear their answers are not really private and be less willing to share. It's critically important that administrators be well trained and that peer nominations be administered using a structured, standardized script so that the accuracy of children's nominations is not adversely impacted.

The psychometric measurement strengths of peer nominations should provide you with considerable confidence regarding the validity and accuracy of the results for a given child. However, sociometrics don't include any built-in ways to check the accuracy of the data. As with other SSA approaches, you can investigate accuracy by gathering data using multiple SSA methods and comparing results. However, this will add time and expense to the overall SSA.

Engaging for Children

If children are provided with a safe, private environment within which to make their nominations, children enjoy participating in this SSA. In fact, the editor's experience administering sociometrics with thousands of children underscores this method's engaging nature. Children appreciate the opportunity to voice their opinion and be heard. Social issues are centrally important to children's school life, so being able to privately share their perspective can be empowering and enjoyable for children. However, if the administrator makes children uncomfortable or does not control the children's behavior in the classroom, children will not feel safe and will dislike the experience.

Ratings of Peer Nominations for SSA

Engaging for children

Overall Ratings

While the quality of data resulting from peer nominations is superior to any other traditional SSA approach, it's simply not a feasible methodology for everyday use. Even computerized software that streamlines the scoring and analysis components is not sufficient for making peer nominations a practical choice for most school settings. The time demands are too high to justify use of sociometrics—time for training, time for setting up the nomination forms, time for data collection with students, and time for data entry are each substantial. In addition, school professionals may be reluctant to use peer nominations because of the sensitive questions posed to students and because of the statistical expertise needed to calculate and interpret the scores.

Use of Peer Nominations for Intervention Planning Purposes

Useful for screening ●

Useful for progress monitoring ●

Useful for intervention evaluation ◐

If peer nominations are used for screening, the benefits likely outweigh the costs. Sociometrics are particularly powerful and useful as a universal screener in that they enable you to understand the relative social strengths and weaknesses of a large number of children with relatively low time and financial cost per student. Peer nominations generate a great deal of information about the entire nominating group so you can identify children at the extremes who are in particular need of intervention. For use as a progress monitoring or intervention evaluation tool, however, sociometrics are an infeasible option for most schools. The only exception would be use of peer nominations to evaluate a universal intervention that involves the entire peer group. In this case, sociometrics would provide a cost-effective way to assess the impact of the universal intervention across all children in a classroom or grade. Currently, this SSA method is rarely used by schools due to its high training and logistical demands for collection, analysis, and interpretation of peer nomination data. As a result, researchers, rather than school personnel, continue to be the primary users of sociometrics.

CHAPTER 9 NOTES

1. Cillessen, A. H. N., van Ijzendoorn, H. W., van Lieshout, C. F. M., & Hartup, W. W. (1992). Heterogeneity among peer-rejected boys: Subtypes and stabilities. *Child Development, 63,* 893-905.

2. Moreno, J. L. (1933). Psychological and social organization of groups in the community. *Proceedings & Addresses: American Association on Mental Deficiency, 38,* 224-242.

3. Terry, R. (2000). Recent advances in measurement theory and the use of sociometric techniques. In A. H. Cillessen & W. M. Bukowski (Eds.), *Recent advances in the measurement of acceptance and rejection in the peer system* (pp. 27-53). San Francisco, CA: Jossey-Bass.

4. Peery, J. C. (1979). Popular, amiable, isolated, rejected: A reconceptualization of sociometric status in preschool children. *Child Development, 50,* 1231-1234.

5. Coie, J. D., Dodge, K. A., & Coppotelli, H. (1982). Dimensions and types of social status: A cross-age perspective. *Developmental Psychology, 18,* 557-570.

6. For each item, children were presented with a roster of all the children in their grade at their school and were asked to nominate all the peers across the grade who matched specific social acceptance and social behavior descriptions (Coie et al., 1982; Crick & Grotpeter, 1995). To assess social status, children responded to two standard positive and negative nominations: (a) children they like the most (liked most), and (b) children they like the least (liked least). To assess social behavior, children nominated peers that fit each of the following five behavioral descriptions (Coie et al., 1982): (a) act like a bully a lot (bully); (b) get picked on or called names a lot (victim); (c) do mean things indirectly, such as spread rumors or organize exclusion (relational aggression); (d) play or work alone a lot (withdrawn), and (e) are often a good leader (leader). Gradewide nominations are the standard for late elementary school grades (Cillessen, Bukowski, & Haselager, 2000). In this study, fifth graders had sufficient contact and familiarity with students in other classrooms, so that grade wide nominations across classrooms were used. Unlimited nominations were also used in this study. Research indicates that unlimited nominations decrease error variance and improve the stability and reliability in the measurement of children's peer relations (Terry, 2000).

For each social behavior item, the number of nominations a child received was summed and standardized (M=50, SD=51) within the school. Thus, children's social behavior was estimated relative to the level of that behavior within their peer group (Coie et al., 1982). Children were assigned to sociometric status groups using the algorithm developed by Coie and colleagues (Coie & Dodge, 1988; Coie et al., 1982). Liked most (LM) and liked least (LL) nominations were totaled and transformed to standard scores (M=0, SD=1) by school (i.e., ZLM and ZLL, respectively). Social preference (SP) was calculated by subtracting the ZLL score from the ZLM score. Social impact (SI) was calculated by adding the ZLM and ZLL scores. SP and SI were then restandardized within each school (i.e., ZSP and ZSI).

The following percentage of the sample was assigned to each group: popular =14% (*n*=120), Controversial=6% (*n*=54), rejected=14% (*n*=123), neglected=10% (*n*=90), average=14% (*n*=119), and unclassified=42% (*n*=375). This distribution closely matches that typically found using Coie's (1982) sociometric classification system. Extending beyond the traditional sociometric classification method (Coie et al., 1982), a new algorithm was used to provide a richer understanding of children's social position within their grade. To be classified within a particular social status group, a child must meet a distinct set of conditions. For example, for a child to be classified as popular, all three of the following conditions must be met:

1. standardized SP score greater than 1 (ZSP41),

2. standardized LM greater than 0 (ZLM40), and

3. standardized LL less than 0 (ZLLo0).

If a child fails to meet just one of these conditions, he or she will not be classified as popular. To measure the strength of a child's classification (i.e., the degree to which a child falls within a status group), we must measure the extent to which each of the conditions that determine that classification are met. For the popular classification, we must calculate the extent to which each child's (ZSP41), (ZLM 40), and (ZLLo0). In fact, each condition that must be met for all six of the social status groups is expressed as a certain standardized score (e.g., ZSP, ZLL, ZLM) being greater than or less than a particular numeric cutoff (e.g.,o1, 40, 4.5). Each condition is expressed in terms of a cumulative density function(CDF) that aggregates the area under the normal curve up to a particular value (an example is available in Hart, 1968). The estimate of the extent to which a given child's score (Zx) exceeds a given cutoff (C) is given by CDF(Zx –C). Conversely, the extent to which a given child's score falls short of a cutoff is given by 1 –CDF(C–Zx).

Statistical Procedures for Calculating Status Group Bias

To illustrate the derivation of these formulas, we show how to derive an estimate for one of the popular status conditions, that is, ZLM40. Another way to express this condition is that the child must have more than average, or mean, number of LM votes. Because our sample distribution of scores only approximates the true population, we can only provide qualified estimates of where the population mean lies. The central limit theorem states that the distribution of sample scores approximates a normal bell-shaped distribution, with our sample mean approximating the population mean. We can use this theorem to estimate likelihood of the population mean being within a particular confidence interval.

The methodology for this is to measure the area under the normal curve between the points that bound the interval (see Berry, 1996, for detailed discussion of this methodology). Usually, we use a fixed confidence coefficient to discover the upper and lower bounds of an interval. But in our case, we know the interval's boundaries and solve for the confidence coefficient. The confidence coefficient (or probability, written P(1)) that a given child's ZLM score is greater than zero is equivalent to the probability that the population mean is less than ZLM, that is, that the population mean mLM lies in an interval between negative infinity and a given child's ZLM score. An algorithm that derives the area under that curve between negative infinity and a given value is called the CDF (see Hart, 1968). Thus, P(ZLM40) is equivalent to the CDF(ZLM).Generalizing, to calculate the probability that the population mean lies some threshold T below the student's score, or P(Zx4T), is given by CDF(Zx –T). Similarly, the P(ZxoT) is given by 1 –CDF(T–Zx). For more information regarding the software used to implement these calculations and how to access this software, contact the first author.

7. Kupersmidt, J. B. & DeRosier, M. E. (2004). How peer problems lead to negative outcomes: An integrative mediational model. In J. B. Kupersmidt & K. A. Dodge (Eds.), *Children's peer relations: From development to intervention.* Washington, DC: American Psychological Association.

8. Cillessen, A. H., Bukowski, W. M, & Haselager, G. J. (2000). Stability of sociometric categories. In A. H. Cillessen & W. M. Bukowski (Eds.), *Recent advances in the measurement of acceptance and rejection in the peer system* (pp. 75-93). San Francisco, CA: Jossey-Bass.

9. Parker, J. G., Rubin, K. H., Erath, S. A., Wojslawowicz, J. C., & Buskirk, A. A. (2006). Peer relationships, child development, and adjustment: A developmental psychopathology perspective. In D. Cicchetti & D. J. Cohen (Eds.), *Developmental Psychopathology, Vol. 1: Theory and Method* (pp. 419-493). Hoboken, NJ: Wiley.

10. Ollendick, T. H., Weist, M. D., Borden, M. C., & Greene, R. W. (1992). Sociometric status and academic, behavioral, and psychological adjustment: A five-year longitudinal study. *Journal of Consulting and Clinical Psychology, 60,* 80-87.

11. Martin, E. (2011). The influence of diverse interaction contexts on students' sociometric status. *The Spanish Journal of Psychology, 14,* 88-98.

12. DeRosier, M. E. & Thomas, J. M. (2003). Strengthening sociometric prediction: Scientific advances in the assessment of children's peer relations. *Child Development, 75,* 1379-1392.

13. Mayeux, L., Underwood, M. K., & Risser, S. D. (2007). Perspectives on the ethics of sociometric research with children: How children, peers, and teachers help to inform the debate. *Merrill-Palmer Quarterly, 53,* 53-78.

14. Hayvren, M. & Hymel, S. (1984). Ethical issues in sociometric testing: Impact of sociometric measures on interaction behavior *Developmental Psychology, 20,* 844-849.

15. Doll, B., Murphy, P., & Song, S. Y. (2003). The relationship between children's self-reported recess problems, and peer acceptance and friendships. *Journal of School Psychology, 41,* 113-130.

16. Olweus, D. (1991). Bully/victim problems among school children: Basic facts and effects of a school based intervention program. In D. Pepler & K. Rubin (Eds.), *The development and treatment of childhood aggression* (pp. 411-448). Hillsdale, N.J.: Erlbaum.

17. Craig, W. M., & Pepler, D. J. (1997). Observations of bullying and victimization on the playground. *Canadian Journal of School Psychology, 2,* 41-60.

18. Foster, S. L., Bell-Dolan, D., & Berler, E. S. (1986). Methodological issues in the use of sociometrics for selecting children for social skills research and training. *Advances in Behavioral Assessment of Children & Families, 2,* 227-248.

19. DeRosier, M. E. (1995). 3-C Program: Final report to the Wake County Public School System.

20. Hymel, S., & Franke, S. (1985). Children's peer relations: Assessing self-perceptions. *Children's Peer Relations: Issues in Assessment and Intervention,* 75-91.

21. Boivin, M., & Bégin, G. (1989). Peer status and self-perception among early elementary school children: The case of the rejected children. *Child Development, 60,* 591-596.

22. Dodge, K. A., & Feldman, E. (1990). Issues in social cognition and sociometric status. *Peer Rejection in Childhood,* 119-155.

23. Weiss, B., Harris, V., & Catron, T. (2002). Development and initial validation of the peer-report measure of internalizing and externalizing behavior. *Journal of Abnormal Child Psychology, 30,* 285-294.

24. Mouton, J. S., Blake, R. R., & Fruchter, B. (1955). The validity of sociometric responses. *Sociometry,* 18(3), 181-206.

25. Eronen, S., & Nurmi, J. E. (2001). Sociometric status of young adults: Behavioral correlates, and cognitive-motivational antecedents and consequences. *International Journal of Behavioral Development, 25,* 203-213.

10

TRADITIONAL BEST PRACTICES FOR SSA

by: Melissa E. DeRosier, Ph.D.

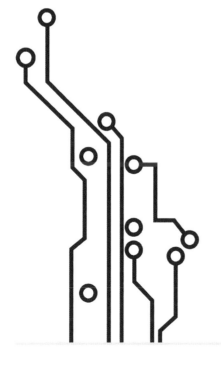

DESCRIPTION

Writing this section of the book was an interesting exercise for the authors. We not only presented a detailed discussion of the four traditional SSA approaches, but we also attempted to quantify the strengths and weaknesses of each. Using a rating scale from 'very good' to 'very poor,' we rated each methodology according to how feasible it is to administer, the utility of its data, the objectivity of its data, and how engaged children are as respondents—key areas you need to consider when selecting an SSA approach. To our knowledge, no one has attempted this type of comparison before. Yet, we found it a very useful way to clearly lay out the relative pros and cons of using each approach.

Of course, a caveat to this entire discussion is that these ratings are only our best judgments, based on the research literature as well as on our clinical experience conducting social skills assessments with children over the years. Others may argue with our ratings. You may have a different experience with these SSA approaches. We only hope that these ratings will be a useful starting place as you consider how to structure your SSA with children.

Finding a Balance

No one has unlimited time, resources, or staffing to conduct the perfect SSA. And, in fact, the perfect SSA does not exist among the traditional options—each has significant strengths and weaknesses. **Table 1** summarizes our ratings for each traditional SSA approach in key areas. To find the right fit for you in your situation, you'll always need to balance among these various factors.

You can find this balance by asking yourself the following questions. First and foremost,

"What is my intervention planning goal?"

As discussed in Chapter 4, always keep your end goal for the assessment in mind. There are three possible intervention planning goals for SSA: (a) conducting a screening to help you identify children with social skill deficits; (b) monitoring whether a child is responding as expected during an intervention; and (c) evaluating whether a child or children actually improve in targeted social, behavioral, or emotional outcomes in response to intervention. Clearly specifying how you plan to use the data will help you identify what information you need to collect. Once the answer to this question is clear, ask yourself the second question:

"How can I gather the most informative and useful data with the time and resources I have?"

Time is a rare and precious commodity within the school setting, so it will often be a driving factor in your SSA selection. How much time do you or other staff have to conduct an SSA? Often, the answer is 'none.' Unfortunately, because time pressures are so high in schools, professionals will often jump to using an approach that yields data quickly, such as brief rating scales or unstructured observations. But, this time savings comes with a heavy price in terms of increased likelihood that your data will be unreliable or inaccurate, and therefore your conclusions will be faulty. If, for example, you use a teacher rating scale as your screening instrument, then you may get a high number of false negatives. So, you'll fail to identify a number of children who are actually experiencing significant social problems and would benefit from intervention.

For most SSA purposes, 'quick and dirty' methods are a waste of the time you spend administering them. Even worse, they'll likely cost you more time in the end than if you had chosen a more accurate, yet more time-consuming approach in the first place. If you consider the example above, children who have social problems but are unidentified are likely to get worse over time, so they'll require more services than if they were accurately identified earlier. And when you find that your intervention doesn't result in the positive classroom outcomes you expected, you'll have to conduct another SSA and likely additional intervention.

Another time pressure in the school setting is that you often need to gather data quickly to meet a deadline, such as completing an IEP (Individualized Education Plan) or deciding on disciplinary action. In these more urgent situations, it's even more crucial that you insist on taking the time needed to use an SSA approach that will generate highly accurate and usable data.

Resources are also precious within schools. We often think of resources as financial, but resources can also be intellectual, staffing, technological, or space related. The actual cost of an SSA involves all of these factors. For example, some SSA options include copyrighted forms, so you must pay for each form you use. Sometimes software is available which costs money to purchase and requires a computer. Some SSA methods require highly trained staff while others do not. Sometimes private office space is needed so the SSA can be conducted one-on-one while other times you can implement the SSA in the classroom.

With limited resources, you may be drawn to inexpensive, simple options. In fact, an Internet search will yield a myriad of free or low-cost rating scales, observational tips, and interview questions you could use. **Be very wary of options that have no research base to support their use.** It is true that research-based SSA methods will be more costly, particularly in the beginning as you spend time and resources getting set up and trained on the system. You'll also have less freedom to change the questions or data collection procedures because the quality of the data depends on standardized administration. However, your SSA will have a much more solid foundation if you carefully select reliable, proven, and established approaches. The resulting data will be more accurate and useful for intervention planning, and in the end, an evidence-based approach will actually be the best use of your limited time and resources.

Review of Ratings

As you look across the ratings in **Table 1**, it becomes clear why **behavioral rating scales** are currently the most widely used SSA method. They're easy to use, relatively inexpensive, and—if administered correctly—produce valuable information quickly. However, our ability to trust the resulting scores can be compromised by potential respondent biases as well as the contextually-generic nature of rating scale questions (see Chapter 6). It's impossible to know how the perspective of the person completing the questionnaire impacts ratings or what particular situations are being used as the basis for those ratings. Perhaps the respondent has particular expectations for 'proper' social behavior. Or, perhaps he's only observed the child in a limited number of social settings. Or, perhaps the child completing the survey is bored or frustrated by question after question, so he just selects responses randomly. The utility and quality of the data will be impacted by these and other respondent-specific factors. You can help mitigate this weakness by gathering rating scale data from multiple respondents, but this process adds time and resource costs to the SSA and there are no clear guidelines to help you interpret differing results across respondents.

It's also easy to see from Table 1 why **peer nominations** are rarely used in the school setting. While the data produced are the most reliable and valid, peer nominations require too much time and too high a level of expertise for most schools to administer (see Chapter 9). Feasibility can be improved with computer software, but the school professional still needs to spend considerable time setting up for data collection and data entry. Plus, because this methodology was developed for research purposes, the resulting scores are not easily understandable without some measure of statistical expertise, which undermines the utility of this approach.

Observations and **interviews** can generate highly useful information about an individual child's functioning in a particular social context (see Chapters 7 and 8). Observations provide a rich picture of the child's social behavior in specific situations at school, so you can clearly understand contextually-relevant antecedents and consequences. Similarly, when you conduct an interview with a child, you can gather much more in-depth, detailed information—particularly the child's thoughts and feelings about

Table 1

Comparison of Traditional SSA Approaches

	Behavioral Ratings	Observation	Interview	Peer Nominations	
				By hand	Software
Feasible to administer	●	◐	○	●	◐
Training/expertise needed	●	●	◐	●	◐
Time efficiency	●	◐	○	◐	○
Cost effectiveness	◐	◐	◐	◐	○
Utility of data	○	◐	○	◐	
Psychometrically sound	◐	○	◐	●	
Norm-based cut-offs	◐	●	●	◐	
Contextually relevant	◐	●	●	◐	
Objectivity of data	◐	○	◐	○	
Standardized measurement	◐	◐	◐	○	
Respondent bias	◐	○	●	◐	
Accuracy checks	◐	◐	●	◐	
Engaging for children	◐	n/a	○	◐	
Useful for screening	◐	○	○	●	
Useful for progress monitoring	◐	◐	○	●	
Useful for intervention evaluation	◐	○	◐	◐	

social situations—than is possible with any other SSA approach. However, this benefit of producing contextually relevant information for a given child is counter-balanced by the fact that these methods provide no norms for comparison. In other words, it's impossible to know how data for one child

compare with data for other same-aged peers in the same context (local norms) or more generally (population-based norms). In addition, with both these SSA approaches, the degree to which the resulting data will be useful or accurate can vary greatly depending on the school professional's level of training as well as on the procedures used to collect the data. If you use a well-established, structured system for conducting the observation/interview and for scoring the data, concerns about validity and reliability of data can be greatly lessened.

Overall, the ease of use and cost-effectiveness of rating scales—provided you're using a research-based measure and administering it properly—make them quite useful for all intervention planning purposes. Observations and interviews are most useful for screening purposes, and usually as a supplement to a broader assessment strategy, such as when you need more detailed information to help you choose which intervention is best for a given child. Data from these methods are particularly helpful as a starting place for intervention planning, but they can also be informative for progress monitoring and intervention evaluation purposes. Peer nominations can be an excellent universal screening tool because they yield a great deal of reliable, valid, and contextually-relevant data about a large number of children within a relatively brief administration time. The cost per child is actually quite low when used for screening and the quality of the data you can gather through this approach makes it worth considering.

Use Cases

Every situation and school setting is different, so you'll have to judge what SSA methods are doable and best for you. Based on the pattern of strengths and weaknesses across the four traditional SSA approaches, here are our recommendations for some sample situations:

- **You need to screen a large number of children**→ collect peer nominations or, if that's not possible, select a brief SSA rating scale with lots of evidence to support its use and ask teachers to complete this scale for all children in their classroom (Note: don't use either of these methods before six weeks into a new school year because it takes this long for teachers and peers to get a reliable picture of children's social functioning.)

- **It's critically important to attain contextually relevant data for a given child** → be sure to include a structured observational coding system

- **You need to determine whether a child is ready for a social skills group** → conduct an interview with the child to evaluate whether she is aware of her social difficulties and is motivated to work on them

- **You want to assess the child's skills in a specific social situation** → conduct a structured naturalistic observation

- **You need to document progress in response to intervention using the most accurate and reliable means possible** → use a rating scale with behaviorally specific questions that directly reflect what is being taught in the intervention

- **You're trying to decide between conducting a pull-out with a subset of children or a universal intervention with the whole classroom** → collect peer nominations or, if that's not possible, conduct an observation of the classroom using a structured time sampling recording system

- **You want to assess whether your intervention resulted in significant change in social functioning for those children who participated** → use well-established rating scale measure(s) with documented reliability and validity with same-aged children

Two common sayings about assessment more generally may be helpful to keep in mind as you select the method or methods to include in your SSA:

The more data, the better.

Trash in, trash out

Though it's more time consuming and costly, it's always best to combine different methods for a more well-rounded and comprehensive SSA approach. More data means you have more information on which to base your intervention planning decisions.

However, not all data are created equal. If you collect data using unreliable, unsubstantiated methods or using inconsistent, faulty procedures, the information you generate will not be informative. To generate the most useful and meaningful data, you need to use well established, research-based, and professionally applied procedures.

PART III

GAME-BASED SOCIAL SKILLS ASSESSMENT

GAME-BASED SOCIAL SKILLS ASSESSMENT

OVERVIEW

Part I of this book defined social skills and their importance across many areas of development. We discussed how poor social skills undermine children's social relationships which, in turn, can foster a number of negative outcomes. Then, in Part II, we examined how children's social skills and social functioning are traditionally assessed. We described behavioral rating scales, behavioral observations, interviewing, and peer nominations, and evaluated the advantages and disadvantages of each.

In Part III, we turn our discussion to a completely new approach to SSA—the use of gaming technology to assess how children solve social problems and respond in social situations within tailored virtual scenes. In the first chapter of this section, we talk about the evolution of computerized assessment methods and why games can be particularly powerful for generating social skill data. The next chapter provides a concrete example of a social problem solving game platform—Zoo U— and discusses the theory and research driving development of the social problem solving scenes. We then summarize the iterative development and testing process that was used to establish the Zoo U software and its underlying scoring rubric. After that, we review the Zoo U assessment reports process followed by a description of the studies we conducted to establish the psychometric soundness of Zoo U. The last chapter of this section evaluates the strengths and weaknesses of a game-based approach to SSA and explores how games move beyond the limitations of traditional SSA methods.

11

USING GAMES FOR SSA

by: Rebecca Sanchez, Ph.D. and Ashley Craig, Ph.D.

DESCRIPTION

If you're reading this book, you understand that assessment of children's knowledge, skills, and abilities is critical for education. Information gained from assessment tells us where children are, so we can help them get where they need to go. In the school environment, there's an increasing push to use technology to better assess children's knowledge and progress in a number of domains. States are under a mandate to implement digital assessments by 2014, and more than 27 states currently have operational or pilot versions of online tests for their statewide or end-of-course exams. In the *2010 National Education Technology Plan,* U. S. Secretary of Education Arne Duncan highlighted this when he called for research about how *"assessment technologies, such as simulations, collaborative environments, virtual worlds, games, and cognitive tutors, can be used to engage and motivate learners while assessing complex skills."*[1]

Clearly, there's strong buy-in for technology-assisted assessment to align with new directions in education. To understand why, let's take a look at how we got here.

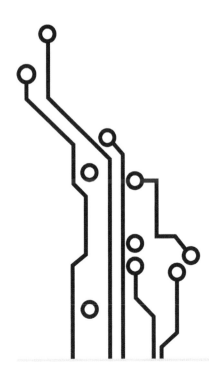

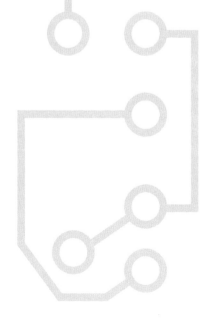

THE MOVE TOWARD TECHNOLOGY-BASED ASSESSMENT

The first steps in technology-based assessment were taken decades ago as educators, administrators, and researchers realized the time, cost, and consistency advantages of computer-assisted assessment over standard paper-based testing. Early computerized assessment came in the form of standard multiple choice items that were scored by—and later actually presented to children on—computers. This method of administration reduced costs for shipping, tracking, and scoring, eliminated human error in scoring, and enabled rapid scoring and return of results.[2-4]

These early assessments, however, were limited in that they could only present simple, static problems (multiple choice or true/false) that focused heavily on fact retrieval. Since then, developments in cognitive science, measurement, and information and communication technologies have enabled more sophisticated methods of assessment. In computerized adaptive testing (CAT), the software adapts or adjusts the type or number of questions presented based on the respondent's answers to prior questions. This important feature of CAT is also found in game-based assessment, which will be addressed at the end of this chapter.

Technology has seen rapid developments since the introduction of CAT in the 1990s, and as a result, the current state-of-the-art assessment can provide more meaningful feedback on multifaceted, hard to measure skills, including social skills. These dynamic assessments can be designed to capture complex processes, such as problem solving strategies and real-time responses to real-world situations.[5] The type and sequence of a child's responses, the amount of time and number of attempts he takes to reach a solution, and his choice of responses to a variety of situations can all be used to understand the child's thinking, identify errors, and provide individual assistance or feedback.

An exciting new vehicle for dynamic assessment is the use of digital games to evaluate children's performance. Game-based assessment can take many forms, from relatively simple games focused on a single skill (such as clicking on the answer to an addition problem in a game-like environment), to immersive virtual environments that require the child to fully engage (such as using his avatar to make a series of choices in a complex situation or ongoing narrative). This latter type of game has great potential for SSA because it requires planning, analysis, and sequential problem solving on the part of the user.

WHY GAME-BASED ASSESSMENT?

Using games or game-like activities for SSA is potentially beneficial for a number of reasons.

Games Share Essential Underlying Characteristics with Assessments

Play is an important element of healthy child development and learning.[6] When children play games, they operate within a *"system in which players engage in artificial conflict, defined by rules, which results in a quantifiable outcome."*[7] The structure of games—that there are rules to follow and an outcome to achieve—provides a way for us to measure knowledge and abilities, making games inherently suited for assessment. We can examine whether and how children use rules and how they reach goals to understand what knowledge they have acquired and what strategies and processes underlie their decision-making.

Games are Engaging and Motivating

It's not surprising that children prefer to participate in games rather than in traditional classroom activities.[8] Teachers have used card games, board games, and role plays for decades to teach children specific skills. And digital games are especially appealing to children today, because technology is a ubiquitous part of life.[9] The tide of professional opinion is beginning to turn from viewing digital games as a distraction in the classroom to an understanding that gameplay through virtual or simulated environments can be a great motivator in the educational process[10] and a valuable part of learning and development.[11] Games can be especially useful for sustaining engagement and motivation for complex, challenging activities.[12,13]

Games Can Provide Powerful Assessment Data

The relatively recent application of digital games to simulate tasks and situations encountered in real life has made it possible to expand their use. Playing a digital game lets a child think, understand, prepare, execute actions, and adjust strategy as needed.[12] Simulation of a situation can add important

context (such as emotion, confusion, ambiguity, urgency) that might impact performance in real-life situations. And while children engage with these virtual environments, we can track their in-game decisions and behavior. For example, we can know exactly where a child moves, what she clicks on, how long she takes to make that click, and the exact sequence of all in-game behaviors. Then we can use this information to make tailored adjustments to the gameplay for each individual child. In other words, state-of-the-art computer assessments can simulate a situation; acquire, filter, and analyze the data; and adapt the scenario or difficulty level based on user performance. Because computers can quickly and easily combine these techniques, they are a natural fit for assessment.[14]

Games are Well-suited for Assessment of 21st Century Skills

There is an increasing emphasis in education on '21st century skills.' *Partnership for 21st Century Skills* (www.p21.org) describes the knowledge and skills children will need to master in order to thrive in their lives and work in the 21st century. For example, children will need to be able to collaborate and communicate with others, integrate and evaluate information, effectively and appropriately use digital technology, and solve real-world problems. Note that many of these skills have a strong social component, and that these skills place a much greater emphasis on learning and working within dynamic systems.

Dynamic assessment of these high-level skills is very difficult with traditional methods but a natural fit for intelligent game-based assessments, which give children the opportunity to demonstrate strategic and critical thinking in authentic environments. It enables us to measure what children know and, perhaps more importantly, what they can do with that knowledge. Designed correctly, digital games can evaluate complex skills such as analysis, synthesis, inference, and evaluation. Games can also assess skills not typically captured in traditional standardized testing, such as communication, collaboration, and context-based decision making, which are of particular importance to SSA. In sum, game-based assessment can advance evaluation of complex skills by using a motivating and engaging platform that can adaptively apply simulation of authentic environments.

Partnership for 21st Century Skills

Learning and Innovation
- Creativity and innovation
- Critical thinking and problem solving
- Communication and collaboration

Information, Media and Technology Skills
- Information literacy
- Media literacy
- Technology literacy

Life and Career Skills
- Flexibility and adaptability
- Initiative and self-direction
- Social and cross-cultural skills
- Productivity and accountability
- Leadership and responsibility

Games are Ideal Vehicles for Formative Assessment

Some methods of evidence-gathering happen at the end of a unit of study—a summative assessment—and assess whether children have reached the intended learning goals. Traditional assessment tends to focus on summative assessment.

Games can easily be used for summative assessments, but they may be especially valuable in formative assessment, since such evaluations can be part of the game experience.[15] Formative assessment (assessment while learning is ongoing) helps us to adjust instruction. When we know where children are having difficulty, we can intervene and provide more focused attention to problem areas. If a particular lesson or instructional method isn't working for a child, we can present it differently, adjust the difficulty of a task, or provide more opportunities for practice. Conversely, if we see that a child has mastered a concept, we can offer new or more advanced challenges.[15-17] Using this adaptive strategy improves children's achievement.[18]

Games Provide Unique Opportunities for 'Stealth' Assessment

When children are aware they're being assessed, they may behave differently than they would in typical circumstances. For example, if a child struggling with impulse control knows she is being evaluated, it's likely she will demonstrate greater control than what parents and teachers see on a day-to-day basis. If that same child is playing a game in which cognitive, social, and or physical impulse triggers are 'invisible' as part of the play, the child is more likely to demonstrate her true behavior pattern. Assessment embedded in gameplay is called 'stealth assessment.'[19] By integrating assessment directly into the game environment, we eliminate observer effects and test anxiety; we can then evaluate intangibles, such as creativity and problem solving. Stealth assessment is a major advantage of game-based assessment and will be described in more detail in the next section.

Stealth Assessment embeds data collection right into game play.

WAYS TO GATHER DATA IN GAME-BASED ASSESSMENT

Assessment can be conducted via games through traditional direct questioning, or alternatively through indirect or stealth means. Whether using direct questioning or stealth assessment, game-based assessment's strength lies in its ability to adapt to individuals.

Direct Questioning

Asking a direct question is a familiar way to assess what a child knows. At any point in the game, the player can be presented with a pop-up question or a series of questions. These can be presented in a number of ways (true/false, multiple choice, or open-ended, such as the examples shown in **Table 1**).

Table 1

Using Direct Questioning We Could Ask:

- You should go past the other kids so you can be first in line. True or False?
- You should:
    - A. touch the children's work in the halls
    - B. keep your hands down
    - C. tap the person in front of you
- How should you behave when walking in the hall?
- Should you talk to your classmate or stay quiet?
- If you see something interesting as you walk past the playground, what should you do?

Direct questioning can provide useful information, and is the method most often used by current educational games, such as Study Island (www.studyisland.com) or Brain Pop (www.brainpop.com). And while direct questioning does have a place in game-based assessments, this method has several disadvantages. It takes the player out of the game experience, thereby compromising the effectiveness of the simulation. In addition, complex skills can be hard to assess in this way. A preschooler may be able to indicate that he shouldn't touch artwork on the walls, but when faced with the temptation, may do so anyway. Direct questioning fails to take advantage of a major advantage of games—the ability to assess without compromising game flow or the child's motivation to continue playing.[14]

This aspect of games also enables us to design games that conduct stealth assessment.

Indirect, or Stealth, Assessment

As mentioned in the previous section, stealth assessment is embedded in the gameplay and often is not detectable by the child.[19] Whereas direct questioning methods can determine children's knowledge of rules or facts (declarative knowledge), game-based evaluations that employ stealth assessment can better determine what children do with those rules (procedural or problem solving knowledge). The use of stealth assessment is increasing as many states are adding performance-based measures as part of their standardized tests or including alternative assessments that require students to apply their knowledge and skills to real-world tasks.[20]

Using stealth assessment can be especially beneficial when evaluating complex knowledge. For example, rather than simply asking the child, *"What are the steps needed to perform this task?"* we can design a game that presents a task and options that enable us to evaluate discrimination, understanding concepts and relationships, use of cognitive strategies, and responses to contextual or other important changes. Or, instead of asking the child, *"How would you solve this problem?"* we can present an in-game problem to be solved. Embedded in the context of the game, the problem and its solutions are less apparent to the child.

By using information about children's actual behaviors, we can set up a virtual environment and manipulate facets of the game to assess children at different levels. For example, we could create a game in which one of the tasks is to walk with a class from classroom to lunchroom. As in a typical elementary school, tempting artwork lines the walls, friends (or enemies!) are walking by in the opposite direction, kids are doing the most interesting things at recess outside the window, laughter is coming from the door to a classroom, and the water fountain beckons. Without asking any direct questions, we can use the child's in-game data to assess a child's impulse control. **Table 2** shows examples of the types of questions that could be answered with stealth assessment.

Table 2

Examples of Indirect Assessment Questions

- Did the child click on the artwork in the hall?
  - » If so, how many times?
  - » How many different pieces of work?
- Did the child talk to other characters in the hall?
  - » If so, for how long?
  - » How many times?
  - » How many characters?
- Did the child try to move ahead of the line?
- Did the child lag behind the line?
- Did the child leave the line to explore other places?

You can see how, compared to direct questioning, stealth assessment can provide a richer, more accurate assessment of a child's likely behavior. A child playing a stealth assessment game would probably be focused on the situation rather than on the question, and, as a result, provide us with a better approximation of how she would actually behave in a similar real-world situation. And based on that in-game behavior, we could make adjustments to the game to further assess the child; this is known as adaptive assessment.

Adaptive Assessment

As mentioned previously, computerized adaptive training (CAT) adapts the level of difficulty and adjusts the specific item presented based on how the person has responded in the assessment to that point. The advantage of CAT is that it uses an underlying measurement model of proficiency—or aptitude—to individualize each person's testing experience.

In this way, CAT addresses one of the major challenges of assessment, namely, creating a measure that appropriately addresses the needs of a group with varying abilities. An assessment that is too easy will not provide good information on the high performers, one that is too difficult won't tell you much about the low performers, and one calibrated to the average child will miss important information about both the high and low performers. Similarly, a game that is too easy or too challenging will quickly lose the engagement of a child. To address this challenge, we can use games to employ adaptive assessment, changing the game to meet the needs of individual children. CAT can be used for both direct questioning and stealth assessment. In direct questioning, we can present questions at a higher or lower difficulty level based on responses to that point. The SAT college entrance exam and the Graduate Record Exam (GRE) are good examples of adaptive testing using direct questioning. A correct response to a question cues the CAT program to present a more difficult item next; an incorrect response prompts a less challenging question to follow. The resulting experience is a unique question set and pattern tailored to each individual, leading to a much more efficient and comprehensive picture of the learner's mastery profile. This means that testing time and burden on the test taker can be reduced, and the test results provide a more accurate and complete picture of each person's comprehension across the entire continuum of learning and mastery.

In stealth assessment, there are a number of ways to adapt the scenario for more fine-tuned assessment. In our impulse control example, if a child was doing well with the baseline scenario, we could increase the difficulty in a number of ways. For example, we could add more distracting items in the hallway or have another character initiate a conversation. Alternatively, a child struggling with the basic scenario could be given in-game feedback and guidance; a virtual teacher could give a reminder to "stay in line." Then, we could assess how the child responded to that feedback to answer questions such as those shown in **Table 3**.

Assessing Child's Response to Feedback

- What happens if the distractions become more or less appealing?

- If a teacher gives a warning about any behaviors, does the child continue?

- If we make it more risky to violate the rules by adding more teachers in the hallway, does the child continue to violate the rules?

- If we make it more difficult to follow the rules by varying the temptations in the hallway, how does the child respond?

By incorporating stealth assessment, game-based adaptive assessments provide not only a more complete picture of child behavior than do traditional assessment methods, but also provide practitioners with a more clearly defined starting point for intervention. Returning to our hypothetical example, by understanding the responses of children to specific adaptations, we can better identify the kinds of accommodations that would be most helpful for any given child. We could remove specific types of distractors from the child's school environment for example. These data could then be incorporated into game-based tutorial systems to provide a complete, efficient, and targeted real-world intervention package.

SUMMARY

Games enable us to collect richer, more informative data than do traditional testing methodologies. By providing a simulation of an event and investigating not only the child's answers, but the strategies, sequences, and timing of actions, and the reactions to different factors, we can understand how the child is likely to perform in similar real-life situations. The information-rich tasks made possible by digital games can help us evaluate and understand complex behaviors, abilities, and knowledge systems in ways simply not possible with traditional testing methods. In the next chapters, we present a concrete example of a digital game-based platform specifically designed to assess children's social skills.

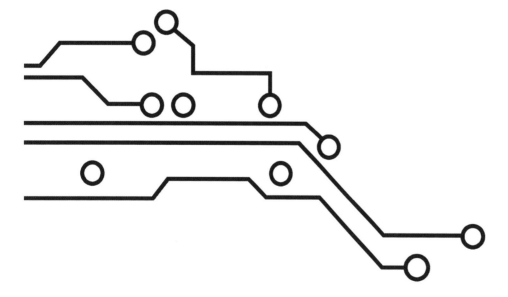

CHAPTER 11 NOTES

1. U.S. Department of Education (2010). *2010 National Education Technology Plan.* Washington, DC: U.S. Department of Education.

2. Bridgeman, B. (2009). Experiences from large-scale computer-based testing in the USA. In F. Scheuermann & J. Bjornsson (Eds.), *The transition to computer-based assessment: New approaches to skills assessment and implications for large-scale testing* (pp. 39-44). Luxembourg: Office for Official Publications of the European Communities.

3. Pollock, M. J., Whittington, C. D., & Doughty, G. F. (2000). Evaluating the costs and benefits of changing to CAA. *Proceedings of the 4th CAA Conference, Loughborough: Loughborough University.*

4. Williamson, D. M., Bejar, I. I., & Hone, A. S. (1999). 'Mental model' comparison of automated and human scoring. *Journal of Educational Measurement, 36,* 158-184.

5. Denham, S. A., Bassett, H. H., & Zinsser, K. (2012). Computerizing social-emotional assessment for school readiness: First steps toward an assessment battery for early childhood settings. *Journal of Applied Research on Children: Informing Policy for Children at Risk, 3.*

6. Ginsburg, K. R. (2007). The importance of play in promoting healthy child development and maintaining strong parent-child bonds. *Pediatrics, 119,* 182-191.

7. Salen, K., & Zimmerman, E. (2004). *Rules of play: Game design fundamentals.* Cambridge, MA: MIT Press.

8. Chin, J., Dukes, R., & Gamson, W. (2009). Assessment in simulation and gaming: A review of the last 40 years. *Simulation & Gaming, 1,* 553-568.

9. North Central Regional Education Laboratory (NCREL) & Metiri Group (2003). *enGauge 21st century skills for 21st century learners: Literacy in the digital age.* Retrieved from http://pict.sdsu.edu/engauge21st.pdf

10. Joyce, A., Gerhard, P., & Debry, M. (2009). *How are digital games used in schools: Complete results of the study.* European Schoolnet.

11. Ke, F. (2009). A qualitative meta-analysis of computer games as learning tools. In R. E. Furdig (Ed.), *Handbook of research on effective electronic gaming in education* (pp. 1-32). New York: IGI Global.

12. Gee, J. P. (2003). What video games have to teach us about learning and literacy. ACM *Computers in Entertainment, 1,* 1-4.

13. Rupp, A. A., Gushta, M., Mislevy, R. J., & Shaffer, D. W. (2010). Evidence-centered design of epistemic games: Measurement principles for complex learning environments. *Journal of Technology, Learning, and Assessment, 8.* Retrieved from http://www.jtla.org

14. Sliney, A., & Murphy, D. (2011). Using serious games for assessment. In M. Ma, A. Oikonomou, & L. C. Jain (Eds.), *Serious games and edutainment applications* (pp. 225-243). London: Springer-Verlag.

15. Shute, V. J., Ventura, M., Bauer, M. I., & Zapata-Rivera, D. (2009). Melding the power of serious games and embedded assessment to monitor and foster learning: Flow and grow. In U. Ritterfeld, M. Cody, & P. Vorderer (Eds.), *Serious games: Mechanism and effects* (pp. 295-321). Mahwah, NJ: Routledge, Taylor and Francis.

16. Murray, T., & Arroyo, I. (June, 2002). Toward measuring and maintaining the zone of proximal development in adaptive instructional systems. *Proceedings of the 6th International Conference for Intelligent Tutoring Systems. Biarritz, France and San Sebastian, Spain.*

17. Murray, R. C., & VanLehn, K. (2006). A comparison of decision-theoretic, fixed-policy and random tutorial action selection. *Lecture Notes in Computer Science, 4053.*

18. Shute, V. J., Hansen, E. G., & Almond, R. G. (2008). You can't fatten a hog by weighing it—Or can you? Evaluating an assessment for learning system called ACED. *International Journal of Artificial Intelligence and Education, 18,* 289-316.

19. Shute, R. J. (2011). Stealth assessment in computer-based games to support learning. In S. Tobias & J. D. Fletcher (Eds.), *Computer games and instruction* (pp. 503-524). Charlotte, NC: Information Age Publishers.

20. Edutopia. (2008). *How should we measure student learning? The many forms of assessment.* Retrieved from http://www.edutopia.org/comprehensive-assessment-introduction

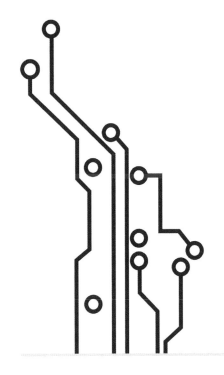

12

ZOO U GAME PLATFORM FOR SSA

by: Melissa E. DeRosier, Ph.D. and Ashley Craig, Ph.D.

DESCRIPTION

The limitations of traditional SSA approaches combined with the real-life barriers schools face in collecting high quality SSA data mean that our social interventions are being hamstrung.

Children who would benefit from social intervention are not being identified.

Our ability to target intervention to specific social skill needs is limited.

Without reliable benchmarks, we can't really know if children benefit from intervention.

Motivated by the belief that effective intervention is possible only with accurate assessment, we at 3C Institute set out to build a more sensitive, effective, and feasible method of assessing children's social skills.

We believe a game platform has the potential to move SSA to a new level—one that's affordable and doable for schools, one where children are actively engaged in the assessment process, one that directly connects data to social intervention, and one where you can clearly establish and monitor goals for intervention.

> Effective intervention is possible only with accurate assessment.

The U.S. Department of Education agreed with our argument. With funding from the Institute of Education Sciences (ED-IES-11-C-0039; ED-IES-10-R-0009), we spent three years developing and testing a game platform for SSA. The finished product, called *Zoo U*, is a web-based game tailored to assess the social skills of 3rd and 4th grade students—children ages 8–12 years.

In this chapter, we describe the social problem solving scenes included in the assessment software, as well as the game mechanics and flow. We also present data from usability testing with children and teachers. The next chapter focuses on how we translate the data captured through *Zoo U* into social skill scores, along with evidence regarding the psychometric properties of these scores.

ZOO U SCENES

Zoo U is a virtual school-like world where children are learning how to be zoo keepers.[1] In large part, this backstory was selected to provide a setting that's similar, but not identical, to a real school setting, in order to present virtual social situations analogous to those commonly experienced by children in elementary school. We felt that presenting a setting too similar to real school life would have two negative consequences: (1) it was likely to be boring for children and (2) some children may have actually experienced the social situations in real life which would bias how they interacted with the software in ways we couldn't know. By setting our social situations in a fantastical zoo keeper training school, we were able to add a bit of fun to the school setting to increase child engagement while also building novel social problem solving tasks that children are not likely to have experienced in real life, such as working with other students to feed and care for the animals.

Figure 1

Opening Screen

In developing the *Zoo U* **social problem solving** (SPS) scenes, we built on educational and developmental theories and empirical research (see Chapters 1-3), and used an approach commonly implemented by educational game designers known as Evidence Centered Design (ECD)[2,3] to adapt that theory and research to a game-based platform. Specifically, ECD requires three components: **competency**, **evidence**, and **task** models. First, we *defined* what **competencies** we wanted to assess as well as the *real-world behaviors* that would provide **evidence** for these competencies. We then, and most importantly, developed **in-game tasks** that we knew from empirical research were *associated* with both the competencies of interest and their related real-world behaviors.

In the case of *Zoo U*, our **competency** model was based on a large body of research identifying specific social behaviors that promote positive peer relations for children in elementary school[4-7] (see Chapter 1), specifically **communication**, **cooperation**, **emotion regulation**, **empathy**, **impulse control**, and **social initiation**. For our **evidence** model, we knew that being able to think through a given social situation, consider alternative problem solving approaches, and evaluate the success of a selected approach for achieving a social goal are critically important for overall social competence.[8,9] Therefore, the **tasks** within *Zoo U* were designed to place children in virtual

Figure 2

Six SPS Scenes

Emotion Regulation · Impulse Control · Communication

Empathy · Cooperation · Initiation

situations that require the application of specific social skills to solve the presented social challenge.

In order to sufficiently cover each of the social skills, we created six SPS scenes, each tailored to target one social skill. **Figure 2** illustrates these six scenes, although in the actual implementation of *Zoo U*, children don't see the labels for the target social skills.

Of course, social skills don't occur in isolation, but rather are interrelated and often go together—it's hard to *cooperate* without *communicating*, for example. So, while a *Zoo U* scene may primarily target one specific social skill, we're actually able to gather data about all six social skills—and social competence more generally—by looking at children's performance across these six scenes. **Table 1** provides a brief summary of each of the six SPS scenes.

Game Mechanics

Zoo U is a single-player point-and-click problem solving game. Each scene employs click-to-move navigation in which the child can move around the scene anywhere he likes by clicking the mouse anywhere on the screen. As the child

Figure 3

Dialog Menu Screenshot

> Do you know what to feed.
> When is recess?
> Can you help me?

moves his mouse around the screen, the cursor changes from the standard arrow to a blue hand when an object or **NPC** (non-player character) is clickable. The child can then simply click to interact with that object or NPC—some of these are clickable because they're important for scene completion while others are included as distractors. When the child clicks on an NPC, his character moves to the NPC and dialog is initiated through a textbox that appears with a list of menu options. **Figure 3** shows a sample screenshot of a dialog menu with an NPC.

For each menu, the child can select from scripted dialog and/or behavioral choices. These choices are randomized so the order changes from one play to the next. In addition, a child's choice in one menu impacts the available choices in subsequent interactions with a particular NPC or in the scene more generally. These alterations in presentation are intended not only to facilitate replay—since children cannot memorize a 'correct' series of responses based on location within the menu—but also to increase children's engagement in the scene, in accordance with the principles of intelligent systems.[10]

Table 1

Summary of SPS Tasks for Each *Zoo U* Scene

Scene 1: Emotion Regulation
Degree to which the child can control what he does and says in an emotionally charged situation

Task:
Bullies in hall are trying to force the child to pay a toll before allowing him to go to his class. Child can choose to be passive (P), aggressive (AG), or assertive (AS) in interactions with the bullies.

Scene 2: Impulse Control
Degree to which the child can stay focused and on-task during problem solving

Task:
Teacher instructs the child to feed the elephant before the class can go to recess. The child must gather information from the clipboard (which provides feeding instructions) and then from the teacher in order to accomplish this task.

Scene 3: Communication
Degree to which the child is able to communicate clearly and respectfully, as well as listen accurately in conversation with another character

Task:
Note on the door indicates the child's class will return at 2:30. Bell rings and the hall monitor informs her that she must get to class. The child must communicate with the hall monitor to find out where her class is and get a hall pass to go and find them.

Scene 4: Empathy
Degree to which the child demonstrates caring for and understanding of another character

Task:
The child is playing 4-square on the playground and there's a boy on sidelines clearly upset. The child needs to understand what is upsetting this boy in a caring and thoughtful way.

Scene 5: Coooperation
Degree to which the child demonstrates team work with another student in order to solve a problem

Task:
The child needs to figure out how to catch the parrot flying around the classroom. In order to be successful, the child must work cooperatively with another character.

Scene 6: Social Initiation
Degree to which the child initiates social play appropriately with other characters

Task:
The child is on the playground and can select to interact with the giraffe or join a 4-square game with three other characters.

We selected point-and-click game mechanics for *Zoo U* based on research on best practices in educational interactive software.[11,12,13] Studies with children have found that this user interface is the fastest and most accurate navigation method for games. In addition, children report that the point-and-click mechanic is the style of interaction that they most prefer in games.

Audio

As the child moves the mouse over a menu choice, he hears the audio of the text for that option. We provide audio for all text in order to minimize literacy requirements as well as help children make fully informed choices. While text-to-speech engines have improved in intelligibility over recent years, they continue to include inexplicable pauses, discontinuities between phonemes and syllables, inconsistent speech patterns, and misplaced word emphases.[14] These audio anomalies can disrupt the natural flow of a scene and distract children from their social problem solving objective. Given our need to emulate natural social interactions, we instead recorded actual human speech for all text within *Zoo U*. We directed professional voice actors to read the passages so that the audio sounds natural for the scene and also portrays the emotion intended.

In addition, when menu dialog is presented to the child, only the text for the first part of each choice is displayed. In part, this is to decrease the amount of clutter on the screen. But, more importantly, it forces the child to listen for clues in the audio in order to discern the exact meaning of each option. In fact, sometimes the text presented on the screen is identical for all options, and the only way to discern meaning is to listen to the audio. This game mechanic is particularly useful when assessing the child's nonverbal communication skills, such as picking out tone of voice or a particular speech pattern when making his menu choice. For example, words spoken in a deep, loud way may signify anger whereas saying those same words in a calm, even tone will not. Similarly, if a menu choice is read with a tremor in the voice, it likely indicates anxiety or fear. Being able to pick up on these types of subtle clues is part of effective social problem solving,[15] so it was important that *Zoo U* be able to assess children's skill in this area.

Graphic Design

It's surprising, in some ways, how much the graphic design of a game impacts whether that game can achieve its intended goals. If the graphic design is too simplistic, boring, or seen as immature, children won't engage with the software. However, if the graphic design is too complex or interesting, children can get confused or distracted from the objective of the game. It's critical in game development to ensure the graphics are *sufficiently engaging without being overly distracting*.[16] This balance can be difficult to achieve.

Similar to modern animated cartoons, such as SpongeBob SquarePants™, we elected to render *Zoo U* in 2.5D, which allows for the appearance of depth and dimension without requiring a 3D virtual environment. 3D environments involve complex mechanics for movement—requiring the child to move her character in three dimensions—that can be visually intensive for children[13] and actually distract them from the problem solving tasks of the environment.[17,18] This side effect of 3D graphics can be particularly problematic for children with attention problems.

Figure 4

Depth Perspective Screenshot

By building *Zoo U* with 2.5D technology we achieve a familiar, visually interesting cartoon feel without the flattened picture effect of older cartoons, while also reducing the visual and cognitive overload that can happen with 3D graphics. For example, **Figure 4** shows the child's character standing next to a chair, which obscures the lower part of his body and creates the perception of depth. For each scene in *Zoo U*, we define a geometrically 'walkable area' using a modified A* algorithm so that the child can freely move about the scene while avoiding collisions with other characters and objects.

In the early testing stages of *Zoo U* we conducted several test groups with children. We were interested in whether *Zoo U*'s colors, settings, and characters as rendered in 2.5D would be sufficiently appealing. We found that children rated *Zoo U* as highly appealing—mean rating of 3.80 on a 4-point scale from 1='Not at all' to 4= 'Very.'[19, 20] However, children approaching adolescence—12 years and older—rated *Zoo U*'s graphic design lower. Therefore, in order to ensure that the graphic design would not interfere with the software's SSA objectives, we restricted *Zoo U*'s target end user group to children between ages 8 and 12 years.

Software Engine

Zoo U is built on 3C Institute's proprietary **intelligent social tutoring system** (ISTS) software engine for game deployment. This engine is built in Adobe Flash Creative Suite (CS) with all software components written in the ActionScript language of Adobe CS. Flash is currently resident on 99% of all computers in the U.S.—or can be downloaded for free—and can be deployed through any standard web browser, including Firefox, Internet Explorer, Chrome, and Safari. Therefore, no significant computer expertise or specialized software is needed by users. Further, while *Zoo U* is currently Flash based, development is underway to port the software to HTML5 web standards for delivery via mobile, desktop, and tablet platforms, including iPad, as of 2014.

We chose to deliver *Zoo U* via the Internet in order to increase accessibility and decrease costs, so that this software can benefit as broad a scope of children as possible. In particular, *Zoo U*'s 2.5D graphics translate into faster load time and greater accessibility for schools that may lack the hardware or software needed to run 3D rendering software.

ZOO U GAME FLOW

Children interact with the *Zoo U* software independently on a computer, completing scenes at their own pace. It's recommended that the child use headphones so she can pay better attention and not disturb others. To complete the SSA, children move through the following components.

Figure 5

Principal Wild Introduction

Welcome to Zoo U -- a school for futue zookeepers. I'm Principal Wild.

Introduction Tutorial

The first time the child interacts with the software, she will click through several introductory screens narrated by Principal Wild in which he describes the backstory of *Zoo U* and gives instructions about how to navigate the software (see **Figure 5**). He tells the child to put on headphones, then explains how to move around a scene, how to find clickable objects and people, and how to listen to and select options within menus. In addition, at the end of the tutorial, Principal Wild emphasizes that the child should *"Make choices in Zoo U just like you would in real life—Do your best!"* The implementation instructions for administrators also emphasize that children should *not* be told that this is a 'game' because doing so may bring certain entertainment gaming expectations. Rather, administrators are asked to tell children that *Zoo U* is an assessment of their problem solving skills and that they should try to do their best.

Avatar Builder

Prior to engaging in the SPS scenes, the child customizes her avatar, the visual representation of herself within the virtual story world. Being able to personalize the avatar's appearance enhances identification with the virtual character, which in turn increases the child's engagement with the software.[11, 21] Children use *Zoo U*'s avatar builder to select their avatar's gender, clothes, hair color and style, and skin color (see **Figure 6**). Once avatar creation is complete, the software engine tracks and renders the avatar's location, directional orientation, locomotion, facial expression, and hand/body position throughout the scenes.

Scene Completion

The software walks children through the six SPS scenes in order from 1 to 6 (see **Figure 7**). As children complete a scene, it becomes locked and can't be completed again and the next scene unlocks for completion. Each SPS scene is thematically consistent with, but independent of the others, so children can complete all scenes in one sitting or break up completion across multiple days. It takes approximately 8-12 minutes for a child to complete one scene, for a total administration time of around one hour to complete the entire assessment.

IMPLEMENTATION

Zoo U can be easily integrated into the classroom setting. It's also possible for other community-based agencies, such as afterschool programs or community youth programs, to use *Zoo U* with one or more children. As a school professional, you can implement *Zoo U* with one child at a time, or you can enable an entire classroom to complete *Zoo U* simultaneously, such as during computer lab. As part of *Zoo U*, schools receive secure login IDs for the *Zoo U* web-based school portal. This portal allows you to deploy the software to children and it gives you access to: (a) **administration instructions** about how to use the software with children; (b) the **Report Center** through which you can monitor each child's completion of *Zoo U* and generate reports regarding child performance; (c) **online help tips** to aid with implementation in schools; (d) **additional resources**, such as links to helpful websites and books to supplement or augment social intervention efforts with children; and (e) **technical support** contact information to access trained technical staff.

USABILITY TEST RESULTS
Testing with School Personnel

During the early stages of *Zoo U* development, we conducted a test with 60 elementary school professionals.[19,20] These professionals included teachers, counselors, psychologists, and administrators. Following an online review, participants completed a survey evaluating *Zoo U*. Ratings were made on a 5-point scale, from 1=Strongly Disagree to 5=Strongly Agree. **Table 2** displays the results across participants, including the mean and standard deviation (in parentheses) for each area assessed, as well as the percent of school staff who selected 'Agree' or 'Strongly Agree'.

Overall, the *Zoo U* software was rated extremely positively. School staff felt that *Zoo U* would be very easy and feasible for them to use in the classroom

Table 2

School Staff Ratings of *Zoo U*		
Zoo U software would be:	**Mean (std)**	**Percentage greater than or equal to 4**
Engaging for students	4.60 (.69)	95%
Easy to use in the classroom	4.43 (.67)	90%
Easy to use with individual students	4.63 (.52)	98%
Feasible for use in schools	4.55 (.62)	94%
Valuable tool for teachers	4.52 (.70)	92%
Valuable assessment tool	4.55 (.59)	95%
Valuable reporting features	4.73 (.48)	98%
More effective than current methods	4.48 (.70)	88%
Highly innovative over current methods	4.67 (.48)	100%

setting and with individual students. They saw it as a highly valuable tool for helping them assess and understand students' social skills. School personnel also liked the idea of a Reporting Center that would let them see each child's progress through the game. All school staff reported that *Zoo U* was highly innovative compared to current alternatives. Following review, several work groups with school staff were conducted to further explore the collected rating scale data. A number of positive comments were shared during these work groups, such as:

> *"Zoo U would be particularly useful because most assessments are based on teacher/parent ratings instead of data collected directly from the student."*

> *"Zoo U would be a nice transition into discussion/ application of skills in a real-life setting."*

> *"Teachers need products like this that are easy to implement and will impact student learning."*

Testing with Children

During initial development we also conducted several tests of the software with upper elementary school children. For example, 3rd and 4th grade students (*n*=44) in one school completed *Zoo U* during their computer lab. We introduced *Zoo U* to the class and then children interacted with the software on individual computers. Research staff observed children and recorded their behavior and comments as they navigated the scenes. After finishing *Zoo U*, children completed a brief survey, rating items on a 4-point scale from 1='Not at all true for me' to 4='Very true for me.' These ratings were similar across 3rd and 4th graders. **Table 3** shows the means and standard deviations for each area rated across all children.

Overall, children thoroughly enjoyed *Zoo U*, rating every area > 3. All children easily—and intuitively—understood how to navigate the software with almost no instruction. In fact, we observed few misunderstandings and almost no requests for technical help. We also found that children were

Table 3

Child Ratings of *Zoo U*

Area rated:	Mean (std)
Fun, interesting	3.90 (.31)
Easy to use and understand	3.95 (.22)
Liked characters and graphics	3.80 (.45)
Want to play more	3.95 (.22)
Overall liked	3.90 (.31)

"That is awesome!"

"When can I play more?"

"Can I do it again?"

highly engaged with the software; 92% were on-task during game play. In fact, after completing *Zoo U* the first time, children were offered the choice of completing *Zoo U* scenes again or engaging with other web-based games for the remainder of the class period. Almost 90% of them chose to play *Zoo U* again. These findings—along with children's positive comments while interacting with the software—show that this social skills assessment platform is appealing and engaging to children.

SUMMARY

We created the game-based *Zoo U* social skills assessment software (using the same theoretical and empirical foundations as traditional SSA) in order to better understand children's social competences in six key areas: impulse control, communication, cooperation, social initiation, empathy, and emotion regulation. By incorporating well-established educational game frameworks and engaging game mechanics found in successful entertainment games, we were able to develop an SSA that appeals to both children and teachers while alleviating the many hurdles associated with traditional SSA methods described in Part I of this book. In Chapter 13, we discuss the metrics that we collect during game play that determine the scoring algorithms for the social skills scores.

CHAPTER 12 NOTES

1. To access a demonstration video and get a trial account of Zoo U, visit: www.3cisd.com/zoou/demo. For subscription information for schools, visit: http://www.3cisd.com/marketplace/catalog/202/Zoo-U-Social-Skills-Assessment

2. Mislevy, R. J., Almond, R. G., & Lukas, J. F. (2004). *A brief introduction to evidence-centered design: CSE Technical Report 632.* Los Angeles, CA: The National Center for Research on Evaluation, Standards, and Student Testing (CRESST).

3. Rupp, A. A., Gushta, M., Mislevy, R. J., & Shaffer, D. W. (2010). Evidence-centered design of epistemic games: Measurement principles for complex learning environments. *The Journal of Technology, Learning, and Assessment, 8* (4). Retrieved January 2, 2014 from http://www.jtla.org.

4. Asher, S. R., & Renshaw, P. D. (1981). Children with friends: Social knowledge and social-skill training. In S. R. Asher & J. M. Gottman (Eds.), *The development of children's friendships* (pp. 273-296). New York, NY: Cambridge University Press.

5. Coie, J. D., Cillessen, A. H. N., Dodge, K. A., Hubbard, J. A., Schwartz, D., Lemerise, E. A.,& Bateman, H., (1999). It takes two to fight: A test of relational factors and a method for assessing aggressive dyads. *Developmental Psychology, 35,* 1179-1188.

6. Dodge, K. A., & Feldman, E. (1990). Issues in social cognition and sociometric status. In S. R. Asher & J. D. Coie (Eds.), *Peer rejection in childhood* (pp. 119-155). New York, NY: Cambridge University Press.

7. Merrell, K. W., & Gimpel, G. A. (1998). *Social Skills of children and adolescents: Conceptualization, assessment, treatment.* Mahway, NJ: Earlbaum.

8. Crick, N. R., & Dodge, K. A. (1994). A review and reformulation of social information-processing mechanisms in children's social adjustment. *Psychological Bulletin, 115,* 74-101.

9. Greenberg, M., Kusché, C., & Riggs, N. (2004). The PATHS curriculum: Theory and research on neurocognitive development and school success. In J. E. Zins, R. P. Weissberg, M. C. Wang, & H. J. Walber (Eds.), *Building academic success on social and emotional learning: What does the research say?* (pp. 170-188). New York, NY: Teachers College Press.

10. Shute, V. J., & Zapata-Rivera, D. (2008). *Educational assessment using intelligent systems.* Educational Testing Service Report No. RR-08-68. Princeton, NJ: ETS.

11. Lester, J., Callaway, C., Gregoire, J., Stelling, G., Towns, S., & Zettlemoyer, L. (2001). Animated pedagogical agents in knowledge-based learning environments. In K. Forbus & P. Feltovich (Eds.), *Smart machines in education: The coming revolution in educational technology* (pp. 269-298). Menlo Park, CA: AAAI/MIT Press.

12. Mott, B., & Lester, J. (2006). Narrative-centered tutorial planning for inquiry-based learning environments. *Proceedings of 8th International Conference on Intelligent Tutoring Systems,* Jhongli, Taiwan, 675-684.

13. Roussou, M. (2005). Learning by doing and learning through play: An exploration of interactivity in virtual environments for children. *ACM Computers in Entertainment, 2,* 1-23.

14. Atkinson, R., Mayer, R., & Merrill, M. (2005). Fostering social agency in multimedia learning: Examining the impact of an animated agent's voice. *Contemporary Educational Psychology, 30,* 117-139.

15. Nowicki, S., & Duke, M. P. (1994). Individual differences in the nonverbal communication of affect: The Diagnostic Analysis of Nonverbal Accuracy Scale. Special Issue: Development of nonverbal behavior: II. Social development and nonverbal behavior. *Journal of Nonverbal Behavior, 18,* 9-35.

16. Pinelle, D., Wong, N., & Stach, T. (2008). Heuristic evaluation for games: Usability principles for video game design. *Proceedings of the SIGCHI conference on Human Factors,* April 5-10, 2008, Florence, Italy.

17. Huk, T. (2006). Who benefits from learning with 3D models? The case of spatial ability. *Journal of Computer Assisted Learning, 22,* 392-404.

18. Paas, F., Renkl, A., & Sweller, J. (2003). Cognitive load theory: Instructional implications of the interaction between information structures and cognitive architecture. *Instructional Science, 32,* 1-8.

19. DeRosier, M. E. (2011). "Using computer-based social tasks to assess students' social skills: findings from the *Zoo U* pilot evaluation. *Zoo U: Final report to Institute for Educational Sciences (IES) at the U.S. Department of Education.* Cary, NC: 3C Institute.

20. DeRosier, M. E., Craig, A. B., & Sanchez, R. P. (2012). Zoo U: A stealth approach to social skills assessment in schools. *Advances in Human-Computer Interaction.* Doi: 10.1155/2012/654791

21. Schroeder, R. (2002). *The social life of avatars: Presence and interaction in shared virtual environments.* Berlin, Germany: Springer.

13

Zoo U
Scoring Metrics

by: Melissa E. DeRosier, Ph.D. and Ashley Craig, Ph.D.

DESCRIPTION

So, how do you translate a game into assessment data? One of the great things about using a game for SSA is that the answer to this question is not obvious—particularly not to children. When you fill out a questionnaire or even participate in an interview, there are always clues as to the 'right' answer, either in the response choices available or in the nonverbal communication from the interviewer. It's not hard to discern the socially acceptable answer to the question *"How often do you pick on or tease others?"* And, it's not hard to pick up on an interviewer avoiding eye contact or changing her tone of voice when she asks you a particularly sensitive question.

But to a child, a game looks like a game. Now, if we tell the child that this game is going to assess his skills—as we do with *Zoo U*—he'll be on the lookout for the right answer. But because the game is fun, he'll be more interested in completing the scenes than trying to figure out what the game is trying to assess. Much like someone who's being videotaped increasingly relaxes and forgets the camera's

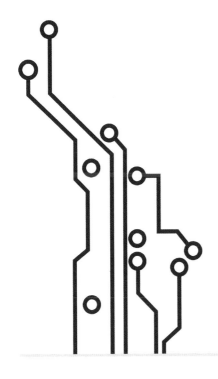

even there, children get immersed in the game and forget it's an assessment. In this way, we can observe the child's naturally occurring behavior in the virtual situation and minimize child reactivity that could bias our results (see Chapter 7). In effect, game-based methods can gather data that reflect the child's real-world social behavior in a manner that approximates the ecological validity of naturalistic observations.

But, again, how do you actually translate data collected within a game into meaningful scores that reflect children's social skills and social functioning? In other words, how can you operationalize social skills assessment within a virtual world? This chapter describes the procedures by which we accomplish this operationalization through *Zoo U*. We describe what we measure and how—without giving away too much of the secret sauce—with examples from *Zoo U* to illustrate each of these methods.

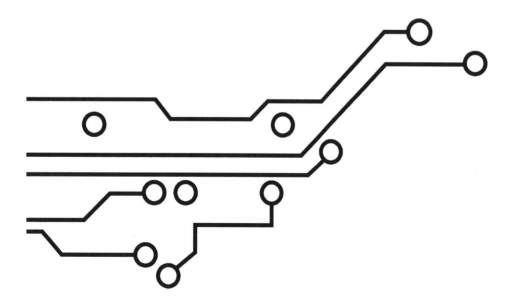

OPERATIONALIZING SSA IN A GAME

The first step to operationalizing game-based SSA—that is, making the social skills concrete and measurable—is to define the behaviors or characteristics that comprise the social skills being assessed. As with any assessment tool, you base these operational definitions on the current body of theoretical and research literature. Part I of this book lays out the literature we drew on when crafting *Zoo U*'s social situations and defining how children would demonstrate positive social skills within those scenes. As discussed in Chapter 12, *Zoo U* is designed to assess children's social competence through the measurement of six core social skills: communication, cooperation, emotion regulation, empathy, impulse control, and social initiation. **Table 1** summarizes those behaviors and characteristics that define social competence for each social skill in *Zoo U*.

The next step in operationalization is to quantify when children do or do not exhibit these behaviors within a given virtual scene. You need a scoring algorithm that defines what's measured and how. In a virtual world, you have many more degrees of freedom regarding what you can measure than is possible with any other SSA approach. This scoring algorithm can consist of scores for menu options plus a wide array of scores for specific in-game behaviors.

Table 1	
Zoo U Operational Definitions	
Social Skill:	**Definition**
Emotion Regulation	• Stays calm when teased • Takes criticism without getting upset • Resolves disagreements calmly • Very good at controlling emotions • Does not escalate situations
Impulse Control	• Follows directions well • Very good at controlling behavior • Stays on task • Avoids distractions • Attends to important cues in his/her environment
Communication	• Is polite • Responds well when others start a conversation • Very good at communicating thoughts to others • Very good at communicating feelings to others • Uses an appropriate tone of voice • Responds to others' questions appropriately • Asks questions appropriately
Empathy	• Good at understanding other children's feelings • Tries to comfort others • Is nice to others when they are feeling bad • Shows concern for others • Aware of others' emotions
Cooperation	• Very good at working with others as a team • Able to recognize appropriate times to cooperate • Participates well in group activities or games • Obeys rules or requests by other children • Doesn't break up, disrupt, or stop group activities
Social Initiation	• Good at initiating play with other children • Joins activities that have already started • Invites others to join activities • Starts conversations with peers

ASSESSING GAME MENUS

As children navigate the social situations in *Zoo U*, the software tracks and scores their choices. Each menu includes scripted dialog and/or behavioral choices. The child can review each of the options and then select what she wants to do or say in that situation. The assignment of scores for menu options is tailored to the social goal of the scene and anchored in the research literature.

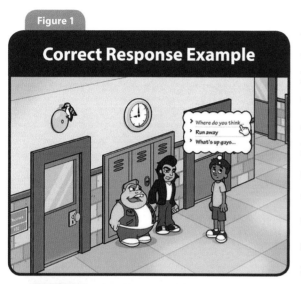

Figure 1

Correct Response Example

> Where do you think...
> Run away
> What's up guys...

Figure 2

Incorrect Response Example

> Can you help me?
> When is recess?
> Do you know what...feed...

Most of the menus in *Zoo U* provide three options, but there could be two, four, or more choices depending on the scene and how refined the scoring needs to be. Typically, we assign a value to each option that represents the 'correctness' of that answer— often a 1 for the correct response and 0s for incorrect responses. For example, in **Figure 1**, the hallway bullies are trying to get the child's avatar to pay a toll. In the assessment of emotion regulation, the child gets a 1 for responding in a calm, assertive manner to this bullying situation, but earns 0 points for selecting either an aggressive response that escalates the situation or a passive response that tries to avoid dealing with it.

Just as in social situations, responses have gradations of correctness. More than one response could be acceptable or one response could be more correct than another. Then, scores for that menu are assigned accordingly. For example, in **Figure 2**, asking Dougie about recess is off-task to solving the problem of figuring out what to feed the elephant. Therefore, in the assessment of impulse control, the child would receive zero credit for selecting that menu option. However, both of the other choices are on-task and directly related to the solving the elephant problem, so the child would receive credit (1 point) for selecting either of those responses.

Beyond the Obvious in Scoring Menus

Of the various scores that can be generated in a game environment, menu options are more easily scored. Children may assume you're scoring their menu choices, as would happen with other rating scales or multiple choice questionnaires. Thus, menu-driven scores potentially suffer from the same social acceptability bias—children may try to pick the most socially acceptable or 'correct' answer regardless of whether that's what they would truly do in that situation.

However, with a game, the child is immersed in a virtual world where his menu choices are integral to his being able to successfully navigate the scene. Over time, he'll be paying less attention to what he thinks you want him to say than to what he truly believes will help him solve the presented social challenge. Further, scoring the child's responses to contextually-specific menus enables you to assess children's social performance or their capacity to apply prosocial skills in a social situation (see Chapter 4). With traditional SSA approaches, you're usually limited to static, contextually-removed survey or interview questions which really only allow you to assess social literacy— or the child's knowledge about social skills. With a game environment, the data you collect through menu choices will more directly reflect the child's ability to problem solve in order to navigate within a given social context—allowing you to actually assess social performance, not just social literacy.

However, even with the advantage of presenting menus in a game-based world, menu choices can still be too obvious for scores to be meaningful. The early attempts at social skill games suffered greatly from this downfall, providing children choices that were dead simple to figure out. If the options are a) hit him back, b) tell an adult, or c) call him a name, even the most antisocial child will know what answer he's supposed to pick. Any resulting score will not indicate anything about that child's actual social skill level or behavior.

A game environment enables measurement of social performance not just social literacy.

Therefore, when formulating your menus and responses, don't underestimate children. Be respectful and ask challenging questions, so the child is required to cognitively engage in the game. If you want to gather meaningful responses from a child, you need to present menus that make the right answer difficult to figure out. Games offer a number of ways to increase subtlety in menu options. For example, you can present different options where each is more or less 'good,' without a clearly poor choice for the presented social situation. Similarly, you can word your options so one choice does not stand out as correct. If your game includes audio voiceover of menu options, you can also get really tricky and present identical options where the distinction is only discernable by listening to tone of voice.

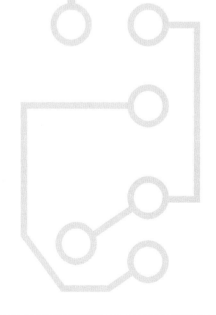

As with real-world social situations, choices in a virtual world influence how others in the scene respond and what options are then available. For example, if you call me a name and I choose to call you a name back, I've now escalated the situation and you're more likely to come back even more aggressively. In contrast, if I had selected a different action—say, standing my ground in an assertive but non-aggressive way, running away, or cracking a joke to break the tension—the response would be different and my subsequent available choices would also be different. A wonderful advantage of a game platform is that you can emulate this naturally occurring sequence of events and then score the sequence itself, not just each individual menu choice. For example, in the hallway bullies scene of *Zoo U* (Scene 1), each menu of dialog includes aggressive, passive, and assertive options. We found in our research that children who escalated this virtual situation by selecting aggressive responses repeatedly were significantly more likely to be seen by teachers as having low emotion regulation skills. Further, this was particularly true if the child's initial choice had been aggressive. Therefore, our scoring algorithm for emotion regulation for this scene captures the sequence of choices made by the child across menus and also gives more weight to the child's first menu choice.

ASSESSING GAME BEHAVIOR

From an assessment perspective, the primary advantage of using a game platform is that it's possible to gather highly detailed and specific data regarding the child's behavior as he navigates virtual social scenes. And, it's practically impossible for the child to recognize what these behavioral indices are. As discussed in Chapter 11, this is called 'stealth assessment' by which assessments are *"woven directly and invisibly into the fabric of the game itself."*[1] Some useful behavioral indices that can be gathered through stealth assessment in a game-based platform include:

- number of times a particular object or character is clicked on;
- amount of time before a specific action is taken;
- percent of time spent in a particular activity;
- order of actions during problem solving; and
- number of clues or prompts by the system needed to solve the problem.

Stealth assessment is intentionally embedded into the *Zoo U* scoring algorithms. For each scene, we integrate specific non-obvious behavioral scoring factors based on the research literature for parallel real-world social situations. Here are some examples of how—and why—we measure behavior in *Zoo U.*

Number of Clicks Example (Figure 3). We know that visual and auditory distractors—colorful objects, loud noise, moving things—interfere with impulse control during problem solving, particularly for children with attention problems. We structured scenes with these types of distractors to purposely measure the degree to which children are distracted and off-task in *Zoo U.* For example, in the elephant feeding scene (Scene 2), how often do children click on the food crates? These crates are distractors because none of these foods are what the elephant eats—which is clear if you try to feed them to the elephant. In our research, we found that children without impulse control problems click on each crate once to see what happens, but then no more. Children with impulse control problems, however, click on these crates 6, 10, even 18 times during the course of completing the scene. So, the total number of times the child clicks on the crates is integrated into our scoring algorithm for impulse control.

Time Spent Before 'X' Example (Figure 4). We know that children who are anxious about joining other children in play or conversation tend to avoid social interaction if they can. Therefore, in *Zoo U,* we include non-social options and measure how long it takes children to join in with other children (equivalent to latency recording in observations; see Chapter 7). For example, in Scene 6, the child can elect to feed the giraffe or join the four-square game already in progress. Our research showed that children who spend more time feeding the giraffe have poorer social initiation skills. Therefore, our scoring algorithm for social initiation includes the amount of time the child elects to feed the giraffe before joining the game.

Time Spent Doing 'X' Example (Figure 5). We know that in order to be a good communicator, you must be a good listener. In *Zoo U,* successfully navigating a social problem often requires listening to what another character tells you. If you miss key information, your pathway through the scene can easily get off-track. For example,

Figure 3

Measuring Number of Clicks

Figure 4

Measuring Latency

Figure 5

Measuring Duration

when talking with the hall monitor in Scene 3, the child must listen carefully in order to know where his class has gone. In our research, we found that children who listened to the hall monitor less had poorer communication skills (equivalent to duration recording in observations; see Chapter 7). Therefore, our assessment of communication in *Zoo U* includes a score reflecting the percent of time the child spends listening to the hall monitor's audio.

Figure 6

Measuring Sequence of Behaviors

Order of Actions Example (Figure 6). We know that cooperation involves give and take between individuals to balance input from more than one person. Children who refuse help and try to stubbornly pursue their own course have poorer cooperation skills than do children who elicit the help of others to solve the problem. In *Zoo U*'s Scene 5, the child must figure out how to catch a parrot flying around the room. Our research shows that children who first independently try to catch the parrot and then seek—and accept—assistance from another child in the room have better cooperation skills. Therefore, our scoring algorithm for cooperation takes into account the order and amount of time spent trying to solve the problem independently versus working cooperatively with the other character.

Figure 7

Measuring Number of Prompts

> Go watch the rabbits.
> Keep playing the game.
> Talk to the kid on the sidewalk.

Number of System Prompts Example (Figure 7). We know that children who are empathetic are very good at recognizing that another child is upset and then initiating caring behaviors. In *Zoo U*'s Scene 4, there is a child sitting on the curb, away from other activities. His posture and face reveal he's upset. The child's avatar is in the middle of a game of 4-square and can choose to keep playing, leave to watch a rabbit race, or approach the upset child on the sidewalk. If the child fails to initiate talking to the upset boy, the software progressively and more explicitly prompts the child to do so—ranging from other characters saying *"I wish we had more players"* to *"Maybe somebody should go talk to him."* In our research, we found that children who require fewer prompts by the system to initiate conversation with the upset boy have higher empathy scores than children who require more prompts. Therefore, the total number of prompts by the system are tracked and included in the scoring algorithm for empathy.

Response Pattern Checks

A related advantage of a game platform is the ability to employ stealth assessment across scenes to identify potential threats to the accuracy of social skill scores. *Zoo U* automatically generates calculations regarding the child's general approach to gameplay in order to gauge the degree to which he may be 'gaming the system' or simply not paying sufficient attention. Six response pattern indices are calculated based on our research showing how these indices negatively impact children's *Zoo U* social skill scores[2] (**Figure 8**).

Figure 8

Response Pattern Indices

Percent audio played	abnormally low percentage of audio for menu choices listened to by the child
Percent speech played	abnormally low percentage of speech bubbles by other characters listened to by the child
Indiscriminant menu selection	abnormally high percentage of menu choices at the identical position, such as always selects the 1st menu option
Antisocial menu selection	abnormally high percentage of menu choices that are the most aggressive or antisocial option available
Random menu selection	selection of menu choices is random
Off-task time	abnormally high percentage of time is spent off-task or not problem-solving focused

When a response pattern check is triggered, the software generates a warning for that child describing how scores may be impacted and providing recommendations for how to proceed with this child. For example, if the percent audio played warning is present, it's recommended that the teacher instruct the child to slow down and listen to all options before making a choice. See

Chapter 14 for a sample screenshot of a report with response pattern warnings for a fictional child. The goal of these response pattern checks is to provide information about the child's overall approach to the assessment. If no response pattern checks are triggered, we can have greater confidence in the resulting data. If one or more checks are triggered, this information can perhaps shed light on some behavioral strategies that may be helpful for working with this child.

Game Logs

As a child interacts with *Zoo U*, every click is recorded and time-stamped through detailed game logs. These data logs record the exact location and time of each mouse click the child makes. As illustrated in **Figure 9**, the log specifies the child's dialog choices (colored in **red**) and behavioral choices (colored in **green**), including clicks to move to a specific location as well as clicks on specific objects or people within the scene. In addition, relevant response pattern data (colored in **blue**) is captured.

Through *Zoo U*'s game logs it's possible to map the exact sequence and timing of each choice made by the child, as well as the amount of time spent in targeted types of gameplay, such as on-task versus off-task behavior. In fact, our system is able to use these logs to replay a scene exactly as the child did, which is extremely helpful for deciphering prosocial versus antisocial or 'system gaming' response patterns. These game logs are translated by the software into relevant scoring variables for each scene according to a detailed codebook. The resulting variables are then exported and used to calculate algorithms for performance in the targeted social skill areas, overall social competence, and response pattern indices.

Figure 9

Game Log Snapshot

2595422: Clicked crate3
2595875: Arrived at crate
2596984: Arrived at elephant
2596984: Running situation panToElephant/1
2603656: Running situation elephantFail/1
2606281: Clicked clipboard
2608734: Arrived at clipboard
2608734: Running situation panToElephant/1
2610125: Running situation clipboard/0
2615641: Clicked directions page
2615641: Running situation clipboard/1
2618484: Clicked directions page
2618484: Running situation clipboard/2
2625891: Clicked directions page
2628188: Clicked to move 936, 406
2630828: Clicked to move 755, 317
2637453: Clicked teacher
2637984: Arrived at teacher
2638375: Running situation askTeacher/1
2642875: Clicked menu option 1, pos: 1, score: G, audio(1): 6.91, audio(0): 0, audio(2): 33.72
2642875: Running situation askTeacher/3
2645375: Running situation askTeacher/6

SUMMARY

Informed by the theoretical and empirical body of literature on children's prosocial skills, we created the game-based *Zoo U* social skills assessment software around virtual scenes requiring children to apply social skills to solve social problems analogous to problems they experience in their everyday lives. By incorporating well-established educational game frameworks with engaging game mechanics found in successful entertainment games, we were able to develop an SSA approach that appeals to both children and teachers, and alleviates many of the logistical hurdles associated with traditional SSA methods. Further, with stealth assessment, we can move beyond simply assessing menu choices to measure complex social behaviors and performance in a specific virtual social context. In effect, games can minimize the negative impact of social desirability bias to yield more accurate and sensitive SSA. The next chapter discusses the various assessment reports and features that are part of *Zoo U*.

CHAPTER 13 NOTES

1. Shute, V. J., & Ke, F. (2012). Games, learning, and assessment. In D. Ifenthaler, D. Eseryel, & X. Ge (Eds.), *Assessment in game-based learning: Foundations, innovations, and perspectives* (pp. 43–58). New York, NY: Springer.

2. Cut-offs for response variables were determined based on Bayesian statistics predicting the confidence interval for the distribution of observed responses to determine a standard reference range. Then, post-hoc Analyses of Variance analyses were used to examine the impact on children's social skill scores at different cut-offs for children with and without teacher-reported social skill difficulties.

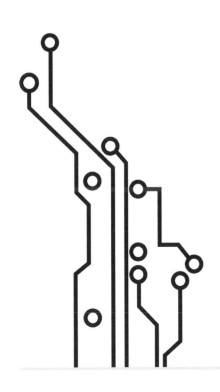

Zoo U
ASSESSMENT REPORTS

by: Melissa E. DeRosier, Ph.D., Chelsea Bartel, Ph.D., and Ashley Craig, Ph.D.

DESCRIPTION

In order for SSA data to be useful for planning an intervention strategy, scores generated through that SSA must be easy to understand and use. Access to high quality, valid data is worthless if it can't be easily translated into concrete, meaningful decisions. For this reason, it's important to consider the quality of the reporting features when selecting an SSA. Its automated data collection and scoring functions give the game platform a leg up in this regard. The computerized nature of games provides the opportunity to automatically generate personalized and customizable reports. However, subject matter experts are still needed to ensure these reports provide information that is easy to understand and helpful for intervention purposes. In our development of *Zoo U*'s reporting functions, we enlisted the help of teachers and other school staff who regularly plan and implement social skills interventions with children. In this chapter, we describe and illustrate the various reporting functions and features that are currently available through *Zoo U*.

ZOO U ADMINISTRATION WEBSITE

Zoo U administrators have access to a secure online administration portal through which they can deploy this SSA with children. As an administrator, you can add children to the system, launch the software for completion by a given child, and view reports of that child's performance. The web portal also provides downloadable administration support tools, including instructions for how to administer the software with children, instructions for how to use the software yourself, and guidelines on how to interpret the data resulting from *Zoo U*. You can monitor children's completion of *Zoo U* as well as generate reports of child performance. **Figure 1** provides a screenshot of the *Zoo U* administration portal for a fictional teacher and children.

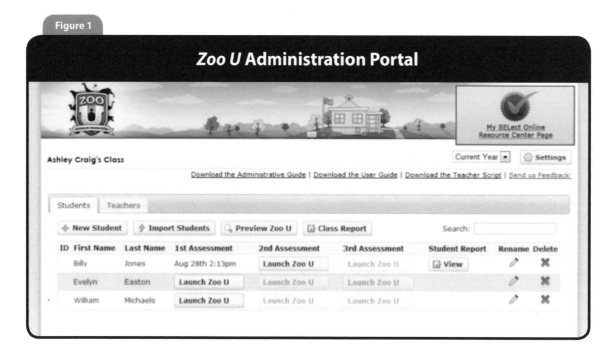

Data Security

Given that data collected through *Zoo U* are of a sensitive nature, it's important to underscore the security features in place to protect these data. *Zoo U* data and reporting functions are fully compliant with federal privacy regulations, including the Family Educational Rights and Privacy Act (FERPA) which protects the privacy of student educational information[1] and the Health Insurance Portability and Accountability Act (HIPAA) which protects the privacy of individuals' healthcare information.[2] *Zoo U* meets the strictest data security standards, including compliance with Title 21 Code of Federal Regulations Part 11. Logins with strong password rule enforcement and expiration schedules consistent with government and industry standards and best practices are required. Protected sections of the website are encrypted during transmission using strong 256-bit SSL transport layer security and trusted certificates. All user accounts are assigned a Globally Unique Identifier (GUID) to ensure the highest level of accuracy for data entry and retrieval. When users access the system, passwords are authenticated against the GUID, so entry is granted only with a perfect match (no 'fuzzy logic'). Data stored online are protected using algorithms and procedures for securing sensitive data consistent with best practices, such as 3DES encryption and separation of encrypted data from keys. A multi-server cloud environment with two independent backup systems is used to ensure comprehensive data accessibility, safety, and recovery.

ZOO U ASSESSMENT REPORTS

Zoo U assessment reports are divided into three sections: (a) Response Patterns, (b) Global Social Competence Score, and (c) Individual Social Skill Scores. This reader-friendly report is modeled after standard universal screening reports.[3, 4] If the child has completed *Zoo U* more than once, the report also documents learning trends over time for both the global and individual scores. You can access these reports at any time for online viewing or download.

Before presenting examples of each section of the *Zoo U* report, we want to emphasize a couple of important points. First, in the calculation of the *Zoo U* social skill scores—both global and individual—there are two possible *norm reference groups* that a child's score can be compared to: (a) our normative national sample of 3rd and 4th grade children or (b) local norms for your organization (see Chapter 4 for a discussion of norms). If more than 20 children in the same grade at the same school have completed *Zoo U*, you can elect for scores to be calculated using your local norms. Essentially, local norms enable you to compare one child's scores to other children within the same location, often a classroom or school. We require 20 'completers,' because computing local norms with fewer than 20 children would not be reliable for any SSA. Therefore, if fewer than 20 children are included, scores for *Zoo U* will only be calculated relative to our national norm sample.

FERPA and HIPAA compliant system
No fuzzy logic

Second, there are both *individual and aggregate report options*. You can create reports for one individual child, which provide detailed information on only that child's performance, or you can run an aggregate report that summarizes the performance across an entire group, such as across all children in a classroom or an entire grade level.

Response Patterns

Response patterns indicate when a child might be 'gaming the system' or just not trying his best, and the *Zoo U* system provides validity scores to indicate when this might be happening (see Chapter 13). In other words, is the child paying attention, responding appropriately, or is he acting in a way that suggests his assessment results might not be an accurate measure of his social skills? Response pattern scores are calculated across all six scenes to indicate the child's overall approach to game play.

Response patterns measure the child's overall in-game behavior and serve as accuracy checks on data.

One type of response that can reduce the accuracy of the assessment is if the child engages in behaviors that are rewarded in entertainment games, but actually undermine the accuracy of scores for an assessment game. We need to ensure these types of behaviors aren't interfering with the goal of *Zoo U*. For example, entertainment games often encourage open exploration where clicking around triggers interesting animations or other rewarding surprises—called 'easter eggs'. For *Zoo U*, we want to make sure children aren't clicking around so much that they aren't really focusing on solving the presented problem.

Also, it's common in entertainment games to just click through dialog or menus to move forward without any real negative consequence. But in *Zoo U*, if a child doesn't take the time to listen to menu options or what other characters say, she's not likely to make well-informed decisions. So, we assess the degree to which children try to rush through scenes without paying adequate attention.

Another area of concern is when the child doesn't take the assessment seriously. She may pick answers at random or deliberately try to 'game the system' by always picking the first response or always picking the worst answer. In *Zoo U*, we want to make sure children are actively engaged in problem solving and really trying.

When one of these response pattern checks is triggered by the system, the software generates a warning describing how scores may be impacted and providing recommendations for how to proceed with this child. For example, if the 'percent audio played warning' is present, we recommend that you instruct the child to slow down and listen to all options before making a choice. **Figure 2** shows an example of a *Zoo U* report with response pattern warnings for a fictional child. Integrating these response pattern checks into the scoring and reporting functions of *Zoo U* provides vital information that increases the confidence with which educators can rely on the resulting data. These reports also give you useful behavioral information about the child that is not available through any other assessment tool.

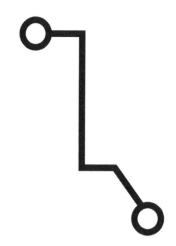

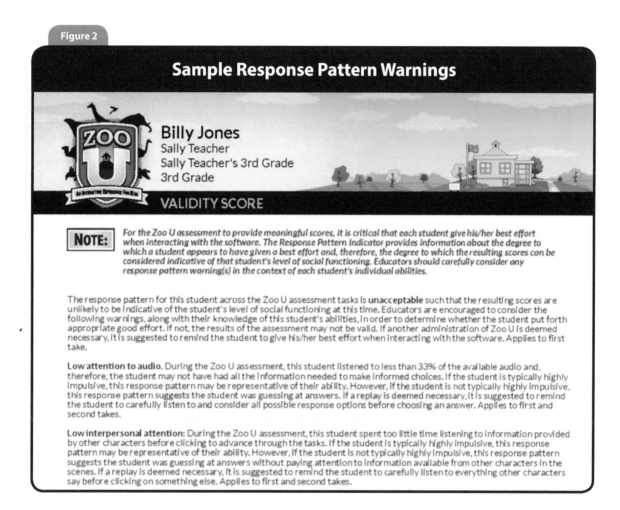

Figure 2

Sample Response Pattern Warnings

Billy Jones
Sally Teacher
Sally Teacher's 3rd Grade
3rd Grade

VALIDITY SCORE

NOTE: *For the Zoo U assessment to provide meaningful scores, it is critical that each student give his/her best effort when interacting with the software. The Response Pattern Indicator provides information about the degree to which a student appears to have given a best effort and, therefore, the degree to which the resulting scores can be considered indicative of that student's level of social functioning. Educators should carefully consider any response pattern warning(s) in the context of each student's individual abilities.*

The response pattern for this student across the Zoo U assessment tasks is **unacceptable** such that the resulting scores are unlikely to be indicative of the student's level of social functioning at this time. Educators are encouraged to consider the following warnings, along with their knowledge of this student's abilities, in order to determine whether the student put forth appropriate good effort. If not, the results of the assessment may not be valid. If another administration of Zoo U is deemed necessary, it is suggested to remind the student to give his/her best effort when interacting with the software. Applies to first take.

Low attention to audio. During the Zoo U assessment, this student listened to less than 33% of the available audio and, therefore, the student may not have had all the information needed to make informed choices. If the student is typically highly impulsive, this response pattern may be representative of their ability. However, if the student is not typically highly impulsive, this response pattern suggests the student was guessing at answers. If a replay is deemed necessary, it is suggested to remind the student to carefully listen to and consider all possible response options before choosing an answer. Applies to first and second takes.

Low interpersonal attention: During the Zoo U assessment, this student spent too little time listening to information provided by other characters before clicking to advance through the tasks. If the student is typically highly impulsive, this response pattern may be representative of their ability. However, if the student is not typically highly impulsive, this response pattern suggests the student was guessing at answers without paying attention to information available from other characters in the scenes. If a replay is deemed necessary, it is suggested to remind the student to carefully listen to everything other characters say before clicking on something else. Applies to first and second takes.

Global Social Competence Score

When a report is generated for a child, his overall level of performance for the global social competence score is displayed. This score reflects a composite performance level across all six social skills. Global scores can range from 0 – 100, with higher scores indicating better overall performance.

Figure 3 shows a sample screenshot for an individual child's report, displaying his global score. As in this example, if a child has completed *Zoo U* multiple times, each of those prior scores will be included in his report.

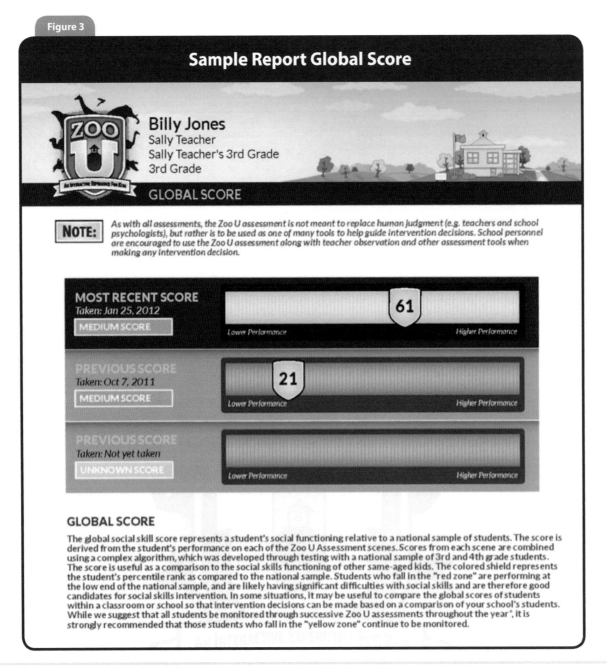

Figure 3

Sample Report Global Score

Billy Jones
Sally Teacher
Sally Teacher's 3rd Grade
3rd Grade

GLOBAL SCORE

NOTE: As with all assessments, the Zoo U assessment is not meant to replace human judgment (e.g. teachers and school psychologists), but rather is to be used as one of many tools to help guide intervention decisions. School personnel are encouraged to use the Zoo U assessment along with teacher observation and other assessment tools when making any intervention decision.

MOST RECENT SCORE
Taken: Jan 25, 2012
MEDIUM SCORE
Lower Performance   **61**   Higher Performance

PREVIOUS SCORE
Taken: Oct 7, 2011
MEDIUM SCORE
Lower Performance   **21**   Higher Performance

PREVIOUS SCORE
Taken: Not yet taken
UNKNOWN SCORE
Lower Performance   Higher Performance

GLOBAL SCORE
The global social skill score represents a student's social functioning relative to a national sample of students. The score is derived from the student's performance on each of the Zoo U Assessment scenes. Scores from each scene are combined using a complex algorithm, which was developed through testing with a national sample of 3rd and 4th grade students. The score is useful as a comparison to the social skills functioning of other same-aged kids. The colored shield represents the student's percentile rank as compared to the national sample. Students who fall in the "red zone" are performing at the low end of the national sample, and are likely having significant difficulties with social skills and are therefore good candidates for social skills intervention. In some situations, it may be useful to compare the global scores of students within a classroom or school so that intervention decisions can be made based on a comparison of your school's students. While we suggest that all students be monitored through successive Zoo U assessments throughout the year*, it is strongly recommended that those students who fall in the "yellow zone" continue to be monitored.

It's also possible to generate an aggregate report for composite scores across a group of children, say all children in the same class. A sample of this kind of combined report for *Zoo U* is shown in **Figure 4**. As you can see from this example, composite scores are divided into three tiers to aid in interpretation of the data.

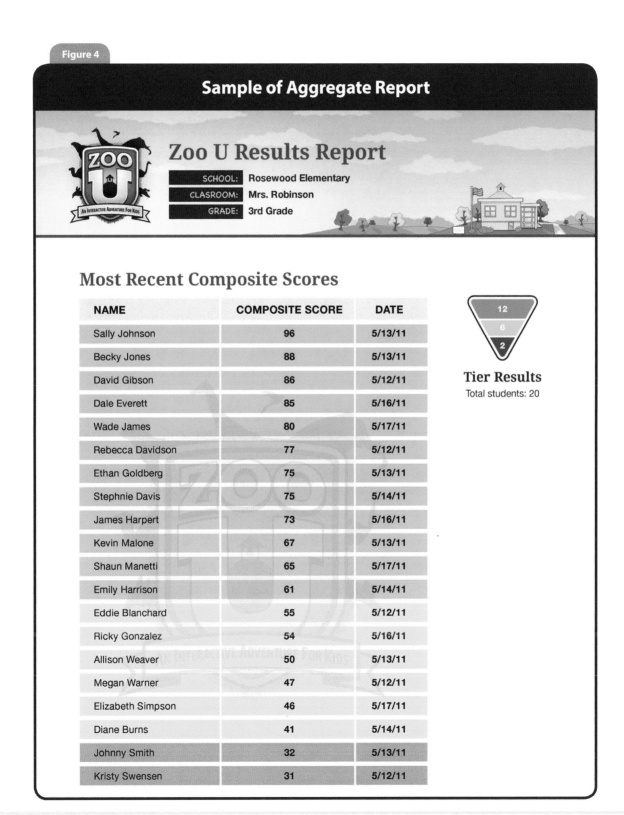

Figure 4

Sample of Aggregate Report

Zoo U Results Report

SCHOOL: Rosewood Elementary
CLASROOM: Mrs. Robinson
GRADE: 3rd Grade

Most Recent Composite Scores

NAME	COMPOSITE SCORE	DATE
Sally Johnson	96	5/13/11
Becky Jones	88	5/13/11
David Gibson	86	5/12/11
Dale Everett	85	5/16/11
Wade James	80	5/17/11
Rebecca Davidson	77	5/12/11
Ethan Goldberg	75	5/13/11
Stephnie Davis	75	5/14/11
James Harpert	73	5/16/11
Kevin Malone	67	5/13/11
Shaun Manetti	65	5/17/11
Emily Harrison	61	5/14/11
Eddie Blanchard	55	5/12/11
Ricky Gonzalez	54	5/16/11
Allison Weaver	50	5/13/11
Megan Warner	47	5/12/11
Elizabeth Simpson	46	5/17/11
Diane Burns	41	5/14/11
Johnny Smith	32	5/13/11
Kristy Swensen	31	5/12/11

12
6
2

Tier Results
Total students: 20

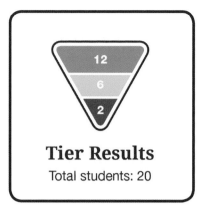

Tier Results

Total students: 20

The red tier represents significant difficulty with social skills. Those children are performing at the low end of the norm sample, and are likely having significant difficulties with social skills. Children with global scores in this range are good candidates for social skills interventions at school and at home.

The yellow tier represents scores falling in the 'at risk' range, suggesting the child may need additional supports to demonstrate competency with social skills. These children are performing a bit below the target range compared to the norm sample, and might be having some difficulties with social skills. Children with global scores in this range should be monitored closely, and would likely benefit from additional supports to improve social skills.

Finally, the green tier represents social skills falling within an acceptable and age-typical range. These children are performing within the ideal range compared to the norm sample, which suggests that their overall social skills are appropriate for their age. Children with global scores in this range do not likely need additional supports or interventions for social skills.

Individual Social Skill Scores

Zoo U also creates reports showing the child's scores in each of the six social skill areas. Again, when more than 20 children in a classroom or other local norm group have completed *Zoo U*, you can use local norms to generate these scores.

There are a couple of options for viewing these results. In the sample report shown in **Figure 5**, you can easily see where a child scores relative to other children in his norm reference group. The graphic of 10 children translates into percentile ranks; if the figure in the graphic is displayed 7th up the line, the child scored at the 70th percentile, or greater than 70% of his comparison peers. Likewise, if the figure representing the child's score is second in the line, the child scored at the 20th percentile, or greater than only 20% of same-aged peers. This report also provides the actual scores in each area. Again, these scores are color-coded into red, yellow, or green tiers so you can easily view how a child performs in a given social skill area. For children who have completed *Zoo U* multiple times, changes in these skill areas can also be seen easily as displayed in the colored bar charts to the right of the figures.

Sample Index Score Report

Billy Jones
Sally Teacher
Sally Teacher's 3rd Grade
3rd Grade

INDEX SCORES

NOTE: The Index scores presented below are designed to inform school personnel about a student's performance in six specific social skill areas. A complex algorithm is used to determine the global score, so although each of these index scores contribute to the global score, they cannot simply be added together to determine the global score. The purpose of these scores is to compare strengths and challenges for each student, and therefore should be used to guide the type of intervention provided to a particular student rather than being the sole basis for determining whether or not intervention is necessary.

Billy Jones has taken and completed ZooU **2** times ➔

	Oct 7, 2011	Jan 25, 2012	Not yet taken
Scene #1 EMOTION REGULATION	5.8	8.2	
In a group of **10**, Billy would be ahead of **2** children and behind **7** children*			
Scene #2 IMPULSE CONTROL	8.9	9.9	
In a group of **10**, Billy would be ahead of **4** children and behind **5** children*			
Scene #3 COMMUNICATION	8.4	8.9	
In a group of **10**, Billy would be ahead of **1** child and behind **8** children*			
Scene #4 EMPATHY	8	12	
In a group of **10**, Billy would be ahead of **9** children and behind **0** children*			
Scene #5 COOPERATION	10.7	11.4	
In a group of **10**, Billy would be ahead of **9** children and behind **0** children*			
Scene #6 INITIATION	8.6	10.5	
In a group of **10**, Billy would be ahead of **7** children and behind **2** children*			

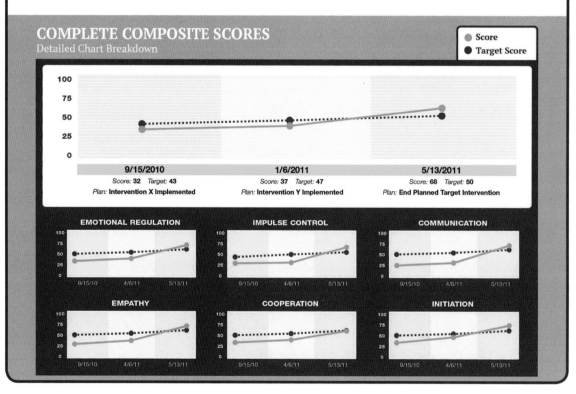

Figure 6

Sample Learning Trend Report

Zoo U Results Report

SCHOOL: Rosewood Elementary
CLASROOM: Mrs. Robinson
GRADE: 3rd Grade

Details for student: Kevin Malone

DATE COMPLETED	9/15/2010	1/6/2011	5/13/2011
Composite Scores	**32**	**37**	**67**
Emotional Regulation	42	43	71
Impulse Control	31	36	55
Communication	26	29	72
Empathy	28	34	69
Cooperation	31	35	57
Initiation	29	40	70

COMPLETE COMPOSITE SCORES
Detailed Chart Breakdown

● Score
● Target Score

9/15/2010	1/6/2011	5/13/2011
Score: 32 Target: 43	Score: 37 Target: 47	Score: 68 Target: 50
Plan: Intervention X Implemented	Plan: Intervention Y Implemented	Plan: End Planned Target Intervention

EMOTIONAL REGULATION

IMPULSE CONTROL

COMMUNICATION

EMPATHY

COOPERATION

INITIATION

Figure 6 shows an alternative display of this information. Here, numerical scores for each social skill, as well as the composite score, are listed for each time *Zoo U* was completed by the child. Line graphs are generated that show overall changes within each skill area over time. With this report, it's easy to see learning trends in social skill competency over time. This type of information is particularly helpful when the child has participated in a social intervention in the interim period, so you can directly examine the degree to which that child has benefited from that intervention and in what areas.

SUMMARY

SSAs are only as good as the data they provide, but those data are really only useful if they are accessible to those who need them for progress monitoring and/or intervention planning. As part of the *Zoo U* software package, we developed automated reporting functions that seamlessly translate *Zoo U*'s sophisticated scoring algorithms into reader-friendly reports to allow teachers and school staff to make informed decisions about both a child's general social competence and specific social skills across six domains. These reports provide not only raw scores, but also percentile information and graphical representations of a child's change in performance over time to aid in progress monitoring. In addition, *Zoo U*'s reports include response pattern warnings that let educators know if a child's style of gameplay may have impacted her performance, and provide suggestions for ways to handle these gameplay issues. And, by capitalizing on the real-time computing power of game technology, teachers who use *Zoo U* for SSA are not only able to evaluate a child's performance relative to a national sample of 3rd and 4th graders, but also relative to their peers at a classroom- or school-level. The next chapter presents the research studies we conducted to help us define and refine the scoring algorithms for each social skill, as well as establish the reliability and validity of these scores, also called psychometric soundness (see Chapter 5).

CHAPTER 14 NOTES

1. See www.ed.gov/policy/gen/guid/fpco/ferpa/index.html for details.
2. See www.hhs.gov/ocr/privacy/ for details.
3. For example, AIMSweb: http://www.aimsweb.com/products/features/data-management-and-reporting
4. For example, DIBELS: https://dibels.uoregon.edu/report/

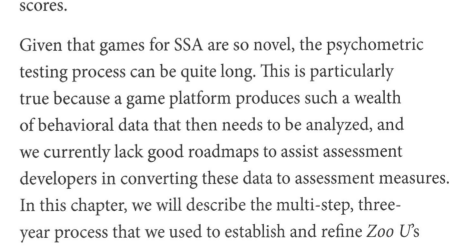

15

Zoo U Foundational Studies

by: Melissa E. DeRosier, Ph.D. and Ashley Craig, Ph.D.

DESCRIPTION

A central aspect of assessment development is establishing psychometric soundness. **Table 1** summarizes some of the more common psychometric properties that sound assessment tools demonstrate.[1, 2] The process needed to establish a new assessment is a long and tedious one that can take many years. The assessment developer must conduct a series of research studies to demonstrate that the new tool is sufficiently reliable and valid to justify its use. Even then, assessment developers often continue to collect data so they can modify and refine the algorithms used to formulate scores.

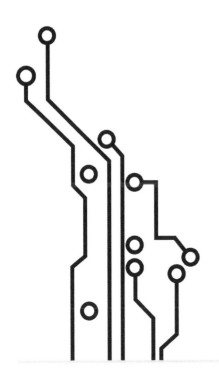

Given that games for SSA are so novel, the psychometric testing process can be quite long. This is particularly true because a game platform produces such a wealth of behavioral data that then needs to be analyzed, and we currently lack good roadmaps to assist assessment developers in converting these data to assessment measures. In this chapter, we will describe the multi-step, three-year process that we used to establish and refine *Zoo U's*

scoring algorithms for use with 3rd and 4th graders. In order to broaden the use of *Zoo U*, we will continue the testing process into the future, including the investigation of how this new game-based SSA method works for diverse samples of children.

Table 1

Definitions of Core Psychometric Properties

Property	Estimates the score's...	Answers the question...
Reliability	Consistency	How likely is it that a child will receive the same score across multiple administrations, over time, or across raters?
Construct Validity	Accuracy	Does the score truly reflect the child's actual skills or level of functioning in that area in the real world?
Content Validity	Completeness	Does the score include or represent all important aspects of this area?
Predictive Validity	Importance	Does the score predict meaningful real-world outcomes?

ALGORITHM DEVELOPMENT

As our first step in establishing the scoring algorithms for *Zoo U*'s six social skills, we conducted a field test with 50 3rd and 4th grade students in one central North Carolina elementary school. An approximately equal number of boys and girls participated in each grade. Students completed the six scenes of *Zoo U* during their computer lab class. Research staff supervised and observed children as they navigated the software. In addition, we asked teachers to independently complete online ratings of the social and behavioral adjustment of the students in their classroom using the *Social Skills Improvement System* (SSIS).[3] The SSIS is a widely used behavioral rating scale with considerable evidence supporting its reliability and validity.[3-6] We asked teachers to complete 40 items covering five SSIS social skill subscales—Communication, Cooperation, Empathy, Self-Control, and Engagement— and the SSIS Hyperactive/Inattentive subscale. Using a 5-point rating scale from 1=*never* to 5=*almost always*, teachers rated the frequency with which each student in their class exhibited specific prosocial (such as 'tries to comfort others') and antisocial behaviors (such as 'uses an inappropriate tone of voice'). Subscale items were averaged to calculate SSIS subscale scores in which higher scores reflect better adjustment in that area (so, items for the Hyperactive/ Inattentive subscale were reverse coded prior to being averaged). We then calculated *Zoo U* scores for each social skill area according to our theoretically-based scoring algorithms and children's performance in each *Zoo U* scene (for review, see Chapter 13).

The question of interest in this test was how well *Zoo U*'s assessment of children's social skills correlated with the established SSIS assessment. Essentially, this was our first step in determining the construct validity of *Zoo U*. We wanted to know if we were on the right track to developing a game-based assessment that reflects children's real-world social behavior. To answer this question, we computed correlations between the *Zoo U* and SSIS subscale scores.[7] These intercorrelations can be found in **Table 2**.

We found that children's performance on *Zoo U* was meaningfully related in expected ways to children's scores on the independent SSIS teacher-report measure. Scales that assess highly similar constructs were significantly and positively related to one another. For example, *Zoo U* Impulse Control was most highly related to SSIS Attentive and SSIS Self-Control, each of which tap into children's ability to regulate their impulses. Empathy and Communication on the SSIS were most highly related to their companion

Content validity

Table 2

Correlations Between SSIS and *Zoo U* Scores

SSIS Subscales:	Impulse Control	Emotion Regulation	Communication	Empathy	Social Initiation	Cooperation
Attentive	.50	.29	.08	.25	.41	.34
Self-Control	.42	.45	.27	.32	.36	.45
Communication	.21	.22	.39	.36	.35	.36
Empathy	.19	.16	.23	.45	.39	.32
Engagement	.12	.23	.49	.37	.31	.39
Cooperation	.33	.28	.23	.40	.47	.40

Note. All correlations ≥ .20 were significant at the *p*<.05 level.

scale scores in *Zoo U*. Similarly, scales that assess more dissimilar constructs were unrelated or less related to one another. For example, *Zoo U* Communication was unrelated to Attentive behavior on the SSIS and *Zoo U* Impulse Control was unrelated to SSIS Empathy and Engagement subscales.

Zoo U scores for Social Initiation and Cooperation were less well-defined constructs compared to the SSIS. Given the complex nature of these social behaviors, this result is not surprising. Initiation and cooperation with others require the interplay of multiple social skills simultaneously. In addition, the SSIS and *Zoo U* constructs differ in important ways, so a direct one-to-one correspondence should not be expected. For example, the SSIS Cooperation scale includes children's social behavior with adults, such as the item 'talks back to adults,' whereas *Zoo U* focuses solely on children's cooperative behavior with other children.

Overall, these promising results for the first iteration of the *Zoo U* algorithms—along with the positive feasibility and usability data presented in Chapter 12—provided considerable support for the viability and potential value of the *Zoo U* software for assessing children's social skills.

ALGORITHM REFINEMENT

Based on the results from our first field test, we modified the *Zoo U*'s scenes and revised our scoring algorithms to better tap into our intended social skill constructs. Then, we conducted a second field test in two schools in central NC. A total of 187 3rd and 4th grade students within 14 classrooms participated with their teachers. Our sample of students was evenly divided across grades and genders. Children came from families representing the full range of socioeconomic status, with about 25% receiving free or reduced lunch. The racial distribution for children was highly diverse with 55% White, 32% African American, 7% Asian American, and 6% multiracial with 27% of Hispanic/Latino ethnicity. As in the first field test, research staff observed children completing *Zoo U* during their regularly scheduled computer lab class.

In this test—as in the first—we wanted to compare *Zoo U* scores with teachers' independent external assessment of their students' social skills. But this time, we wanted to gather teacher opinions of social behaviors that more closely mapped onto the social skill constructs assessed in *Zoo U*. Therefore, we consulted established social skill rating scale measures, including the Teacher Checklist,[8] the Social Skills Improvement System[3], and the Social Competence Scale-Teacher Version,[9] to create the Social Skills Behavior Inventory (SSBI).[10] This teacher rating scale includes 34 items across six social skills subscales—Communication, Cooperation, Empathy, Initiation, Impulse Control, and Emotion Regulation. The SSBI presents behavioral descriptors (such as 'gets distracted easily,' 'good to have in a group,' 'tries to comfort others') and teachers rate the degree to which each descriptor is true of each student in their class. Ratings are made on a 5-point scale from a low of 'never true' to a high of 'almost always true.' Subscale items were averaged to calculate SSBI subscale scores in which higher scores reflect higher social skills in that area. Internal consistency of the teacher-report SSBI was excellent with a mean Cronbach alpha (α) of .86 across the six subscales and the measure worked equally well for both 3rd and 4th grade students.

Intercorrelations Between Zoo U and SSBI

First, we computed correlations between the *Zoo U* social skill scores and the SSBI subscale scores. **Table 3** displays these results. This test achieved greater differentiation across the individual *Zoo U* social skill scores. Each *Zoo U* score was significantly correlated with its analogous teacher-rated SSBI subscale and this correlation was greater than most other intercorrelations. This finding provides evidence of *Zoo U*'s construct validity in that related areas were most highly associated with one another (convergent validity) and more dissimilar areas were less associated with one another (discriminant validity).

Construct
validity
=
Convergent and
Discriminant
validity

Table 3

Correlations Between SSBI and *Zoo U* Scores

SSBI Subscales:	Impulse Control	Emotion Regulation	Communication	Empathy	Social Initiation	Cooperation
Impulse Control	.29***	.31***	.15*	.16*	.17*	.16*
Emotion Regulation	.15*	.30***	.08	.17*	.25**	.17*
Communication	.26***	.28***	.20**	.19*	.27***	.20**
Empathy	.26***	.22**	.10	.23**	.24**	.17*
Social Initiation	.17*	.14*	.08	.15*	.27***	.18*
Cooperation	.23**	.31***	.12	.17*	.16*	.21**

Note. ***p<.0001, **p<.01, *p<.05 level.

Social skill areas were related to one another in expected ways. For example, being able to talk to and understand other children—communication—is an essential component of both social initiation and cooperation. Therefore, it makes sense that the *Zoo U* Communication score is highly related to both the Social Initiation and Cooperation subscales of the SSBI. Similarly, both impulse control and emotion regulation require the ability to control your impulses, but emotion regulation is specific to emotionally charged situations. Therefore, it makes sense that the *Zoo U* Emotion Regulation score is equally related to both the Impulse Control and Emotion Regulation SSBI subscales, whereas the *Zoo U* Impulse Control score is more highly related to the SSBI Impulse Control subscale than it is to the SSBI Emotion Regulation subscale.

Intercorrelations Among Zoo U Scores

In developing *Zoo U*, we intended the six individual scores to be meaningfully related to one another—and when combined, reflect a child's overall social competence—but we also expected each score to independently reflect a distinct aspect of social competence. To examine how these six scores were related to one another, we computed correlations among the six scores. As can be seen in **Table 4**, *Zoo U* scores were related to one another in meaningful and expected ways. For example, it's not surprising that impulse control was correlated with emotion regulation. However, as expected, these scores were clearly not redundant with one another. No correlations were excessively high and the pattern of intercorrelations supported each *Zoo U* score as an independent social skill competency.

Table 4

Intercorrelations Among *Zoo U* Scores

	Emotion Regulation	Communication	Empathy	Social Initiation	Cooperation
Impulse Control	.23**	.07	.24**	.15*	.21**
Emotion Regulation		.20**	.16*	.26**	.09
Communication			.10	.19*	.07
Empathy				.14*	.16*
Social Initiation					.21**

Note. **p<.01, *p<.05

In addition, we expected that, when combined, the six *Zoo U* scores would provide a reliable estimate of children's overall social skill level. In other words, we expected the six scores to hang together to form one overall social competence construct. To test this, we computed the Cronbach alpha statistic across the six individual scores. The result was an alpha of .76, indicating acceptable internal consistency and supporting *Zoo U*'s ability to reliably measure children's overall social competence. This alpha level is particularly good given only six scores were included in the calculation (internal consistency generally increases with the number of items). Because the alpha was only moderately high, we have support for the fact that the six scores are not redundant with one another, but rather are independent facets of an overall construct.

Demographic Differences in Zoo U Scores

We want *Zoo U* to be equally useful for assessment with both boys and girls and for children across the 3rd and 4th grades. Therefore, we needed to understand whether and how the *Zoo U* scores differ across our two grades or for children of different genders. We conducted an analysis of variance (ANOVA) comparing *Zoo U* scores by gender and grade level. The only area in which we found a grade difference was Cooperation—3rd graders scored significantly higher in cooperation (mean = .15) than did 4th graders (mean = -.12). For all cases except Social Initiation, females scored significantly higher on *Zoo U* than did males. These demographic differences in social skill levels are similar to what has been found for other social skill assessment tools.[3,11,12]

Reliability

Establishing Cutoffs for Zoo U Scores

One of the goals of *Zoo U* is to determine cutoff scores that identify children who have poor social skills relative to their same-age peers. Establishing cutoffs to categorize children into social skill levels makes interpreting and using assessment results easier. For example, if we're able to reliably identify children who struggle with particular social skills, we can implement targeted social skill interventions to improve those skills. As a first step in this process for *Zoo U*, we examined the distribution of scores in our sample for each *Zoo U* score and categorized children into low (≤ 25th percentile), moderate (middle 50th percentile), or high (≥ 75th percentile) performance categories for each of the six social skills.

We then conducted ANOVAs to examine whether the teacher's report of children's social skills—using the SSBI—differed significantly by these categories. In other words, we tested whether children in the three *Zoo U* performance categories were significantly different from one another in their teacher-rated SSBI scores for the same social skill area. Results revealed significant differences across categories for all social skill areas. We then computed means per category and conducted post hoc mean comparison tests[7] to determine how these categories differed from one another. **Table 5** summarizes these results. The superscripts in this table indicate which categories **within a row** are significantly different from one another. So, if two categories in a row have the same letter, these were not significantly different from one another. But, if the letters are different across categories for that row, these categories were significantly different.

Predictive validity for social behavior

Table 5

Means and Mean Comparisons for Teacher-rated SSBI Social Skills by *Zoo U* Categories

Social Skill Area	Zoo U Category		
	High	**Moderate**	**Low**
Impulse Control	.38[A]	-.04[B]	-.21[C]
Emotion Regulation	.24[A]	-.01[A]	-.38[B]
Communication	.17[A]	.00[AB]	-.19[B]
Empathy	.34[A]	-.12[B]	-.17[B]
Social Initiation	.20[A]	-.04[A]	-.42[B]
Cooperation	.20[A]	.05[AB]	-.22[B]

Note. Means within a row with different superscript letters are significantly different from one another.

Overall, categories using these percentile-based cutoffs were effective in identifying children who were seen by their teachers as higher or lower in that social skill area, respectively. For example, children who scored in the high category for *Zoo U* Impulse Control were rated by teachers as significantly higher than children in the moderate category who, in turn, were rated by teachers as significantly higher than children in the low category. Children in the moderate category for *Zoo U* Communication were not significantly different from children in either the high or low categories, but children in the low category were significantly lower on teacher-rated communication skills than were children in the high category. These results indicated that different levels of *Zoo U* performance are meaningfully related to teacher's external views of children's social skills, providing further support of *Zoo U*'s construct validity. These significant differences also indicate that local norms for *Zoo U* performance scores can be effective for identifying children who struggle with social skills more than their peers at school (see Chapter 4 for a discussion of norms).

FURTHER ALGORITHM REFINEMENT

We conducted a third field test to evaluate *Zoo U* with a broader selection of schools and teachers. The participating sample included 289 3rd and 4th graders in 27 classrooms across 12 states. The sample was evenly divided across genders and grades. We also wanted to compare data collected in the fall versus spring of the school year, so we could examine whether *Zoo U* performance was different at these two time points. Therefore, 48% of classrooms (n=139 students) participated in the fall and 52% (n=150 students) participated in the spring.

Similar to the other field tests, teachers independently completed the SSBI for each student in their class. While all students in the class could complete *Zoo U*, teachers only rated 10 to 14 randomly selected students from their class in order to decrease the data collection burden on teachers. We only collected and analyzed *Zoo U* data for those students also rated by the teacher.

Using the 5-point scale of 'never true' to 'almost always true,' teachers rated children for each of the SSBI social skill subscales (as described above) as well as additional SSBI subscales assessing children's adjustment for school-related outcomes. These outcome-focused SSBI subscales included Academic Performance, Internalizing Problems, Externalizing Problems,

and Disruptive Behavior Problems. Internalizing Problems include items for social withdrawal, social anxiety, and loneliness at school. Externalizing Problems include items for bullying, leaving others out on purpose, and acting aggressively with peers. Disruptive Behavior Problems include items for disturbing others, disrupting class, and bothering other children when they're trying to work. The Academic Performance subscale assesses how well children perform in core subjects and the ease with which they learn and perform academically compared to their peers. In addition, teachers provided data regarding incidents of discipline problems for each student, including in-school and out-of-school suspensions.

Demographic Comparisons

To examine whether the relations among *Zoo U* scores and SSBI scores varied by gender or grade level, we ran correlations separately for boys versus girls, for 3rd grade versus 4th grade, and for fall versus spring. Then, we looked for differences in the strength of intercorrelations across these groups.

For **gender**, Zoo U worked similarly for males and females—the associations between *Zoo U* and SSBI scores showed a highly similar pattern of intercorrelations for both boys and girls in the sample. The only exception to this pattern was Impulse Control which showed a stronger correlation for females. In other words, *Zoo U* performance for Impulse Control was more strongly related to teacher ratings of impulse control for girls. However, the correlation for males continued to be significant.

Across **grades**, several differences in the pattern of correlations were present. Three *Zoo U* scores—Emotion Regulation, Communication, and Social Initiation—showed stronger correlations for 4th graders than for 3rd graders. So, children's performance on *Zoo U* was more strongly correlated with teacher ratings in these three social skill areas in the older grade. In contrast, Empathy on *Zoo U* showed a stronger correlation for 3rd graders. So, teacher ratings of empathy were more strongly related to *Zoo U* performance for empathy for children in the younger grade.

When comparing **fall** and **spring**, we found that *Zoo U* Emotion Regulation and Impulse Control worked better in the fall whereas *Zoo U* Empathy and Social Initiation worked better in the spring. In other words, teacher ratings were more strongly correlated with *Zoo U* performance in the corresponding

Reliability

skill area at these different time points. These differences may be indicative of differences in teachers' ability to easily, and quickly, observe these social skills. Problems with impulse control are more obvious and quickly evident, so teachers may be able to reliably record children's skills in these areas in the fall. In contrast, Empathy and Social Initiation are more complex social behaviors that may be more difficult to observe at school, so it may take longer for teachers to accurately assess children's skills in these areas. Communication and Cooperation worked equally well at each time point.

While further investigation is needed to determine the underlying causes fueling these demographic differences, these early results suggest that it could be valuable to adjust the underlying scoring algorithms for different demographic groups. This is a focus of our ongoing research with *Zoo U*, including the establishment of national norms for different genders and age groups (see Chapter 4 for a discussion of norms).

Prediction of School Outcomes

In order to examine whether children's performance on *Zoo U* was significantly related to their real-world adjustment at school, we conducted ANOVAs with *Zoo U* scores predicting the teacher-reported SSBI school outcome subscales. We ran these analyses separately by gender and grade.

The pattern of results was highly similar for boys and girls. Only a few gender differences were found when analyses were conducted separately by gender. And these differences likely reflect gender differences in the school-based outcomes rather than gender differences in *Zoo U* performance *per se*. For example, *Zoo U* more strongly related to internalizing problems for girls

Predictive validity of real world outcomes

Table 6

Significant Prediction of School Outcomes by Grade Level

SSBI School Outcome Subscale	Impulse Control	Emotion Regulation	Communication	Empathy	Social Initiation	Cooperation
Internalizing behavior problems			4th	4th	4th	
Externalizing behavior problems	3rd & 4th	4th		3rd & 4th	3rd & 4th	
Disruptive behavior problems		4th	4th		4th	
Discipline actions			4th	3rd & 4th	4th	3rd
Academic performance	3rd & 4th			4th	3rd & 4th	3rd & 4th

than for boys and we know that girls are more likely, in general, to exhibit internalizing problems to a greater extent than boys.[13, 14]

Table 6 displays the grades for which each *Zoo U* score significantly predicted (*p*<.05) that school outcome.

Findings revealed that each outcome area was predicted by *Zoo U* in meaningful ways. Children with internalizing behavior problems at school were more likely to show poor communication, empathy, and social initiation skills. Children with poor impulse control were particularly likely to exhibit externalizing behavior problems at school. Children who lacked prosocial initiation skills were likely to disrupt other children in the classroom. Disciplinary actions were particularly likely for children who scored lower on empathy. And, children who were able to control their behavior, initiate appropriately with peers, and cooperate well with peers were most likely to perform well academically.

There was variability in the predictive strength of *Zoo U* across the two grades. In particular, *Zoo U* scores for Communication and Emotion Regulation significantly predicted outcomes only for 4th graders. Internalizing and Disruptive Behavior Problems were also only related to *Zoo U* scores for 4th graders. It's unclear whether this differential pattern by grade is due to developmental differences for these outcomes—such as, children exhibit more of these problems in 4th grade—or developmental differences in *Zoo U* performance. There does seem to be evidence that *Zoo U* is more strongly related to outcomes for older children. When analyses were further broken down by fall versus spring, the predictive strength of *Zoo U* tended to be stronger in spring compared to fall. For example, Social Initiation was more highly related to externalizing problems in the spring for both 3rd and 4th graders. A goal of our continuing research on *Zoo U* is to examine whether our underlying scoring algorithms need be adjusted to increase sensitivity in the prediction of school-based adjustment problems, particularly internalizing behavior problems.

SUMMARY

We created the game-based *Zoo U* social skills assessment software in order to provide a more feasible, usable, and effective SSA approach. Our initial set of field tests provides strong support for the psychometric soundness of this new SSA approach. Children's performance on *Zoo U* was related in meaningful and expected ways to the teacher's independent report of social, behavioral, and academic adjustment at school.

Given that a psychometrically sound game-based assessment tool for SSA has never been developed before, the strength and utility of *Zoo U* as an SSA approach is truly remarkable. Clearly, you can reliably and validly assess many things in a game beyond simple menu choices. With stealth assessment, you can collect a wealth of meaningful data on social behavior while simultaneously minimizing the impact of social desirability biases. And these data can clearly be related to meaningful real-world social behavior and school-based outcomes. When you combine reliable, valid scoring algorithms for measuring children's social competence with the engaging, cost-effective, and feasible nature of a game-based platform, the potential for games as SSA is significant.

The current *Zoo U* scoring algorithms are based on these iterative test samples to date and were calculated to maximize construct validity for children of both genders across 3rd and 4th grades. Schools across the United States are currently using *Zoo U* to help them identify children with social skill problems and track progress in response to social skills intervention. Of course, we are continuing our research process to refine and improve our underlying scoring algorithms. Our long-term goal is to maximize sensitivity and accuracy of measurement for different development age groups so we can attain accurate and sensitive assessment of intended constructs for all children. Because *Zoo U* is deployed over the Internet, all refinements and improvements that we make are automatically integrated into the software and made available for users.

CHAPTER 15 NOTES

1. Kline, P. (1998). *The new psychometrics: Science, psychology, and measurement.* London, UK: Routledge.

2. American Educational Research Association, American Psychological Association, & National Council on Measurement in Education. (1999). *Standards for educational and psychological testing.*

3. Gresham, F., & Elliott, S. N. (2008). *Social Skills Improvement System (SSIS) Rating Scales.* Bloomington, MN: Pearson Assessments.

4. Elliott, S. N., Gresham, F. M., Frank, J. L., & Beddow, P. A. (2008). Intervention validity of social behavior rating scales features of assessments that link results to treatment plans. *Assessment for Effective Intervention, 34,* 15-24.

5. Gresham, F. M., Elliott, S. N., Cook, C. R., Vance, M. J., & Kettler, R. (2010). Cross-informant agreement for ratings for social skill and problem behavior ratings: An investigation of the Social Skills Improvement System—Rating Scales. *Psychological Assessment, 22,* 157-166.

6. Gresham, F. M., Elliott, S. N., Vance, M. J., & Cook, C. R. (2011). Comparability of the Social Skills Rating System to the Social Skills Improvement System: Content and psychometric comparisons across elementary and secondary age levels. *School Psychology Quarterly, 26,* 27-44.

7. Coolican, H. (2009). *Research methods and statistics in psychology.* New York, NY: Routledge.

8. Coie, J. (1990) *Teacher checklist.* Unpublished manuscript.

9. Gornall, M. E. (1980). *Validity of the Kohn Social Competence Scale for use with elementary school children.* (Unpublished master's thesis). The University of British Columbia.

10. DeRosier, M. E., Craig, A. B., & Sanchez, R. P. (2012). Zoo U: A stealth approach to social skills assessment in schools. *Advances in Human-Computer Interaction.* doi:10.1155/2012/654791

11. Romer, N., Ravitch, N. K., Tom, K., Merrell, K. W., & Wesley, K. L. (2011). Gender differences in positive social–emotional functioning. *Psychology in the Schools, 48,* 958-970.

12. Matthews, J. S., Ponitz, C. C., & Morrison, F. J. (2009). Early gender differences in self-regulation and academic achievement. *Journal of Educational Psychology, 101,* 689-704.

13. Merrell, K. W., & Dobmeyer, A. C. (1996). An evaluation of gender differences in self-reported internalizing symptoms of elementary-age children. *Journal of Psychoeducational Assessment, 14,* 196-207.

14. McClure, E. B. (2000). A meta-analytic review of sex differences in facial expression processing and their development in infants, children, and adolescents. *Psychological Bulletin, 126,* 424-453.

ADVANTAGES OF GAMES OVER TRADITIONAL SSA METHODS

by: Ashley Craig, Ph.D., Melissa E. DeRosier, Ph.D., and Rebecca Sanchez, Ph.D.

DESCRIPTION

Part II of this book detailed the most common traditional methods for social skills assessment, including rating scales, observations, interview methods, and peer nominations. Each of these methods has a long-standing and well-regarded history in school, clinical, and research settings. Now, emerging consensus about the importance of social skills for learning and work, combined with the rapid pace of technology development, provides an unprecedented opportunity for a significant overhaul of the traditional assessment paradigm.[1]

In Part III of this book, we introduced digital games as one such technological innovation that holds promise for effective assessment, and demonstrated our successful application of game technology (*Zoo U*) to the incredibly nuanced domain of children's social skills. Much like naturalistic observations, digital game-based assessments place the child directly into an environment while someone—in the case of game-based assessment, the

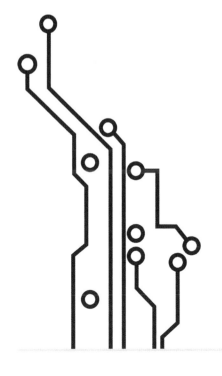

software—observes. Some virtual environments allow the child to simply explore, while others, such as *Zoo U*, ask the child to actively solve specific social problems. Although our understanding of game-based assessments is still in its infancy, early research from other domains[2] and our own experience developing game-based social skills assessment platforms suggests that this new SSA approach has many advantages over traditional assessment methodologies. In this chapter, we summarize the strengths and caveats of game-based SSA in the areas of administration feasibility, data utility and accuracy, and child engagement.

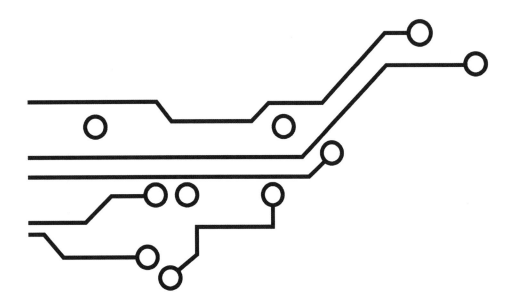

STRENGTHS AND WEAKNESSES

In the following review of the relative strengths and weaknesses of using game-based assessments for SSA, we address how practical this approach is to administer, the quality of the resulting data—in terms of both accuracy and usefulness—and how engaged children are likely to be as respondents. To help guide our discussion, we provide summary ratings in each area and then present the rationale behind these ratings. At the end of this discussion, we also provide overall ratings (our best judgment based on available evidence) to summarize how effective we believe game-based assessments are for intervention screening, progress monitoring, and evaluation (see Chapter 4).

Rating Legend

◗ = **Very good in this area**

◖ = **Generally good**

○ = **Generally fair**

◖ = **Generally poor**

● = **Very poor in this area**

Feasibility of Administration

One of the major advantages digital game-based SSA offers over traditional methods is the practicality of administration. For example, if you think back to Chapter 7, one of the major drawbacks of observational methods is the amount of training required to objectively note and accurately rate the real-time behaviors of children in order to generate useful data. Digital game-based assessments automate this process by incorporating both the notation and rating process into the game software itself. As a result, minimal if any training is required to administer game-based SSA once children have been added to the system.[3]

Well-designed game-based SSAs should be essentially 'plug and play' for professionals, making them not only feasible but also incredibly time efficient. For example, as part of the *Zoo U* software, we give providers easy 24/7 access to all needed training, support, and resources in order to quickly and easily use *Zoo U* with children, interpret the resulting data, and assist with intervention planning.

As with any SSA, the time required to administer digital game-based SSA will vary, but in the case of *Zoo U* we've found that children take approximately 45 to 60 minutes to complete the six social problem solving scenes. This time requirement is on par with the time required for many traditional SSA methods. But unlike traditional methods, game-based assessments can be administered to multiple children simultaneously. In other words, in the same

> **» WARNING**
>
> *The ratings in this chapter reflect the authors' opinions, based on our experience and understanding of the literature. Proceed with caution.*

amount of time it takes to assess the social skills of one child using traditional methods, it's possible to gather data about the social skills of an entire classroom of children using game-based assessment. The time efficiency of game-based SSAs is only restricted by the number of computers available at any given time.

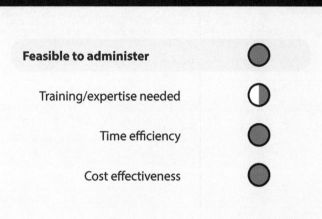

Ratings of Game-Based SSA

Feasible to administer	◐
Training/expertise needed	◐
Time efficiency	◐
Cost effectiveness	◐

The time efficiency of digital game-based SSAs can also translate into significant cost savings. It's hard to estimate the average cost per child due to the limited number of game-based SSAs currently on the market, but given the quality of data that can be generated about children's social behaviors relative to the time required for training and administration (see Chapter 11), game-based SSAs offer an excellent return on investment. For example, a one-year subscription for full access to *Zoo U* and all of its 24/7 web-based support tools is currently $49.95 for a school-wide license agreement.[4] For this small fee, a school can assess up to 300 students. Even compared to the most inexpensive of traditional SSA methods, digital games offer a significant cost-reduction in staff time as a result of the savings in training, administration, and scoring.

Utility of Data

The utility of data that can be gathered from game-based social skills assessments is largely dependent upon the quality of the in-game social simulation, the specificity of in-game choices, and the accuracy with which

Ratings of Game-Based SSA

Utility of data	◐
Psychometrically sound	◐
Norm-based cut-offs	◐
Contextually relevant	◐

these choices are recorded and scored by the software. In other words, like all SSAs, game-based methods need to have strong psychometric properties, including both validity and reliability. Validity refers to the degree to which an assessment is measuring what you intend to measure. Reliability refers to the ability of an assessment to measure a skill consistently, both over time and across people.

In Chapter 7, we describe a number of potential threats to validity, including poorly defined behavioral definitions (that is, which specific behaviors will be observed), responder reliability, and biased expectations. The majority of these validity threats are due to the possibility of human error. For example, a rater can drift from the operational definition of the targeted social behavior when she is recording a child's responses to interview questions, the child's behavior in a naturalistic observation, or even when recounting the child's past behaviors. These drifts may be due to observer or respondent bias, fatigue, or simple recording errors. Digital game-based SSA approaches essentially eliminate the human error found in traditional methods because the underlying software provides unbiased documentation of child behaviors. With game-based SSA, there's no drift in the application of behavioral definitions, because the software records and evaluates all children and all behaviors with the same fatigue- and error-free rubric.[3]

Of course, game-based SSAs are not completely without human error. One particular place where human error is cause for concern is in the designing stage of the social problem solving scenarios. Well-designed game-based SSAs should rely heavily on subject matter experts—experts in child social development, education, child mental and behavioral health—to develop the content and scoring procedures that are the foundation of the virtual SSA environment.[5] This may be more challenging relative to traditional SSA methods due to the necessary interdisciplinary nature of digital game development.

Careful attention must also be paid to the balance of assessment and entertainment. If the assessment is not planned carefully, undue focus may be given to the gaming experience, which may introduce unnecessary cognitive demands, inadvertently interfering with the assessment of children's social skills.[6] For example, 3-D environments, while immersive for entertainment games, introduce spatial reasoning requirements that may detract from effective social problem solving.

Of course, social skills experts can differ in their views of the kinds of social problems children should be able to solve, how these scenarios should be translated into virtual social problem solving scenarios, what behaviors are or are not appropriate in these social interactions, and the threshold of behaviors that are indicative of social skills problems, just to name a few. Thus, even though the computer software inherent in game-based SSAs may be capable of error-free recording and scoring of in-game behaviors, human bias in defining the underlying scoring rubrics can threaten the validity of

game-based SSAs, and thus should be closely monitored in the planning and iterative development stages. To ensure that a game-based SSA is measuring social skills performance appropriately, validity should be established by correlating the results of these assessments with existing standardized assessments. Chapter 13 provides an example of the psychometric testing process we used to establish the scoring algorithms for *Zoo U*.

The utility of assessment data can also be assessed based on the ability and accuracy of an SSA to rank an individual child against her peers. To accomplish this, SSAs must include cut-off information based on norm-referenced estimates at either the local or population level, or both (see Chapter 4 for discussion of norms). When traditional SSAs are administered, they must be hand-scored and then those scores must be compared to reference tables that provide information about relative rankings. This process is both time consuming and error-prone.[7] Further, traditional SSAs generally only provide population-based norms; if local norms are needed, additional resources, including time and expertise, are required. In contrast, with a simple click, game-based SSAs can generate rankings based on both population and local norms in real time, in both individual and aggregated report formats.

Lastly, utility of data collected from SSAs should have strong ecological, or face, validity. Ecological validity is one of the most basic and intuitive forms of validity in that its only requirement is that the test—whether items on a rating scale or a social problem solving scene in a game-based SSA—appears at face value to measure what it claims to measure.[8] In other words, SSAs should reflect real-world behavior. Game-based SSAs, like *Zoo U*, should be developed specifically to provide game-based social problem solving scenarios analogous to real-life situations that children encounter. There is a caveat to ecological validity, however. While it's important that in-game social problems be clearly linked to the social skills being assessed, the intention should not be so clear that children knowingly adjust their behavior to, in effect, 'play to the test.' But when assessment designers strike the right balance, this type of contextually-relevant assessment can maintain ecological validity akin to naturalistic observations and to a degree, well beyond behavioral ratings scales. As a result, game-based SSAs are able to optimize the measurement of children's social skill competence.

Accuracy of Data

Successful social skill intervention hinges on the implementation of quality assessments, and as noted throughout this book, SSA approaches are only as good as they are accurate. Game-based assessment methods shine particularly well in this category for many of the reasons outlined above, but most importantly because they are inherently consistent.[9] Once developed, the in-game social scenarios are delivered in the same way every time, every child's choice is measured by the same ruler, and there is no effect of observer or respondent biases impacting a child's score.

In addition to consistency, game-based SSAs may provide more accurate data because children can be unaware, or less aware, that their social skills are being assessed. When a child completes a self-report rating scale or is aware that her behavior is being observed, social desirability bias often influences the resulting data.[10] In other words, the child may try to answer questions or act in a way that she believes will be seen positively. In particular, the child may over-report what is perceived to be 'good behavior' or under-report 'bad behavior.' Games can go a long way to reduce respondent bias by making the assessment disappear behind an interactive and engaging format children are very familiar with (stealth assessment, see Chapter 11).[11] Even if children are told in advance that they are being assessed, this primary objective is likely pushed aside quite quickly as they focus on the game.

This is not to say that game-based SSAs are free of respondent bias. Whereas social desirability is a concern for traditional methods, of larger concern to game-based assessment methods is that children will take the gameplay aspect too literally, reverting to gameplay behavior that's acceptable and encouraged in popular entertainment games, but produces adverse consequences for assessing social skills. For example, in entertainment games it's very common to reward exploration and off-task behavior with additional in-game achievements called 'easter eggs,' but making an SSA game too open for exploration could detract from a child's engagement with the presented social problem. It's critical to design game-based assessments so that social assessment and gameplay are not at odds with each other.

Ratings of Game-Based SSA

Objectivity of data	●
Measurement	●
Respondent bias	●
Accuracy checks	●

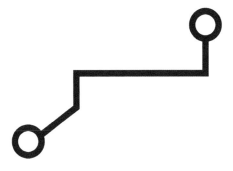

One way to guard against the problems associated with respondent bias is to include accuracy checks as part of the SSA. Traditional SSAs may include additional items to assess social desirability or bias, but in game-based assessments these checks can be embedded into gameplay itself. For example, games have the power to automatically generate calculations regarding the child's general approach to gameplay, gauging the degree to which she may be 'gaming the system' or simply not paying sufficient attention. Developers of SSA games can translate how these patterns of in-game behavior may influence the scores, and provide recommendations for how assessment administrators should proceed with an individual child. For example, in *Zoo U*, if a child's gameplay indicates that she isn't listening to menu options before making a selection, a response pattern warning is included in the child's report with a suggestion to the teacher to instruct the child to complete the assessment again, this time slowing down and listening to all options before making a choice (See Chapter 14). Because it's possible to integrate response pattern checks like these directly into scoring and reporting functions in game-based assessments, this approach to SSA can provide a wealth of information not available through other assessment tools. This additional information provides professionals with more confidence in the resulting data about a child's social behaviors.

Ratings of Game-Based SSA	
Engaging for children	

Engaging for Children

When children are the respondents for an interview or rating scale, both the feasibility of administration and the quality of data generated can be affected by their engagement in the assessment process.[12, 13] For example, it may be difficult to elicit responses from an uninterested, unmotivated child, so administrators may get only limited data and the validity of those data may be questionable. In contrast, an engaged child will be more willing to provide responses and those responses are likely to be more accurate and useful.

A desire for alternative tools that provide rich, accurate data and also increase child engagement has led to transdisciplinary interest in computer games for assessment and learning.[14] In fact, comprehensive in-game modeling of an individual child's knowledge and skills is becoming more common as intelligent tutoring systems research and technology are increasingly applied to computer games (see Chapter 17).[15-17]

A major advantage of game-based SSAs is their engaging quality. Game-based SSAs leverage children's predilection for and familiarity with computers to provide an enjoyable, interactive platform to assess social skills.[18, 19] Activities that support basic human needs for competency, autonomy, and relatedness are intrinsically motivating and foster enhanced participation in these types of game-based assessments.[20, 21]

Overall Ratings

When designed by a team of well-trained subject matter experts, computer scientists, and animators all sensitive to the nuances of social skills for specific populations, digital games can be a tremendously powerful SSA tool. Games can mitigate many of the challenges associated with traditional SSAs, particularly those that impact efficiency of administration, accuracy of data, and child engagement. While useful for all three SSA purposes, games have a great ability to assess a large number of children simultaneously at low cost, making them ideal for screening purposes. Games can be quite effective for quickly identifying specific children with social skill deficits and helping professionals plan appropriate social interventions. And, because games are capable of tracking a child's change over time due to the ability of robust software to store gameplay history (see Chapter 14 for an example), they can be very useful for progress monitoring and intervention evaluation.

Use of Game-Based SSA for Intervention Planning Purposes

Useful for screening

Useful for progress monitoring

Useful for intervention evaluation

Table 1

Comparison of Traditional and Game-Based SSA Approaches

	Behavioral Ratings	Observation	Interview	Peer Nominations		Games
				By hand	Software	
Feasible to administer	●	◐	○	●	◐	●
Training/expertise needed	●	●	◐	●	◐	◐
Time efficiency	●	◐	○	◐	○	●
Cost effectiveness	◐	◐	◐	◐	○	●
Utility of data	○	◐	○	◐		○
Psychometrically sound	◐	○	◐	●		○
Norm-based cut-offs	◐	●	●	◐		◐
Contextually relevant	◐	●	●	◐		●
Objectivity of data	◐	○	◐	○		●
Standardized measurement	◐	◐	◐	○		●
Respondent bias	◐	○	●	◐		●
Accuracy checks	◐	◐	●	◐		●
Engaging for children	◐	n/a	○	◐		●
Useful for screening	◐	○	○	●		●
Useful for progress monitoring	◐	◐	○	●		◐
Useful for intervention evaluation	◐	○	◐	◐		◐

SUMMARY

Although the field of game-based SSA is in its infancy, **Table 1** shows that games hold a great deal of promise for overcoming many of the challenges associated with traditional SSA approaches. Games such as *Zoo U* allow for an engaging yet controlled simulation of contextually-relevant social problems for a child to solve, providing the administrator the opportunity to go beyond simple knowledge testing to a more in-depth assessment of a child's applied social skills. To get equally high quality data from traditional methods is generally too time- and cost-prohibitive. Game-based SSAs significantly reduce the burden placed on administrators by allowing simultaneous assessment of many children and automatically scoring and reporting their progress. Moreover, these capabilities ensure a level of accuracy not generally possible with other SSA approaches. With all of these advantages, game-based SSAs are poised to make the goal of universal assessment and regular progress monitoring more attainable in a variety of domains and settings. And, as will be explained in the next chapter, SSA games can be integrated with game-based tutorial systems to deliver a unique, individualized, and adaptive intervention experience.

CHAPTER 16 NOTES

1. Denham, S. A., Bassett, H. H., & Zinsser, K. (2012). Computerizing social-emotional assessment for school readiness: First steps toward an assessment battery for early childhood settings. *The Journal of Applied Research on Children: Informing Policy for Children at Risk, 3*(2).

2. Mayrath, M. C., Clarke-Midura, J., Robinson, D. H., & Schraw, G. (Eds.). (2012). *Technology-based assessments for 21ˢᵗ century skills: Theoretical and practical implications from modern research.* Charlotte, NC: Information Age Press.

3. Clarke-Midura, J., Code, J., Dede, C., Mayrath, M., & Zap, N. (2012). Thinking outside the bubble: Virtual performance assessments for measuring complex learning. In M. C. Mayrath, J., Clarke-Midura,. D. H. Robinson, & G. Schraw (Eds.), *Technology-based assessments for 21ˢᵗ century skills: Theoretical and practical implications from modern research* (pp. 125-147). Charlotte, NC: Information Age Press.

4. For *Zoo U* subscription information: http://www.3cisd.com/marketplace/catalog/202/Zoo-U-Social-Skills-Assessment

5. Zyda, M. (2005). From visual simulation to virtual reality to games. *Computer, 38,* 25-32.

6. Zapata-Rivera, D., & Bauer, M. (2012). Exploring the role of games in educational assessment. *Technology-based assessments for 21st-century skills: Theoretical and practical implications from modern research* (pp. 147-169). Charlotte, NC: Information Age Press.

7. Merrell, K. W. (2001). Assessment of children's social skills: Recent developments, best practices, and new directions. *Division of Psychological & Quantitative Foundations, 9,* 3-18.

8. American Educational Research Association, American Psychological Association, & National Council on Measurement in Education. (1999). *Standards for educational and psychological testing.*

9. Kiili, K. (2005). Digital game-based learning: Towards an experiential gaming model. *The Internet and Higher Education, 8,* 13-24.

10. Paulhus, D. L. (1991). Measurement and control of response bias. In J. P. Robinson, P. R. Shaver, & L. S. Wrightsman (Eds.), *Measures of personality and social psychological attitudes* (pp. 17-59). San Diego: Academic Press.

11. Shute, R. J. (2011). Stealth assessment in computer-based games to support learning. In S. Tobias & J.D. Fletcher (Eds.), *Computer games and instruction* (pp. 503-524). Charlotte, NC: Information Age Publishers.

12. Christian, B. J., Pearce, P. F., Roberson, A. J., & Rothwell, E. (2010). It's a small, small world: Data collection strategies for research with children and adolescents. *Journal of Pediatric Nursing, 25,* 202-214.

13. Enzmann, D. (2013). The impact of questionnaire design on prevalence and incidence rates of self-reported delinquency: Results of an experiment modifying the ISRD-2 questionnaire. *Journal of Contemporary Criminal Justice, 29,* 147-177.

14. Shute, V. J., & Ke, F. (2012). Games, learning, and assessment. In D. Ifenthaler, D. Eseryel, & X. Ge (Eds.), *Assessment in game-based learning* (pp. 43-58). New York, NY: Springer.

15. Cheong, Y., Jhala, A., Bae, B., & Young, R.M. (2008). Automatically generating summaries form game logs. In *Proceedings of AIIDE-08* (pp. 167-172).

16. Rowe, J., & Lester, J. (2010). Modeling user knowledge with dynamic Bayesian networking interactive narrative environments. *Proceedings of the Sixth Annual AI and Interactive Digital Entertainment Conference* (pp. 57-62). Palo Alto, CA.

17. Tveit, A., & Tveit, G. B. (2002). Game usage mining: Information gathering for knowledge discovery in massive multiplayer games. *Proceedings of the International Conference on Internet Computing (IC'2002), session on Web Mining.*

18. Gee, J. (2003). *What video games have to teach us about learning and literacy.* New York, NY: Palgrave.

19. Prensky, M. (2007). *Digital game-based learning.* New York, NY: Paragon House Publishers.

20. Chirkov, V. I., & Ryan, R. M. (2001). Parent and teacher autonomy-support in Russian and U. S. Adolescents: Common effects on well-being and academic motivation. *Journal of Cross-Cultural Psychology, 32,* 618-635.

21. Jang, H., Reeve, J., Ryan, R. M., & Kim, A. (2009). Can self-determination theory explain what underlies the productive, satisfying learning experiences of collectivisticly oriented Korean students? *Journal of Educational Psychology, 101,* 644-661.

PART IV

MOVING FROM ASSESSMENT TO INTERVENTION

IMPLICATIONS FOR INTERVENTION

OVERVIEW

We know that social skills matter. In Part I of this book, we detailed how children's social skills directly impact the quality of their social relationships which, in turn, impact their academic, emotional, social, and behavioral adjustment. Part II discussed how traditional approaches to SSA in schools—rating scales, interviews, behavioral observations, sociometrics—suffer from a range of psychometric limitations and logistical demands that undermine their regular use. SSA through a validated game platform offers a valuable alternative. In Part III, we described one of these SSA games, Zoo U. We talked about how and why Zoo U is a particularly powerful tool for collecting and analyzing social skill data with children.

We now turn our attention to the real purpose of this book— improving the effectiveness of social intervention with children. As we've pointed out throughout this book, the first step in effective intervention is effective assessment. Only through careful identification using validated assessment methods, can you lay the necessary foundation for successful intervention.

In this last part, we present several examples of how game-based SSA data can be translated into social intervention for children. We first discuss how the gaming environment can be extended to an individualized, adaptive social tutoring tool with data continually informing and personalizing instruction for maximum learning. The second chapter presents how game-based SSA data are a perfect fit for informing the Response to Intervention (RtI) and Multi-Tiered Systems of Support (MTSS) approaches that schools use to implement and assess social and behavioral interventions with children. The next chapter discusses how administrators can help parents understand the data that is generated through Zoo U, extending social intervention efforts into the home environment. The last chapter of this section considers how games can be used across different sub-populations of children. We've focused our discussion in this book on typically developing children, so we also need to consider the ways that games—and Zoo U specifically—can be used with children who have autism spectrum disorders.

Our hope is that this section will help clarify how games can be used to benefit children—not only for engaging, effective SSA, but also for engaging, effective social intervention.

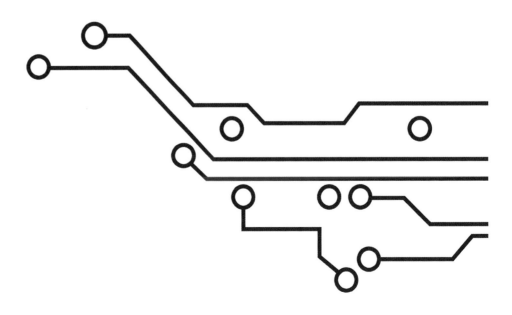

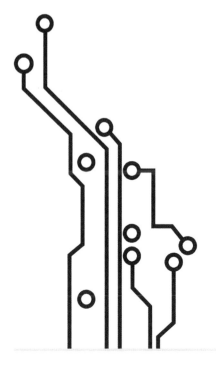

17

SCAFFOLDED SOCIAL TUTORING

by: Jim Thomas, Ph.D.

DESCRIPTION

In this chapter we change our focus from assessment to tutoring. We consider tutoring to be a specialized form of teaching—teaching that is informed and guided by an evolving understanding of what a particular student knows and needs to know. High quality assessment of student knowledge and skills is therefore a cornerstone of good tutoring.

In the case of *Zoo U*, what we have discussed in Chapters 12 through 16 is just part of a larger system, called the *Zoo U Intelligent Social Tutoring System (Zoo U ISTS)*. The first six scenes (as we have described previously) serve as the assessment component. The aim of the second component is to teach children how to improve and apply their social skills. *Zoo U ISTS* uses the assessment component to intelligently guide children through 30 more scenes, adapting the level of difficulty to ensure the learning experience is challenging enough to keep them from getting bored, but not so challenging that they are likely to become confused or frustrated. The goal is to allow each student to learn social skills at his own pace, so that he can achieve mastery as efficiently as possible while minimizing stress and maximizing transfer of learning into the real world.

To achieve this goal, we drew upon decades of research and practice in a number of scientific fields. The following sections describe the influences of education theory on tutoring, explore how principles informed by theory are incorporated into a computer-based **intelligent tutoring system (ITS)**, and review some learning technologies specific to digital games. In this chapter, we pull these strands together to show how *Zoo U ISTS* integrates an ITS within digital game technology to deliver individualized, adaptive tutoring of social skills in settings that are analogous to real life.

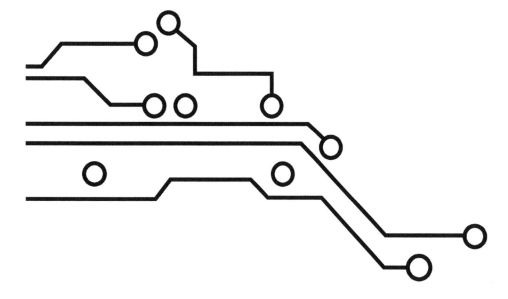

THE HEART OF TUTORING: ADAPTING TO INDIVIDUAL LEARNERS

So what is so special about tutoring? In the following subsections, we compare tutoring with teaching, discuss a guiding principle of tutoring called the Zone of Proximal Development, and describe how tutoring concepts have been implemented in intelligent systems.

Comparing Tutoring with Teaching

We're loosely defining tutoring as the subset of teaching situations that arise when a single teacher works with a single student for some period of time. Whereas classroom teachers are typically engaged with many students at once, a tutor can devote her full attention to a single student, tailoring her instruction and delivery exactly to the particular needs of the individual student. Similarly, the tutoring context demands more attention from the student, who is keenly aware that the teacher is speaking just to him and will be asking questions to check for understanding and ensure he's learning. This additional two-way attention can vastly improve learning effectiveness. A prominent early study[1] found that the mean learning gains derived from expert one-on-one tutoring were two standard deviations higher than the mean gains for conventional classroom instruction. That is to say, the average learning gains of the tutored child corresponded to the 95th percentile of a similar group of children taught through typical classroom instruction. Note that a recent re-evaluation of this study and subsequent studies has found that the mean effect size of human tutoring is actually 0.79, less than two standard deviations, but still substantial.[2]

The problem with tutoring is that we have a lot more students than teachers. Rare are the contexts in which every student can be assigned a dedicated human tutor for all instruction. A possible, and intriguing, answer to this problem may be found in the use of technology, which can be imbued with sufficient intelligence to guide students the way that human tutors do. This idea has given rise intelligent tutoring systems (ITSs). Computer-aided instruction has existed in a variety of forms for several decades, but ITSs are different in that they are informed by research on human tutoring processes. A key component of this research is the concept of the Zone of Proximal Development.

> Mean learning gains derived from expert 1-1 tutoring are around 2 standard deviations higher than the mean gains for conventional classroom instruction.

Tutoring Sweet Spot: The Zone of Proximal Development

Learning theorist Lev Vygotsky provided a theoretical explanation for the efficacy of tutoring in his description of the Zone of Proximal Development, or ZPD. Vygotsky described the ZPD as *"the distance between the actual development level as determined by independent problem solving and the level of potential development as determined through problem solving under adult guidance or collaboration of more capable peers."*[3] The ZPD is often described as the area between what a student can perform on her own, and what she can do with an engaged tutor. **Figure 1** depicts the ZPD as encompassing increasingly difficult challenges as the student becomes more capable. Students who encounter instruction below their ZPD have little to learn from it and may become bored. Students pushed to perform above their ZPD may become confused and frustrated. To maximize learning effectiveness, instruction must be confined within the individual ZPD of each learner (not too easy, not too hard).

Human tutors are very well positioned to continually assess student capability and adapt the level of instruction accordingly.

Figure 1

The Zone of Proximal Development

CONFUSION

Difficulty

ZONE OF PROXIMAL DEVELOPMENT

BOREDOM

Student Capability

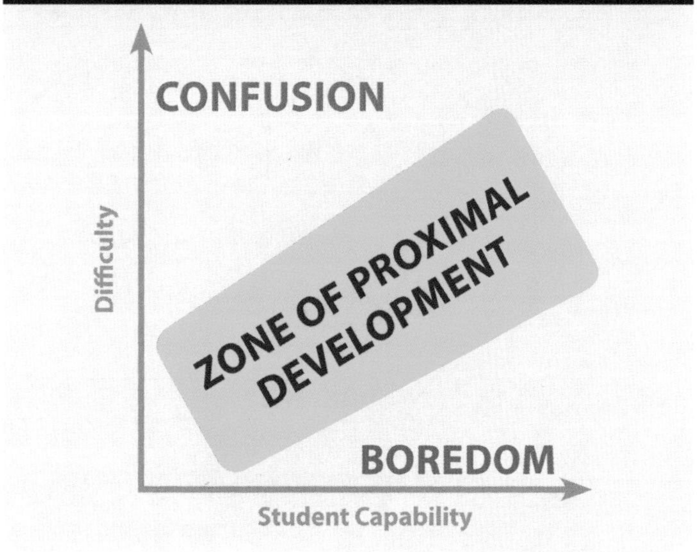

ZPD: A Guidepost for Intelligent Tutoring Systems

The ZPD concept suggests a mechanism to guide intelligent tutoring systems in selecting the most appropriate tutoring actions. Once an ITS is able to dynamically and accurately assess student capability, it can then use algorithms to keep students within the ZPD by modulating instructional difficulty, just as human tutors do. A computer-based system has an advantage over traditional classroom instructors—it can focus its full and undivided attention on the individual student. In fact, studies have shown that well-constructed intelligent tutoring systems that focus on helping children complete homework problems are approximately as effective as human tutors assigned the same task.[4] The enduring challenge for these systems is to dynamically assess and adapt to changes in the student's knowledge and behavior to keep them learning in the zone between boredom and frustration. The following section dives a bit deeper into how these systems work.

INDIVIDUALIZATION AND SCAFFOLDING IN INTELLIGENT TUTORING SYSTEMS

Much of intelligent tutoring system research focuses on two related goals. The first goal is to increase the accuracy of the assessments of what the student knows. These assessments are then used to build a **student model**. The second major goal is to use the student model to adapt the tutoring to the needs of individual learners through a process called **scaffolding**.

Modeling Student Knowledge through Continuous Assessment

Just as a human tutor closely observes the behavior of each student to assess what the student does and does not know, and what she can or cannot perform, an intelligent tutoring system assesses student behavior and uses those assessments to develop a persistent view of student knowledge and capability. That persistent view is the **student model**, a data construct internal to the ITS that is customized to the individual learner. Student models come in a variety of forms. The most common form of student model is called a **knowledge-tracing model**,[5] in which a body of knowledge or skills is represented as a hierarchy that aggregates specific concepts into those that are progressively more general. For each component of the model, the system maintains an estimate of the student's current proficiency or level of knowledge. For example, a simple student model of arithmetic might consist of just addition, subtraction, multiplication and division. If a student correctly performs nine out of ten addition problems presented by the ITS, but fails to successfully complete any of the subtraction, multiplication, or division problems, the system would record a high proficiency for addition and a low proficiency for the other three skills in that student's model.

Real student models can be much more detailed. Models can include both assessments of knowledge as well as assessments of commonly held incorrect beliefs or 'mind bugs.' Many systems proactively build all the possible classes

Student model
=
ITS internal view of the student's knowledge and capability

of errors students may encounter so that the intelligent tutor can respond to those errors with specific and useful help. For example, consider the problem of three column subtraction. The procedures for subtracting from a three digit number can be described in just a handful of rules. Yet one of the earliest intelligent tutoring systems in this domain found as many as 121 distinct bits of knowledge associated with common misconceptions about three column subtraction.[6] Two of these erroneous knowledge components are depicted in **Figure 2**: the 'Borrow-Across-Zero-Over-Blank' bug occurs when a student skips to the next place value to decrement rather than decrementing the zero. This is distinct from the 'Don't-Decrement-Zero-Over-Zero' bug, where the student fails to borrow from a zero that is placed over a zero. Either bug yields an incorrect answer to the problem.

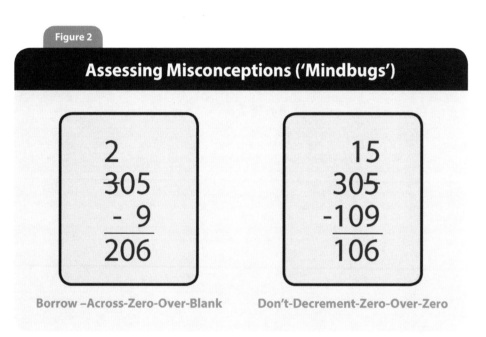

Figure 2

Assessing Misconceptions ('Mindbugs')

Borrow –Across-Zero-Over-Blank

Don't-Decrement-Zero-Over-Zero

Armed with a precise and complete model of student knowledge, an ITS can adapt its instruction in a variety of ways. It can provide specific hints or prompts to directly instruct the student on particular concepts. It can efficiently guide the student to concept mastery by focusing practice on the particular concepts in which the student is weakest. It can anticipate errors that are highly correlated across different problem types and provide the student with additional instruction or help in advance of presenting those problems. It can ensure that core concepts are well understood before presenting the student with more abstract concepts that build on those specific core components. A truly intelligent tutoring system should exhibit all of these behaviors, often referred to as **scaffolding**, in adapting to the needs of an individual learner. Clearly, precise assessment and modeling of knowledge allows the system to provide the student with useful help and guidance.

Using Scaffolds to Adapt Tutoring

Scaffolding is a metaphorical term for learning support processes first introduced by Wood, Bruner, and Ross.[7] The word 'scaffold' was chosen to convey that the supports provided by tutors are temporary constructs to be removed or 'faded' as the student gains proficiency, just as scaffolds used on construction projects are temporary supports that are built up and then removed over the course of work.

For intelligent tutoring systems, Murray and Arroyo[8] define scaffolding as exactly the assistance required to keep a student in the ZPD. They describe this goal as giving assistance *"in order to keep the learner at their leading edge - challenging, but not overwhelming them."*[9] They further refine the definition of the ZPD as, *"neither a property of the learning environment nor of the student; it is a property of the interaction between the two."*[10] The role of the tutor is to ensure that the learner is not overly confused by tasks that are too difficult or overly bored by tasks that are too easy. Either condition can lead to frustration, distraction or disengagement. As skills are mastered, scaffolding assistance is faded to ensure that learners do not become bored.

Some systems scaffold only when learners explicitly request help, others only when a student makes a mistake. Scaffolding may take the form of dynamic adaptation to individual needs or it may be a static calibration that sets a difficulty level for some duration of the learning exercise. Many systems add scaffolds but fail to fade them after students improve. Even the nature of what is being scaffolded varies. Systems can scaffold student understanding of domain knowledge, particular mechanics of the system itself, or meta-cognitive processes (learning about one's own learning).

Not all of scaffolding in ITS is associated with didactic guidance. Scaffolding, according to Murray and Arroyo,[8] can include providing hints to the user, sequencing the content in a way that helps understanding, and giving feedback and opportunities for practice. Hints are defined as *"problem solving assistance that gives information or focuses attention in ways that improve the chances that the learner will be able to solve a problem."* In keeping with

Scaffolding = temporary supports that are removed as student knowledge is constructed

Piaget's[11] stages of development (concrete thinking develops first, followed by more abstract, formal reasoning), hints can be given in two different levels of granularity. Less advanced learners are more efficient when first presented with more concrete hints; more advanced learners are more efficient when the system first supplies formal hints.

A comprehensive analysis of scaffolding across a subset of ITS systems that focus on discovery-based learning of science[12] distinguishes between three distinct scaffolding techniques: **sense-making**, **process management**, and **articulation and reflection**. Sense-making scaffolds help the user by providing visual organizers, text descriptions, audio overlays, multiple views, and manipulable representations of concepts. Process management scaffolds include checklists of required tasks, navigation aids for tools and tasks, and automatically organizing student work products (journals, for instance). Students can be encouraged to articulate and reflect through tools for self-explanations, self-monitoring, and by reiterating knowledge they have learned.

Zoo U ISTS employs scaffolds from each of these three categories to focus learning and to adapt to individual student needs. Sense-making scaffolds are pervasive in *Zoo U ISTS* through characters who comment on the social situation at hand and can prompt the student toward fruitful action. Similarly, articulation and reflection scaffolds are embedded in many scenes as the student's avatar engages in an internal dialog to lead the student to consider particular ideas. For example, in a scene designed to teach empathy, the avatar says *"I wonder why Sarah is sitting alone,"* prompting the student to consider the same question.

An example of a process management scaffold in *Zoo U ISTS* is the notebook (**Figure 3**). The notebook is used in scenes where the student is asked to follow multi-step procedures. This scaffold lessens the cognitive load associated with following procedures so that children can focus on the pedagogical heart of *Zoo U ISTS*: the acquisition of social skills. The notebook is available to all children encountering this scene; the system adapts by displaying blinking arrows that point toward the notebook to those children who seem to require prompting.

Figure 3

Zoo U ISTS – Process Management Scaffolding

Zoo U ISTS employs individualized articulation and reflection scaffolding in several scenes that teach reflective listening and use of 'I Statements' to communicate feelings. For example, a game where the student selects from a list of expected responses is dynamically adjusted to include a higher or lower ratio of correct answers to incorrect answers, depending on the current skill level of the student.

Didactic Scaffolding

A common framework for didactic instruction is to begin with help that is general and less directive, then move toward more explicit help if the child continues to struggle. A common progression in intelligent tutoring systems is to first *prompt*, then *hint*, then *teach*, and finally *do* the action the child is intended to take. A *prompt* message generally highlights information that was already available to the student to draw her attention to a particular concept. A *hint* provides partial information of what is required to solve the problem. It may remind the student of a particular procedure to be employed, or simply underscore information the student needs to consider. Moving beyond hints, a system that decides to *teach* the student a particular concept will provide all the information the student needs to complete the particular problem, possibly using an example. If the student still cannot complete the problem after prompt, hint, and teach, the system may choose to simply *do* the problem for the student, filling in the answer with or without an accompanying explanation.

A quintessential example of this progression is found in Murray and VanLehn's fixed-strategy intelligent tutor, which *"followed a strong successive explicitness constraint: it always provided a help message that was minimally more explicit than any help already provided. In other words, first it provided a prompt message, then hint, then teach, before bottoming out with do."*[13] Another ITS called AutoTutor[14] employs a sophisticated model of the typical dialog elements between tutors and learners to provide nuanced forms of verbal assistance that blur the lines between prompts and hints. Feedback can be positive ('That's right'), negative ('Not quite'), or neutral ('Uh-huh'). Hints may be 'pumps' for more information 'What else?', or for specific information. Hints may take the form of questions about content, assertions about content, or specific corrections to erroneous content supplied by the student. AutoTutor provides not only information, but emotional support, motivation, and feedback.

Prompt
↓
Hint
↓
Teach
↓
Do

Didactic scaffolding in *Zoo U ISTS* takes several forms. In many scenes, characters with pedagogically useful information will share it more freely with children who have not yet demonstrated mastery of the particular skills in a given scene. In other cases the scope of choices presented to the student is narrowed and the differentiation between choices is magnified. For example, **Figure 4** shows two different views in the *Zoo U ISTS* that teach empathy. The screen capture on the left shows a configuration of the game for a lower performing student; the screen capture on the right shows a game set up for a higher performing student. The challenge for the student is to imagine how the characters are feeling in the scene that was just depicted, then click on all the words and all the facial expressions that match those feelings. Note how the higher performing student is confronted with more possible choices, and more ambiguity between choices.

Figure 4

Zoo U ISTS – **Didactic Scaffolding**

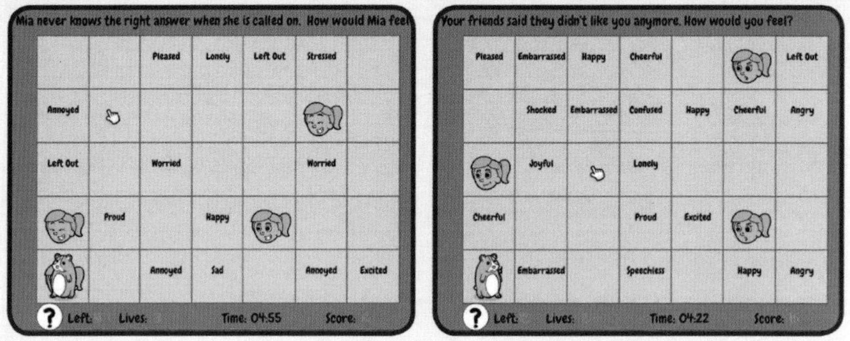

TUTORING AND DIGITAL GAMES

Concurrent with advances in intelligent tutoring systems, the digital game industry has developed a plethora of ways to teach people how a game is played.[15] Long gone are the days when a player was expected to sit down and read a manual before playing. As games become progressively more complex and diverse every year, a game that is not clever and effective in teaching its players how to use it will not sell. As the game industry has eclipsed the financial might of Hollywood (Grand Theft Auto 5 garnered over $1 billion in sales in just its first three days),[16] the Darwinian pressure of high-stakes investment has driven game designers to continually advance the learning mechanisms embedded in games. This section details some of the ways game-based learning overlaps and extends the learning theory that underlies intelligent tutoring systems.

Crafting the Optimal Gameplay Corridor

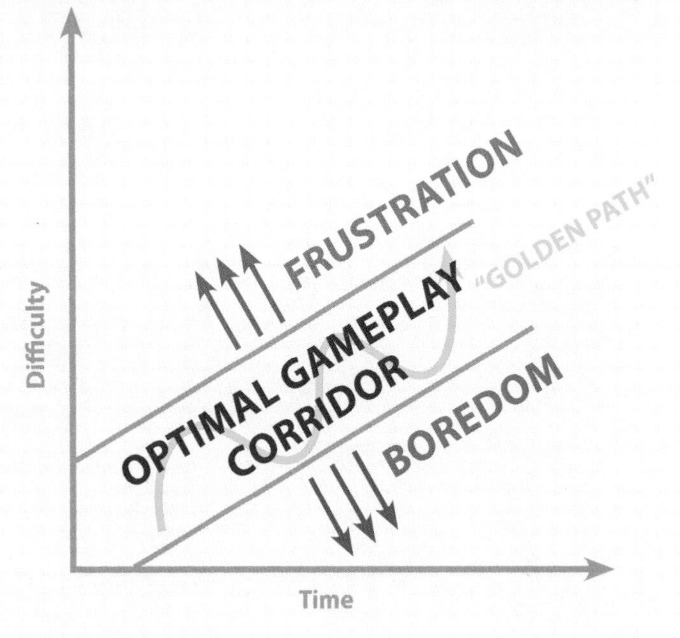

The core conceptual models posited by games and ITSs to guide exploration are remarkably similar. Game designers describe a goal of leading the player along a sinuous 'golden path'[17] that moves through an 'optimal game play corridor,'[18] as shown in **Figure 5**. Too challenging, and the player moves toward increasing frustration. Not challenging enough, and the player loses interest. Game industry insiders generally credit psychologist Mihaly Csikszentmihalyi's ideas on 'flow'[19] as inspiration to their understanding of guided learning. While there is little doubt that Csikszentmihalyi's study of Vygotsky helped form this concept in similar terms to the ZPD shown in Figure 1, the idea that it is desirable not only to keep the student in the zone but to modulate the student's challenge between the upper and lower boundaries of that zone is an advance from the game design community that has yet to be fully appreciated by ITS researchers. *Zoo U ISTS* guides the player through the optimal gameplay corridor by adjusting the difficulty level in each scene based on student performance.

Figure 5

The Optimal Gameplay Corridor

The Language of Learning Principles in Games

Within game design, the dynamic balancing of player autonomy and game structure has spawned a set of concepts and conventions. For example, one of the guidance techniques found in nearly all games is **staggered instruction**. As games have become more complex, designers can no longer afford to tell the player everything they need to know at the beginning of the game. It would take too long and it would be too difficult for the player to remember it all. Instead, a bootstrapping approach is followed. The player is given just enough overt information and training to get started. As new challenges are encountered, the player is given additional information *just-in-time* to confront those challenges. *"In essence, a game manual has been spread throughout the early episodes of the game, giving information when it can be best understood and practices through situated experience."*[20]

Gee[15] identifies 36 distinct learning principles exemplified in games. These include the **incremental principle**, where designers thoughtfully order learning situations so that specific cases encountered early in the game can be usefully generalized in more complex cases later. A corollary is the concentrated sample principle, where the learner is presented early on with an abundance of the fundamental signs and actions relevant to the domain to give them practice and accelerate their mastery. The **achievement principle** dictates that learners at all levels of skill receive awards customized to their growing skill and mastery to signal ongoing success. Echoing the descriptions of the ZPD, the **regime of competence principle** of game design says that the learner *"gets ample opportunity to operate within, but at the outer edge of, his or her resources, so at those points things are felt as 'challenging' but not 'undoable'."*[15] The crucial insight is that the incredible success of the learning technologies embedded in games is not accidental, but rather hinges on a core set of identifiable learning principles.

Although these principles are exemplified in games in thousands of different ways, designers have coalesced on a manageable set of conventions across and within game genres. For example, the incremental principle is evident in a few distinct conventions: progressively more difficult game levels, quantification of your character's level combined with level-restricted challenges, and locked geographic zones that cannot be escaped until particular skill mastery is achieved.

Figure 6

Zoo U ISTS employs many of the principles and mechanisms of game-based learning. The incremental principle drives the organization of the game into six distinct series (one for each key social skill) that progress in difficulty and intensity across five levels. The achievement principle drives the awarding of coins to children as they perform each substantive action in the scene. As the student achieves a certain number of coins, subsequent action sequences are unlocked (**Figure 6**). At the end of each scene, the child can view his coin totals and choose to get pedagogical feedback from Principal Wild for each segment of the scene.

Other examples of game-design scaffolding in *Zoo U ISTS* include a scene in which less skillful children are given more time to complete a task than are more highly skilled children. In another scene designed to challenge the child's emotion regulation skills, a mini-game is manipulated behind the scenes to force the student to either lose or win. As a challenge for the child to practice impulse control, another scaffold varies the number of animated distractors in a scene based on the current skill level of the student.

Social Scaffolding in Games

For teaching social skills, games have one huge advantage over both human and typical intelligent tutoring systems: they can feature multiple characters with whom the user can interact. A student's relationship with an ITS is highly constrained: the hints and prompts given by the system must preserve conventions of honesty, sincerity and correctness or the student would lose faith in its usefulness. In contrast, games allow for multiple characters that have varying degrees of social mastery, self-awareness, and alignment with the goals of the student. Characters can supply both positive and negative examples of social behavior and challenge the student in situated contexts that mirror the real world. Furthermore, games allow children a safe place to explore the consequences of different social choices without the burden of those consequences persisting for days, months, or years. Therefore, because it combines an ITS and a game, *ZooU ISTS* can offer opportunities for social learning not possible anywhere else.

An example of social scaffolding that would be difficult or impossible to achieve outside of a game context is *Zoo U ISTS*'s ability to dynamically select the genders of characters with whom the student interacts. As shown in **Figure 7**, *Zoo U ISTS* chooses the genders of the non-player characters (NPCs) that populate each scene at run-time, based on both the gender of the child *and* the child's current level of social skill mastery as it has evolved throughout the game. Children at the target age range of *Zoo U ISTS* generally find it easier to initiate social interactions with same sex peers, and are less threatened by negative feedback or teasing from other sex peers. Therefore, in initiation scenes, like the one shown in Figure 7, the game matches the gender of the student to the gender of the NPC in cases where the student has yet to show mastery, but chooses NPCs of the other gender for more advanced children. Conversely, where characters are teasing or antagonistic, the system

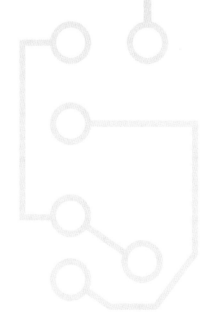

makes the situation more difficult by choosing to depict NPCs of the same gender as the child, or less difficult by mismatching the genders.

Figure 7

Zoo U ISTS – Social Scaffolding Using Gender

Another form of social scaffolding common across many scenes in *Zoo U ISTS* is to modulate the phrasing, tone of voice, and facial expressions of game characters to indicate higher or lower degrees of affinity and/or goal alignment between those characters and the child. Most scenes have multiple, socially-differentiated versions of most of the lines of dialog. In the example below, if the player chooses a non-cooperative response at one point in one particular scene, an in-scene character named José will respond in one of three highly-differentiated ways depending on how the student has performed to that point:

- **José**: *"Oh, I thought they'd be cool. I guess you have a better idea?"*
  Expression: hurt

- **José**: *"I thought they'd be cool! I bet you don't have a better idea anyway."*
  Expression and tone of voice: angry

- **José**: *"As if you even know what's cool. You think you have a better idea?"*
  Expression: angry; tone of voice: snarky.

Thus, each of the scenes in *Zoo U ISTS* is populated with characters who can respond differently based on both the tutorial needs of and the social choices made by the student.

SUMMARY

This chapter described how intelligent tutoring systems effectively teach through adaptation to individual students' needs and skills. The cornerstone supporting such individual adaptation is the accurate assessment of student knowledge and skills. We showed how the powerful assessment tool embedded in *Zoo U* has been harnessed in the *Zoo U ISTS* to teach social skills through dynamic scaffolding to meet the learning needs of individual children.

CHAPTER 17 NOTES

1. Bloom, B. S. (1984). The 2 sigma problem: The search for methods of group instruction as effective as one-to-one tutoring. *Educational Researcher, 13,* 4-16.

2. VanLehn, K. (2011). The relative effectiveness of human tutoring, intelligent tutoring systems, and other tutoring systems. *Educational Psychologist, 46,* 197-221.

3. Vygotsky, L. S. (1978). *Mind in society: The development of higher psychological processes* (p. 86). Cambridge, MA: Harvard University Press.

4. VanLehn, K. (2011). The relative effectiveness of human tutoring, intelligent tutoring systems, and other tutoring systems. *Educational Psychologist, 46,* 197-221.

5. Corbett, A. T., & Anderson, J. R. (1994). Knowledge tracing: Modeling the acquisition of procedural knowledge. *User Modeling and User-Adapted Interaction, 4,* 253-278.

6. VanLehn, K. (1990). *Mind bugs: The origins of procedural misconceptions.* Cambridge, MA: The MIT Press.

7. Wood, D., Bruner, J. S., & Ross, G. (1976). The role of tutoring in problem solving. *Journal of Child Psychology and Psychiatry, 17,* 89-100.

8. Murray, T., & Arroyo, I. (2002, January). Toward measuring and maintaining the zone of proximal development in adaptive instructional systems. In *Intelligent Tutoring Systems* (pp. 749-758). Berlin: Springer.

9. Murray, T., & Arroyo, I. (2002, January). Toward measuring and maintaining the zone of proximal development in adaptive instructional systems. In *Intelligent Tutoring Systems* (p. 751). Berlin: Springer.

10. Murray, T., & Arroyo, I. (2002, January). Toward measuring and maintaining the zone of proximal development in adaptive instructional systems. In *Intelligent Tutoring Systems* (p. 751). Berlin: Springer.

11. Piaget, J. (1976). *Piaget's theory* (pp. 11-23). Berlin: Springer.

12. Quintana, C., Reiser, B. J., Davis, E. A., Krajcik, J., Fretz, E., Duncan, R. G., ... & Soloway, E. (2004). A scaffolding design framework for software to support science inquiry. *The Journal of the Learning Sciences, 13,* 337-386.

13. Murray, R. C., & VanLehn, K. (2006, January). A comparison of decision-theoretic, fixed-policy and random tutorial action selection. In *Intelligent Tutoring Systems* (pp. 114-123). Berlin: Springer.

14. Graesser, A. C., Lu, S., Jackson, G. T., Mitchell, H. H., Ventura, M., Olney, A., & Louwerse, M. M. (2004). AutoTutor: A tutor with dialogue in natural language. *Behavior Research Methods, Instruments, & Computers, 36,* 180-192.

15. Gee, J. P. (2003). *What video games have to teach us about learning and literacy.* New York, NY: Palgrave Macmillan. 207-212.

16. Graser, M. (2013, September 18) 'Grand Theft Auto V' earns 800 million in a day, more than worldwide haul of 'Man of Steel', *Variety.* Retrieved from http://variety.com/2013/digital/news/grand-theft-auto-v-earns-800-million-in-a-day-more-than-worldwide-haul-of-man-of-steel-1200616706/

17. Bateman, C. (Ed.). (2006). *Game writing: Narrative skills for videogames.* Boston, MA: Charles River Media.

18. Masuch, M. (2007, August). *Is this the real thing? Realism and fun in computer games.* Invited lecture at North Carolina State University, Raleigh, NC.

19. Csikszentmihalyi, I. S. (Ed.). (1992). *Optimal experience: Psychological studies of flow in consciousness.* Cambridge, MA: Cambridge University Press.

20. Gee, J. P. (2003). *What video games have to teach us about learning and literacy* (pp. 133-137). New York, NY: Palgrave Macmillan.

18

ASSESSMENT AS A COMPONENT OF INTERVENTION PLANNING IN SCHOOLS

by: Janey Sturtz McMillen, Ph.D.

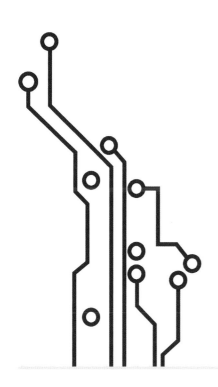

DESCRIPTION

In Chapter 4, we learned that data collected through social and behavioral assessment are primarily used for three purposes in guiding the intervention planning process: (1) screening (identifying children with specific skill deficits), (2) progress monitoring (monitoring how a child's skills or behaviors change during an intervention), and (3) evaluation (to learn whether a child shows improvement in target outcomes after participating in an intervention). Due to federal initiatives that require schools to implement more proactive approaches to match children's needs with the type and intensity of intervention they receive (such as the No Child Left Behind[1] and Individuals with Disabilities Education Improvement Acts[2]), there has been an increasing interest in using data to guide and evaluate the intervention process. These initiatives are often based on the 'dual-discrepancy' model which emphasizes the importance of measuring not only a child's achievement level, but also the level and rate of his response to intervention.[3] It's necessary to know whether the child falls below his peers in achievement as well as whether he responds as expected to appropriate intervention. In this chapter, we discuss how assessment is therefore an integral component of intervention planning in schools.

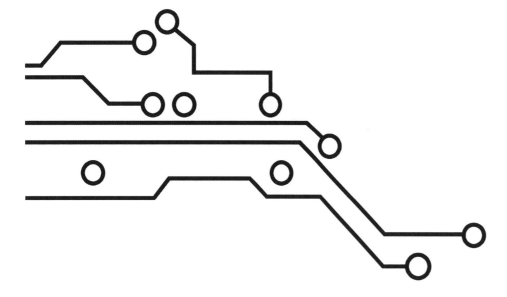

RESPONSE TO INTERVENTION

One of the more popular proactive approaches is **Response to Intervention (RtI)**, a framework for developing and implementing multi-tiered systems of support in schools. An essential assumption of RtI is that all children can learn and will do so if given the right opportunities. These opportunities are typically provided through three tiers of interventions of increasing intensity based on the level of a child's skill deficits.

Most children (approximately 80%) succeed in **Tier 1**, which provides universal, school-wide preventive interventions. Children in Tier 1 receive differentiated supports personalized as much as possible within the general classroom setting to produce the best results. In **Tier 2**, a smaller group of children (about 15%) who require additional help receive more intensive, individualized interventions and close progress monitoring in addition to the core supports provided to all children in Tier 1. Finally, **Tier 3** delivers high-intensity, longer duration, individualized interventions and frequent—often daily—progress monitoring to the approximately 5% of children who require significant support beyond what is provided in Tiers 1 and 2.

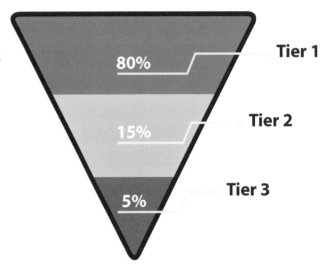

Children move between the tiers in both directions as indicated by assessment data. The goal is for the vast majority of children (80% or more) to be performing at expected skill levels within the core intervention—universal school-wide preventive interventions. While the progress of all children should be monitored regularly and skills instruction modified accordingly, some children have greater needs than others. The tiered model is used to adjust the level of resources to fit these varying levels of need. This emphasis on resource allocation is a large part of what distinguishes RtI from other change models.[4-5]

While the application of RtI can vary considerably across school settings, there are three common components: (1) matching interventions to a child's needs, (2) frequently monitoring a child's progress during an intervention, and (3) adjusting what is done with a child based on data from that progress

Universal interventions are those in which all students are exposed to a core social and behavioral curriculum to prevent the development of problem behavior and to help identify students whose behavior is not responsive at this Tier 1 level.

monitoring. In order to match intervention to a child's needs, educators should first collect social and behavioral assessment data to help identify children with specific skill deficits. Screening is the most typical method of gathering these data.

Screening

Although many school settings have adopted screening tools for academic performance, **few schools use social or behavioral screeners.**[6] Further, while screening for academic performance is based on benchmark standards clearly defined by state and federal mandates, screening for social and behavioral performance is significantly more challenging. This is because social and behavioral performance norms vary greatly depending on the setting and individuals involved.[7] For example, expectations for children's behavior differ if they are at home with family members, on the playground with peers, or in a community library with a mix of adults and children. An additional complication is the lack of brief, inexpensive, social and behavioral screening measures that are reliable and valid.[8] The screeners must be efficient enough to assess children with minimal cost and schedule disruption, but powerful enough to predict meaningful outcomes. This is particularly problematic in large service settings, such as schools, in which educators may want to screen all children.

Figure 1 shows three sets of tools commonly used by schools. **Permanent products** are data that already exist, such as records of school attendance or discipline/suspension rates. These data can be useful in identifying existing behavior problems, particularly when used as a screening tool. Often, educators use a history of a high number of office discipline referrals (ODRs) relative to the rest of the school's population to identify students needing more support. One recommended guideline for interpreting ODR data is that children who receive 0 to 1 ODRs per year do not need support beyond universal school-wide preventive interventions, while children who receive 2 to 5 ODRs per year are recommended for Tier 2 interventions and children with 6 or more ODRs per year receive Tier 3 or intensive individualized behavior service plans.[9] Educators also use records of poor school attendance, frequent tardiness, and poor academic performance as indicators to identify children who are at risk for poor social and behavioral outcomes.[10]

Figure 1

Social and Behavioral Screening Tools

Permanent products

Educator nomination strategies

Computer adaptive testing

While ODRs may be an efficient way to identify children with high rates of externalizing behaviors, they're not sufficient for identifying all children needing support for social or behavioral problems. Children with internalizing behaviors—such as social anxiety, social withdrawal, or depression—or less severe externalizing behaviors are often not identified by ODRs.[11] This means more systematic screening methods should be used to proactively identify these at-risk children. **Educator nomination strategies** can help in this regard.[3] There are three steps in this process. First, educators identify children who are at high risk based on specific externalizing and/or internalizing behavior. For example, *"identify the children in your class who play or work alone most of the time."* In the second step, educators complete behavioral rating scales for the identified children to determine if further assessment is needed. For those children who appear to be most at risk, the third step involves direct observation of these children's social and behavioral performance at school. While educator nomination strategies are a more proactive method for identifying children, the starting place is the educator's reported opinion which, as discussed in Part II of this book, can suffer from a number of biases. In addition, direct observation can be time consuming and expensive.

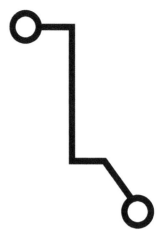

It's possible to gather self-report screening data directly from children using **computer adaptive testing** (CAT) that employs item response theory (see Chapter 11 for more information). CAT has been gaining popularity in recent years because it allows enough data to be gathered to draw reliable conclusions without creating undue burden on children or staff. CAT can collect sufficient data for highly reliable results in a relatively short time by selecting items as the test progresses based on the pattern of the child's answers. When CAT is normed—either to national or local distributions— and validated, it can serve as an excellent screening tool, and the efficiency of computer testing makes administration highly practical and useful for schools. Unfortunately, the majority of available CAT programs target academic rather than social and behavioral performance.

The majority of available CAT programs target academic rather than social and behavioral performance.

Progress Monitoring

Once screening data are gathered and children in need of supports are identified, the next step is to use a problem-solving model to select beneficial interventions. This requires matching effective interventions to specific child difficulties and then setting goals for improvement. In order to determine if a child benefits from an intervention, the dual discrepancy model requires measuring not only the child's achievement levels, but also the level and rate of her response to intervention. Regardless of which tier of intervention a child is receiving, data will need to be gathered to monitor her progress to ensure that she's benefiting at an appropriate rate. The frequency of progress monitoring increases in proportion to the intensity of service provision: weekly or biweekly for Tier 1 interventions to daily for Tier 3.[12]

One challenge to progress monitoring is the **testing effect**—if a child completes the same measure multiple times in quick succession, his performance will be influenced by familiarity with the content and may not indicate true benefit from the intervention.[12] By using measures that have alternate forms and are comparable in difficulty, evaluators can look at how the child performs over time to quantify the rate of response to intervention.[13] Intervention providers can then use this information to identify whether or not adjustments are needed, such as in the case of inadequate responsiveness (see Chapter 4).

Effective progress monitoring measures should also be short and easy to administer without specialized training. Many of the current measures used for academic progress monitoring are based on child mastery of a series of short-term instructional objectives—an approach known as 'mastery measurement.' These measures—sometimes referred to as curriculum-based or criterion-referenced—are based on the planned educational content for a school year and designed to match each step in that sequence. While these measures meet the criteria for being short and easy to administer, mastery measurement is problematic for monitoring social and behavioral progress. As mentioned earlier in this chapter, social and behavioral performance norms vary significantly depending on the setting and individuals involved. While there may be general behavioral expectations for a setting or general social norms based on child development, there's no standardized social educational content on which to base the measurement. Similarly, although educators could use social literacy-based probes to assess what the child knows about expected social or behavioral performance, children's actual social behavior can lag behind newly acquired social knowledge. Further, even if the child's performance does improve, he still must overcome reputational biases within his peer group to generalize and maintain these new social and behavioral skills.

Another challenge to progress monitoring is distinguishing between the types of behavior to be targeted at the different tiers. For Tier 1, the measure should be applicable to *all* children and strive to meet a social-behavioral norm. For Tier 2, the measure should be targeted at *individual* child behavior goals rather than at a norm. This means the behaviors are individually scaled and the starting point—or current level of performance—is toward the bottom of the measurement scale. The benefits of this scaling method are that it (a) allows for monitoring growth, (b) allows for a task analysis of the steps needed to achieve the goal, and (c) provides a concrete example of successive approximations.

The most frequently used methods for monitoring social and behavioral performance in schools are permanent products, behavior rating scales, systematic direct observation, daily progress reports, functional behavioral assessments, and computer adaptive testing. (See **Figure 2**). In addressing the multiple challenges outlined above, each of these methods has advantages and disadvantages.

As described earlier, **permanent products** are data that already exist. Before exerting substantial effort to 'reinvent the wheel,' educators should first consider permanent products. Because they don't require additional data collection and there's no training required for use, permanent products may be most useful for progress monitoring when resources—such as time and money—are limited and/or the information is sufficient to make sound judgments about intervention. However, even though permanent product data produce readily accessible information, these data generally don't specify the duration, frequency, and intensity of a particular problem behavior or the environment in which it typically occurs. Thus, these data may present only superficial insight with regard to the monitoring for intervention.

Typically completed by a teacher or parent, **behavior rating scales** provide more global estimates of children's behavior along various dimensions. As discussed in Chapter 6, the advantages of behavior rating scales are that they require very little training for the rater, often have demonstrated good reliability and validity, are relatively inexpensive and time efficient, and provide global information about individual behavior. Unfortunately, these scales are problematic when used for progress monitoring. In particular, while social and behavioral rating scales are appropriate for evaluating change in a

Task analysis is the process of breaking a skill into smaller, more manageable steps in order to teach the skill.

Successive approximations shape a student's behavior by positively reinforcing any response that comes close to the desired one.

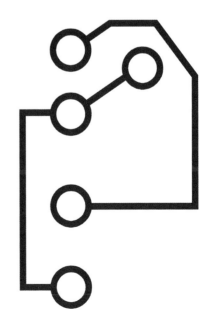

Figure 2

Social and Behavioral Monitoring Tools

Permanent products

Behavior rating scales

Systematic direct observation

Daily progress reports

Functional behavioral assessments

Computer adaptive testing

pre/post fashion over several weeks or months, progress monitoring requires multiple brief interval snapshots of a child's behavior. Most behavior rating scales are not designed to be used in this fashion—the resulting scores aren't sensitive enough to demonstrate change over brief time spans and they may be artificially inflated due to testing effects. Further, like permanent product data, behavioral rating scales don't indicate what factors are contributing to the child's behavior change.

Systematic direct observation has historically been considered the gold standard for social-behavioral assessment because it lends itself to reliable and accurate measurement with information collected as the behavior actually occurs. As discussed in Chapter 7, it requires a trained observer to identify and operationally define a behavior of interest, use a system of observation—typically momentary time sampling and frequency counts—in a specific time and place, and then score and summarize the data in a consistent manner.[14] Observers usually conduct multiple observations in order to maximize the reliability of the measure. The advantage of direct observation is that it can provide a reliable snapshot of multiple behaviors occurring within a discrete amount of time, making it useful for identifying and monitoring target behaviors during intervention. However, this method also has several drawbacks. In addition to being time consuming, direct observation requires the presence of an independent observer, which creates the potential for reactivity; that is, an observer's presence can alter the behaviors of the child under observation, other children, and the teacher.[9]

Daily progress reports have been used to rate key behaviors, share information with parents, educators, and the child, and monitor the effects of an intervention.[9] Evaluators give the child a numeric rating (such as 0, 1, 2) on predetermined behavioral goals throughout the school day. For example, *"how much did the child interrupt another child during class time?"* At the end of the day, educators calculate the percentage of points and measure progress over time to determine if the child is meeting his goal. A major advantage of daily progress reports is that they provide a resource-efficient method of estimating behavior change over time.[15] The two largest drawbacks to this method are that it takes a considerable amount of time from the educator and it can suffer from respondent biases similar to any behavioral rating scale.

Functional behavioral assessments (FBA) aim to understand why a child continues to engage in problem behavior. For example, a child may continue a problem behavior in order to escape a difficult task, attract peer or adult attention, or gain permission to do a desired activity. Conducting FBAs typically involves reviewing records, interviewing teachers, parents, and students, conducting direct observations, and synthesizing this information to develop a behavioral hypothesis.[16] Educators can use FBA information to develop a behavior intervention plan for actively teaching the child prosocial ways to achieve the same goal. An FBA can also involve rearranging the environment to support or encourage appropriate behavior and ignore problem behavior.[17] However, in addition to being a time consuming process, the FBA approach does not clearly define—or quantify—the targeted behavior, making it less than ideal for progress monitoring.[18]

Computer adaptive testing is growing in popularity due to the advantage of test-retest reliability and lower testing effects. Using item response theory, CAT uses advanced techniques to measure the difficulty of each test item, as well as the probability a child at that achievement level will get the item correct. The test 'knows' the difficulty level of items and matches them to the child's previous performance, so scores are always comparable on the same scale. This adaptive nature allows the assessment to be repeated as often as necessary for progress monitoring while still retaining statistical reliability and change sensitivity. In this way, computer technology allows continuous monitoring that provides useful, psychometrically sound indicators of progress. Another advantage of CAT is the option for 'practice progress monitoring.' Within the RtI model, measuring the underlying tasks that contribute to skill growth is extremely valuable, as is gauging child progress toward goals. Through technology, task measurement and monitoring of personal goals can take place daily, providing continuous data to show how the child is progressing, and allowing for real-time use of the data for decision-making.

Evaluation

In addition to monitoring child progress during implementation of an intervention, it's essential to evaluate whether a child shows improvement in target outcomes after participating in an intervention. This is particularly important if educators need data to document progress toward goals within student support team (SST) interventions and/or individualized education plans (IEP) for children receiving special education services. A major

Figure 3

Social and Behavioral Evaluation Tools

Permanent products
Behavior rating scales
Daily progress reports
Computer adaptive testing

challenge in evaluation is always time efficiency—how to gather enough data to draw reliable conclusions without creating an undue burden on children or educators. Generally, the more items presented within an assessment, the greater its reliability and precision. This is why classical norm-referenced tests take so long—they must administer a significant number of items at a variety of levels to place the child accurately. Their length—and the difficulty of creating multiple equivalent forms from a huge amount of statistical data—are why classical norm-referenced tests are not very useful for measuring short-term behavioral growth. Instead, administrators typically conduct RtI evaluations using permanent products, behavior rating scales, daily progress reports, or computer adaptive testing. (See **Figure 3**)

Permanent products data are best for evaluation when gross indicators—such as number of school absences—are sufficient for evaluating intervention outcomes—such as an intervention to remediate poor school attendance. The advantage of permanent products is their time and resource efficiency, but low specificity and sensitivity limits their usefulness for evaluation.

Behavior rating scales can provide strong estimates of a child's social behavior across multiple dimensions. But, they're often not sensitive to change over time, such that interventions of shorter duration may not show significant impact on child outcomes. The fact that data come from teacher or parent report of student behavior, rather than actual behavior, is also problematic, as discussed previously.

Although educators use **daily progress reports** more frequently as a progress monitoring tool, they can also use them for evaluation by comparing the child's points percentage before and after the intervention. This is an effective method of estimating behavior change over time and useful for evaluating intervention outcomes.[18] However, similar to behavior rating scales, the reports reflect the rater's view of the child's behavior rather than actual behavior.

Evaluation using **CAT** can eliminate redundant questions at too-high or too-low levels in order to zero in on the child's correct performance range. Results can often be generated in ten minutes or less with reliability equal or superior to paper tests.[19] Further, reliability is greater for CAT than it is for traditional tests when assessing children far below—or above—expected achievement for their grade level.[20] The ability of CAT to keep scores on the same scale is particularly useful for comparison across time points. Therefore,

CAT is perfectly suited for repeated use throughout the school year, reliably measuring growth from test to test. Tests that are developed to be vertically equated across grades also allow valid comparisons of children's scores as they progress through multiple years—a particular issue with children who require more than a year of interventions to reach expected performance. Lastly, a unified database of assessment results can be extremely valuable when documenting and communicating intervention decisions to parents, a legal requirement of RtI.[21]

SUMMARY

In recent years, there's been an increasing interest in using data to guide the intervention planning and assessment process due to federal initiatives requiring schools to match the type and intensity of intervention to children's actual needs.[3] These initiatives emphasize a 'dual-discrepancy' model[4] in which evaluators use a problem solving approach to determine if a child benefits from implemented interventions. This determination is accomplished by measuring not only achievement levels, but also the level and rate of the child's response to intervention. Within the RtI framework, educators use social and behavioral assessment data to help identify children with specific skill deficits (screening), monitor whether a child's skills or behavior change during an intervention (progress monitoring), and evaluate whether a child shows improvement in target outcomes after participating in an intervention (evaluation). Traditional social and behavioral assessment methods for intervention screening, monitoring, and evaluation have both advantages and disadvantages, as discussed in detail in Part II of this book.

Of those currently available social and behavioral assessment methods, only computer adaptive testing (CAT) can be accurately used for screening, progress monitoring, *and* evaluation purposes. CAT is most frequently applied through traditional computerized testing forms—such as sequential multiple-choice items. Consider the SAT as a prime example of this. For social skills assessment, CAT in this self-report questionnaire format can be useful for assessing children's social literacy. However, only when CAT is applied within a game-based world—as it is within *Zoo U*—can social performance indices also be assessed. As described throughout this book, *Zoo U* dynamically adapts the child's experience based on her responses within tailored virtual social problem solving situations—akin to CAT—and

Dual discrepancy model

=

measure of child's achievement level

+

his rate of response to intervention

adjusts the scoring indices for more sensitive assessment of the child's ability to perform socially.

The *Zoo U* assessment software offers a highly innovative alternative to achieve the screening and evaluation goals of RtI for social skills assessment. As discussed in detail in Chapter 16, the practical, statistical, and engagement advantages of the *Zoo U* assessment make it ideal for schools to quickly and easily identify children in need of social and behavioral intervention. The assessment can also be administered repeatedly, in three month intervals, to demonstrate growth and change in social competency over the school year. When social interventions are implemented between these intervals, *Zoo U* can be a powerful evaluation tool by documenting growth for the same child using the same standardized norms.

With regard to progress monitoring, the *Zoo U ISTS* described in Chapter 17 enables schools to not only administer a social intervention through an engaging, adaptive, game-based platform, but also continually measure the child's progress. The *Zoo U* social tutoring software is ideal for accomplishing the 'mastery measurement' needed for RtI progress monitoring. For each social problem solving scene, children's criterion-referenced performance is assessed. Children's progress towards social skills mastery is documented and reported in real time for easy monitoring of progress by educators. Adjustments to social intervention—such as additional trials on *Zoo U ISTS* scenes or supplemental in-person activities—are directly informed by the child's ability to perform socially within the *Zoo U* virtual world.

The authors of this book know of no other game-based software that can achieve all three RtI goals in the social behavioral realm. *Zoo U* is the first to offer schools a feasible, engaging, and psychometrically sound alternative to traditional RtI approaches for SSA. While we don't expect—or wish— for games to completely replace traditional RtI methods, we do believe that games are the wave of the future. The cost-benefit ratio for games is remarkable compared to that for traditional assessment methods (see Part II of this book). *Zoo U*—and other intelligent game-based social skills applications that follow—provides schools with an unparalleled powerful RtI tool.

CHAPTER 18 NOTES

1. No Child Left Behind (NCLB) Act of 2001, Pub. L. No. 107-110, § 115, Stat. 1425 (2008).

2. Individuals with Disabilities Education (IDEA) Act of 2004, Pub. L. No. 101-476, 104 Stat. 1142 (2004).

3. Sandomierski, T., Kincaid, D., & Algozzine, B. (2007). Response to intervention and positive behavior support: Brothers from different mothers or sisters with different misters? *Positive Behavioral Interventions and Supports Newsletter, 4*, 1–4.

4. Fuchs, L. S. (2003). Assessing intervention responsiveness: Conceptual and technical issues. *Learning Disabilities: Research & Practice, 18*, 172-186.

5. Batsche, G., Elliott, J., Graden, J. L., Grimes, J., Kovaleski, J. F., Prasse, D., ... Tilly, W. D. (2005). *Response to intervention: Policy considerations and implementation.* Alexandria, VA: National Association of State Directors of Special Education, Inc.

6. Burns, M. K., & Gibbons, K. (2008). Response to intervention implementation in elementary and secondary schools: *Procedures to assure scientific-based practices.* New York, NY: Routledge.

7. Lane, K. L., Little, M. A., Casey, A. M., Lambert, W., Wehby, J. H., Weisenbach, J. L., & Phillips, A. (2009). A comparison of systematic screening tools for emotional and behavioral disorders: How do they compare? *Journal of Emotional and Behavioral Disorders, 17*, 93-105.

8. Gresham, F. M. (2004). Current status and future directions of school-based behavioral interventions. *School Psychology Review, 33*, 326-343.

9. Riley-Tillman, T. C., Kalberer, S. M., & Chafouleas, S. M. (2005). Selecting the right tool for the job: A review of behavior monitoring tools used to assess student response to intervention. *The California School Psychologist, 10*, 81-91.

10. Horner, R. H., Sugai, G., Todd, A. W., & Lewis-Palmer, T. (2005). School-wide positive behavior support. In L. Bambara & L. Kern (Eds.), *Individualized supports for students with problem behaviors: Designing positive behavior plans* (pp. 359–390). New York: Guilford.

11. Walker, H. M., & Shinn, M. R. (2002). Structuring school-based interventions to achieve integrated primary, secondary, and tertiary prevention goals for safe and effective schools. In M. R. Shinn, H. M. Walker, & G. Stoner (Eds.), *Interventions for academic and behavior problems: Vol. II. Preventive and remedial approaches* (pp. 1-26). Bethesda, MD: National Association of School Psychologists.

12. McIntosh, K., Campbell, A. L., Russell, D., & Zumbo, B. D. (2009). Concurrent validity of office discipline referrals and cut points used in schoolwide positive behavior support. *Behavioral Disorders, 34*, 100-113.

13. Fuchs, D., Compton, D. L., Fuchs, L. S., Bryant, J., & Davis, N. G. (2008). Making "secondary intervention" work in a three tier responsiveness-to-intervention model: Findings from the first grade longitudinal reading study of the National Research Center on Learning Disabilities. *Reading and Writing Quarterly: An Interdisciplinary Journal, 21*, 413–436.

14. Fuchs, L. S., & Fuchs, D. (2008). The role of assessment within the RTI framework. In D. Fuchs, L. S. Fuchs, & S. Vaughn (Eds.), *Response to intervention: A framework for reading educators* (pp. 27–49). Newark, DE: International Reading Association.

15. Salvia, J., & Ysseldyke, J. E. (2004). *Assessment* (9th ed.). Princeton, NJ: Houghton Mifflin.

16. Fuchs, L. S., & Stecker, P. M. (2003). *Scientifically based progress monitoring.* Washington, DC: National Center on Student Progress Monitoring. Retrieved May 15, 2013 from http://www.studentprogress.org/library/Presentations/ScientificallyBasedProgressMonitoring.pdf.

17. VanAcker, R., Boreson, L., Gable, R. A., & Potterton, T. (2005). Are we on the right course? Lessons learned about current FBA/BIP practices in schools. *Journal of Behavioral Education, 14*, 35-56.

18. Chafouleas, S. M., Riley-Tillman, T. C., Sassu, K. A., LaFrance, M. J., & Patwa, S. S. (2007). Daily behavior report cards (DBRCs): An investigation of consistency of on-task data across raters and method. *Journal of Positive Behavior Interventions, 9*, 30–37.

19. McMaster, K. L., & Wagner, D. (2007). Monitoring response to general education instruction. In S. R. Jimerson, M. K. Burns, & A. M. VanDerHeyden (Eds.), *Handbook of response to intervention: The science and practice of assessment and intervention* (pp. 223–233). New York: Springer.

20. Renaissance Learning. (2009). *Making RtI work: A practical guide for using data for a successful "Response to Intervention" program.* Wisconsin Rapids, WI: Renaissance Learning Inc.

21. Zirkel, P. A., & Thomas, L. (2010). State laws and guidelines for implementing RTI. *Teaching Exceptional Children, 43*, 60–73.

19

BRIDGING TO HOME

by: Chelsea Bartel, Ph.D. and Lorraine Taylor, Ph.D.

DESCRIPTION

So far, we've highlighted the strengths of *Zoo U* as a tool for social skills assessment (SSA) with particular focus on the school setting. In this chapter, we discuss how *Zoo U* data can provide parents and caregivers with information and resources to support children at home. First, we review the importance of regular assessment of social skills and the relationship between assessment and intervention. Second, we explore how teachers and other educators can partner with parents and caregivers to understand and use SSA data. Third, we provide case examples to demonstrate how educators can work with parents to use *Zoo U* data at home. After reading this chapter, you should have a clear understanding of how this innovative assessment approach can enhance partnerships between educators and parents by giving both parties clear, accessible data and achievable intervention recommendations.

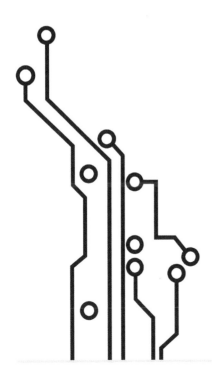

ASSESSMENT AS A STARTING POINT

Many parents are accustomed to cursory reports on their child's behavior, often via a report card and measured by items such as 'maintains attention to tasks' or 'gets along with peers.' These broad-scale, periodic reports are prone to problems, such as teacher bias in rating the student and vague or absent explanations about what exactly is meant by each rating. In addition, notes on behavior are often overlooked when presented to parents along with academic grades. Recent emphasis on 'common core' academic standards has resulted in most student report cards conveying little information about social skills or needs, leaving parents with only the most general understanding of their child's social functioning. Educators typically have more frequent contact with parents of children who engage in socially inappropriate or disruptive behaviors, in the form of a call from the teacher or principal about a child's bad day, a note home, or even suspension/expulsion discussions. However, these types of communication don't tell the complete story about a child's social skills. Sharing vague behavioral data on a report card, or reporting to parents in a reactive manner only after behaviors become disruptive, can leave parents unaware of their children's social needs and leave them feeling blindsided when problems erupt.

Schools and, increasingly, parents, are becoming familiar with the Response to Intervention (RtI) framework for assessing academic skills and selecting evidence-based interventions to meet students' needs (see Chapter 18). A critical piece of RtI is universal assessment of academic skills.[1] This means that two or three times each academic year, every student completes a series of brief assessments to demonstrate functioning across academic areas including fluency and comprehension in reading and mathematics. The assessment measures are standardized, which allows educators to accurately measure academic growth and to quickly determine which students are not demonstrating mastery of the curriculum. When children do not meet established criterion levels, educators intervene to provide that child with additional supports to meet the need. This model is appealing in its simplicity and focus on data-driven decision making. RtI allows educators to identify needs early and intervene as needed.

What is Common Core?

"The Common Core State Standards provide a consistent, clear understanding of what students are expected to learn, so teachers and parents know what they need to do to help them. The standards are designed to be robust and relevant to the real world, reflecting the knowledge and skills that our young people need for success in college and careers."

- Common Core State Standards Initiative

Although RtI has been widely adopted and embraced as a useful model for assessing and addressing academic needs, its counterpart for measuring and intervening with behavioral concerns has been less successful. This model, called Positive Behavioral Interventions and Supports (PBIS), is designed to mirror RtI—including its core features of universal assessment and data-based intervention.[2] PBIS is considered a 'best practice' model for schools to use when intervening with student behaviors.[3] However, it's implemented less frequently than RtI, and schools vary widely in their ability to implement the PBIS model as designed.[4] One of the hindrances to implementation of PBIS is that there are far fewer easy-to-use, standardized assessments available to universally measure behavior and social skills than there are to measure academic skills, making data collection and interpretation difficult.[5] When measures are not available or demand too much training or time to administer, data on student behavior are less reliable and valid, which undermines intervention efforts. *Zoo U* is innovative and timely, filling the need for a valid measure of social skills that is feasible to deliver to all children within a school setting at multiple time points throughout the year. When educators measure behavior with the same frequency as they do academic skills, they emphasize the importance of assessing and teaching the whole child.

Getting reliable and valid data is especially important when what's being assessed is difficult to measure or can go unnoticed until real problems emerge. This is often the case with social skills, which can be overlooked for far too long in an environment of academic pressures. Interventions designed to help children whose social skills are not up to par are only effective if they target the child's true skill deficits, making assessment the starting point for action. Next, we discuss how educators can team with parents to interpret *Zoo U* data and from there, intervene to help the child.

IMPORTANCE OF CONSULTATION

In order to effectively communicate assessment results to parents, it's important for educators to understand how consultation works and what factors lead to the best outcomes for students. Consultation is a well-established practice that is essential in schools, and at its core is an organized and systematic approach to problem solving.[6] Consultation occurs when two or more professionals—at least one with specialized knowledge in the area of

Positive Behavioral Interventions and Support (PBIS)
=
Universal assessment
+
Data driven intervention

need—meet to discuss the needs of another person.[7] For example, a teacher and a school psychologist meet and develop plans to help a child learn to greet other children appropriately. Likewise, when a teacher or other educator meets with a parent to discuss strategies for improving a child's social skills, the consultation can occur either at that time, or later between the teacher and another professional. Susan Sheridan and her colleagues at the University of Nebraska developed a consultation model called Conjoint Behavioral Consultation (CBC), in which a consultant meets with the teacher and parents together, and all parties discuss the child's needs and together plan interventions.[8] This model has been demonstrated to contribute to favorable outcomes for children.[9]

A consultation framework can provide a foundation for educators to help them interpret and discuss the results of *Zoo U* with parents. Teachers should first review and discuss the report with a mentor, school psychologist, or school counselor so that both parties can glean information and plan possible interventions to help the child. In a traditional consultation model, this meeting would occur before the parent is present. However, the CBC model provides support for the idea of including the teacher, an additional educator (such as a school psychologist or behavior support personnel), and the parent together in the same meeting. Regardless of which consultation model you wish to use, the most important thing is to review the assessment data in advance and have a plan for sharing it with parents. In the next section, we walk through the *Zoo U* assessment reports in detail and provide tips for sharing results with parents and teaming with parents to implement interventions at home to improve children's social skills.

CONSULTATION MODEL
Review *Zoo U* SSA data in advance and have a plan for sharing with parent

SHARING ZOO U ASSESSMENT DATA WITH PARENTS

Zoo U assessment results are divided into five sections: (a) Validity; (b) Global Scores; (c) Index Scores; (d) Detailed Individual Results; and (e) Class-wide reports. These sections were reviewed in detail in Chapter 15, and here we focus discussion on how you can use these automatically generated reports to communicate and collaborate with parents regarding their child's social skills strengths and weaknesses.

Response Patterns

Zoo U automatically generates calculations on the child's general approach to the game and, on an individualized report, displays warnings if the child's overall game play may negatively influence scores. Sample reports are provided to accompany the Case Examples later in this chapter. You can also refer to Chapter 14 for additional sample reports.

When reviewing the validity data with parents, educators can use the guide below:

I. Determine whether any response pattern checks were triggered.

If yes:

- Read all triggered checks and ensure you understand their meaning.
- Do these patterns of performance match with what you know about the child? Or do you think the child interacted with Zoo U in a way that does not reflect her actual social performance?
- Explain to parents which checks were triggered and what that could mean.
- If you determine the child's results likely are invalid, do not share additional scores with parents.

If no:

- Explain to parents how validity is measured in the Zoo U stealth assessment system.
- Note that this child's scores appear to be a valid measure of her social skills.

II. Ask parents for their reactions regarding validity scoring and answer any questions.

Global Social Competence Score

The *Zoo U* global report displays the child's performance on the composite social competence score. Performance is compared to a normative national sample of 3rd and 4th grade children, or teachers can select to use local norms so the child's performance is determined relative to other children in that classroom or grade level. Global Social Competence scores range from 0–100, with higher scores indicating better performance. As discussed in Chapter 14, scores are divided into three tiers for ease of interpretation: the red tier represents significant difficulty with social skills, the yellow tier represents falling in the 'at risk' range—suggesting the child needs additional supports to exhibit competence with social skills—and the green tier represents social skills falling within an acceptable or age-typical range.

When reviewing Global Social Competence score data with parents, educators can use the guide below:

I. Where does this child's composite score fall?

Red tier

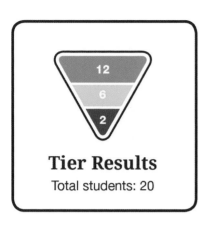

Tier Results
Total students: 20

• Explain to parents that their child is performing at the low end of the norm sample, and is likely having significant difficulties with social skills.

• Explain that you'll go into detail about exactly which social skills their child is struggling with.

• Share that children with global scores in this range are good candidates for social skills interventions at school and at home.

Yellow tier

• Explain to parents that their child is performing a bit below the ideal range compared to the norm sample, and might be having some difficulties with social skills.

• Explain that you'll go into detail about exactly which social skills their child is struggling with.

• Share that children with global scores in this range should be monitored closely at school and at home, because they might benefit from some additional supports to improve social skills.

Green tier

• Explain to parents that their child is performing within the expected range compared to the norm sample, which suggests the child's overall social skills are age appropriate.

• Explain that you'll go into detail about how their child performed in each of the six social skill areas.

• Note that children with global scores in this range don't appear to need additional supports or interventions for social skills at this point. However, every child has strengths and weaknesses and may still benefit from supports in specific skill areas.

II. Ask parents for their reactions regarding the Global Social Competence Score and answer any questions.

Individual Social Skill Scores

Index scores display the child's performance for each of the six specific social skill areas assessed by *Zoo U* (see **Table 1**). Performance is compared to a normative national sample of 3rd and 4th grade students, or teachers can select to use local norms so the child's performance is determined relative to other children in that classroom or grade level. Global scores range from 0–10, with higher scores indicating better performance.

Table 1

Definitions and Examples of the Six Social Skills Assessed by *Zoo U*

Emotion Regulation

The ability to respond to life with a range of emotions that is socially acceptable and flexible to allow or delay outwardly expressing emotions, depending on the situation.

Children with good emotion regulation can: stay calm when teased, take criticism without getting upset, resolve disagreements calmly, control their emotions, and keep things cool when situations are getting hot.

Impulse Control

The ability to resist temptations, urges, or impulses.

Children with good impulse control can: follow directions well, control behavior, stay on task, avoid distractions, and pay attention to important cues in the environment.

Communication

The ability to share and receive information through the exchange of thoughts, messages, or information, by speech, visual, signals, writing, or behavior.

Children with good communication skills can: be polite, respond well when others start a conversation, share their thoughts with others, share their feelings with others, use an appropriate tone of voice, respond to others' questions appropriately, and ask questions appropriately.

Empathy

The ability to recognize and share in others' feelings.

Children with good empathy skills can: understand other children's feelings, try to comfort others, be kind to others when they are feeling bad, show concern for others, and be aware of others' emotions.

Cooperation

The ability to work or act together with other people toward a common goal, for mutual benefit.

Children with good cooperation skills can: work with other children as a team, recognize appropriate times to cooperate, participate well in group activities or games, obey rules or requests by other children, and refrain from breaking up, disrupting, or stopping group activities.

Social Initiation

The ability to start a social interaction with others.

Children with good social initiation skills can: invite other children to play with them, join in activities that have already started, and start conversations with peers.

When reviewing Index Score data with parents, educators can use the following guide:

I. Explain that *Zoo U* measures six social skills that are key to children's social, behavioral, and academic success.

II. Clearly explain each social skill and where the child's score falls. Use the 'Red tier,' 'Yellow tier,' and 'Green tier' notes from the Global Social Competence Score section above as a guide for explaining the child's score on each index. You can use the information in Table 1 to help you explain what's meant by each of the six social skills labels.

III. Ask parents for their reactions regarding the Index Scores and answer any questions.

Detailed Individual Results

Zoo U also allows teachers to create reports showing child's exact numerical scores along with charts depicting progress over time. We do not recommend sharing the numerical scores with parents; since the raw scores are not placed within a meaningful context, they can be misinterpreted. However, the charts can be shared as a useful tool for helping parents see their child's skill level relative to same-age peers. Additionally, these charts indicating change in the child's scores over time can also be a useful visual tool to help parents see their child's progress in relation to target scores for each skill.

Class-wide Reports. Teachers can use the class-wide report to see the relative overall social performance of children across the entire class. The class-wide report should not be shared directly with parents, as it contains identifying data on other children in the class. However, teachers can talk about how the child is performing relative to the other children, if desired, though names or other identifying information for the other children should not be used.

Before reviewing these data with parents, teachers should have a plan for exactly which results to highlight. Are there areas of concern based on assessment scores? Do these areas correspond with what the teacher and/or the parent already know about the child, or is this new information? Research-based practice would incorporate consultation between the teacher and another school professional before or during the parent meeting to review results. Next, we present two examples of how teachers have shared *Zoo U* assessment data with parents.

We do not recommend sharing the numerical scores with parents; since the raw scores are not placed within a meaningful context, they can be misinterpreted.

Case Examples. The two case examples presented here can serve as a guide for teachers preparing to share *Zoo U* assessment data with parents. In these examples, we focus on how the teachers and parents interact when the data are shared for the first time. Prior to discussions with parents, the teachers reviewed the assessment results and consulted with other educators to gather intervention ideas.

Case Example A: Raymond

Raymond, an academically advanced 3rd grade boy, has been struggling to make friends at his new school. His teacher notices his failed attempts at engaging with his peers in conversations and is concerned about Raymond becoming isolated. Despite these social difficulties, Raymond excels in his academic work. He's an exceptional writer and seems to particularly enjoy his language arts work. Raymond's teacher considers him to be in the yellow zone, or at risk, in terms of his overall social skill competence.

Bridging the Gap to Home: During a parent-teacher conference, Raymond's teacher first shared the validity (reponse patterns) report with Raymond's parents. The validity report showed no flagged areas, and the teacher explained that *Zoo U* is a good way to accurately measure Raymond's skills. She then shared the Index Score report, showing Raymond's parents where his scores fell across all six assessed social skills. She did not share the global score, which was in the green zone, because she planned to move to his area of need quickly so that there would be time to discuss it. Raymond's parents noticed that all of his scores fell in the green zone with the exception of Social Initiation. Raymond's teacher explained what that skill means, and gave his parents time to ask questions about this skill. Raymond's parents quickly asked what could be done to help Raymond develop stronger social initiation skills. His teacher then outlined the in-class strategies that she planned to use to help Raymond make more effective social initiations with his peers—a plan she developed in consultation with the school psychologist.

Raymond's parents were mildly concerned about this social issue, but since Raymond's academic work was on track, they were not alarmed. The teacher recommended that they work with Raymond at home to reinforce classroom strategies for engaging with peers. The teacher shared a list of conversation starters for Raymond to use in class, and discussed the importance of Raymond practicing conversation skills at home. She emphasized that parents can use these same conversation starters with each other and with Raymond, modeling this process. Raymond's parents were relieved to discover this area of need, and they reported that it helped them to understand why he was having difficulty making friends at his new school. The teacher and parents agreed to meet again in a few weeks to see how the conversation starters exercise was going and discuss any additional interventions.

Case Example B: Mallory

Mallory is a 4th grade student who is having a difficult time getting along with her peers and following instructions in class. She is slightly behind in her academic work and struggles to complete assignments. In addition to almost daily conflicts with her classmates, Mallory often fails to comply with teacher directions and is resistant to following instructions.

Bridging the Gap to Home: During the parent-teacher conference, Mallory's teacher began by explaining the use of the *Zoo U* assessment tool and sharing the validity report, which showed no areas of concern. He then shared the global report which showed that Mallory's overall social skills score fell at the low end of the yellow zone. He explained that this global score was derived from subscales measuring six specific social skills, and emphasized that Mallory had strengths and weaknesses across those skill areas. Throughout the conversation, Mallory's teacher remembered what his mentor had told him during their consultation before the parent-teacher conference: be sure to include positive stories about Mallory in order to not overwhelm her mother with negative reports. Moving on to the index score report, the teacher explained that Mallory's performance on the assessment placed her in the red zone for cooperation and impulse control, the yellow zone for communication and emotion regulation, and the green zone for social initiation and empathy. He shared specific examples of Mallory's struggles with social skills in the red and yellow areas, and outlined a plan involving small-group and individual sessions with the school counselor to target the identified areas of need.

After hearing about Mallory's classroom struggles, her mother was concerned but resistant to the teacher's evaluation. She was somewhat defensive about her daughter's behaviors and explained how she wanted Mallory to be a strong girl who wouldn't let people take advantage of her. The teacher validated the mother's perspective and talked about the balance between independence and cooperation. The teacher highlighted Mallory's strengths in empathy and social initiation, giving specific examples of how Mallory excelled in those areas. He also shared more information about the role of cooperative learning in the classroom (such as group projects and partnered reading assignments) and that Mallory would have to learn to cooperate so that she could succeed in school. The teacher also provided contact information for the school counselor to facilitate communication between Mallory's mother and the counselor who would be the primary interventionist in this case. By emphasizing the notion of parents and teachers as partners, Mallory's teacher was able to allay the mother's concerns and strengthen their alliance in helping Mallory succeed in school.

SUMMARY

Because we know that the negative consequences of social skills deficits are far-reaching (see Chapter 3), the importance of addressing this area of children's development is paramount for children's present and long-term success. It is essential for teachers to partner with parents in order to improve outcomes for children struggling with social skills. In order to effectively help their child, parents must be fully informed not only about the treatment plan, but also about their child's specific social skills strengths and needs. In this chapter, we provided a clear guide for understanding *Zoo U* assessment data and described the details that teachers and others educators should focus on when sharing *Zoo U* data with parents and caregivers. The case examples we provide bring together the topics discussed in this chapter and can be used as models for teachers as they prepare to share data with parents. When you have these structured, data-driven conversations with parents, you build the parent-teacher partnership and emphasize the importance of social skills. By using the resources provided with *Zoo U* as well as the information provided in this chapter, teachers can effectively communicate with parents and caregivers about children's social skills strengths and needs.

CHAPTER 19 NOTES

1. Reschly, D. J., & Bergstrom, M. K. (2009). Response to intervention. In T. Gutkin & C. Reynolds (Eds.), *The handbook of school psychology* (4th ed., pp. 434-460). Hoboken, NJ: John Wiley & Sons.

2. Scott, T. M. (2001). A schoolwide example of positive behavioral support. *Journal of Positive Behavior Interventions, 3,* 88-94.

3. Algozzine, K., & Algozzine, B. (2010). Classroom instructional ecology and school-wide positive behavior support. *Journal of Applied School Psychology, 24,* 29-47.

4. Recent survey data reveal that RTI is implemented in approximately 94% of elementary schools in the United States, as reported by Spectrum-K12's (2011) Response to Intervention Adoption Survey. PBIS, however, is currently implemented in approximately 27% of elementary schools in the United States (according to Swain-Bradway, J., Swoszowski, N. C., Boden, L. J., & Sprague, J. R. (2013). Voices from the field: Stakeholder perspectives on PBIS implementation in alternative educational settings. *Education and Treatment of Children, 36* (3), 31-46.).

5. Kincaid, D., Childs, K., Blase, K. A., & Wallace, F. (2007). Identifying barriers and facilitators in implementing schoolwide positive behavior support. *Journal of Positive Behavior Interventions, 9* (3), 174-184.

6. Bartel, C. M. (2012). Understanding verbal interaction patterns in problem-solving team meetings using the Consultation Analysis Record. (Doctoral dissertation). Retrieved from ProQuest Dissertations and Theses (Accession Order No. 3538259).

7. Caplan, G. (1963). Types of mental health consultation. *American Journal of Orthopsychiatry, 33,* 470-481.

8. Sheridan, S. M., & Kratochwill, T. R. (2007). *Conjoint behavioral consultation: Promoting family-school connections and interventions* (2nd ed.). New York, NY: Springer.

9. Sheridan, S. M., Eagle, J. W., Cowan, R. J., & Mickelson, W. (2001). The effects of conjoint behavioral consultation: Results of a 4-year investigation. *Journal of School Psychology, 39,* 361-385.

Informing Treatment of Children with Autism Spectrum Disorders

by: Deb Childress, Ph.D. and Melissa E. DeRosier, Ph.D.

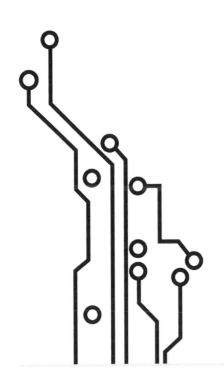

DESCRIPTION

For years, technology has been used to improve the quality of life of people with a wide range of developmental, learning, and physical disabilities. Technology-based tools hold great appeal for users of all ages due to their flexibility, portability, and ease of use. Children tend to be drawn to technology, and this is no less true for children with disabilities. In addition to its engaging nature, technology can level the playing field for children who struggle with learning, and do so in a way that doesn't add to the stigma that can be associated with other types of supports or interventions. For example, test taking accommodations (such as text-to-speech or synchronized highlighting) increase accessibility for children with learning disabilities, and can be built into software so they aren't obvious to others and the child doesn't stand out as different.

In this chapter, we describe a sub-group of children who struggle with social skills—children with Autism Spectrum Disorders (ASD). We first examine the ways in which our discussion of social skills and social skills assessment in this book can be applied to this sub-population of children. We then discuss how games can be a particularly effective means of engaging children with ASD in social skills assessment.

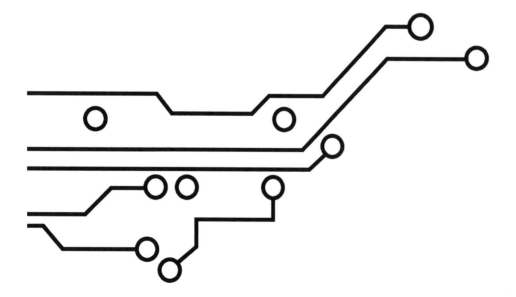

SOCIAL SKILLS AND AUTISM SPECTRUM DISORDER

Autism spectrum disorder (ASD) is a neurodevelopmental disorder involving impairment in reciprocal social interaction and communication, and repetitive and restricted interests. Social dysfunction has been a core component of the diagnosis since it was first described by Leo Kanner in 1943.[1] Kanner's case study of 11 children provided the original description of autism:

> "The outstanding, 'pathognomonic,' fundamental disorder is the children's *inability to relate themselves* in the ordinary way to people and situations from the beginning of life (…) This is not, as in schizophrenic children or adults, a departure from an initially present relationship; it is not a 'withdrawal' from formerly existing participation. There is from the start an *extreme autistic aloneness* that, whenever possible, disregards, ignores, shuts out anything that comes to the child from the outside." (p. 242)

Since Kanner's first paper, thousands of articles on the cause, developmental trajectory, and treatment of social deficits found in ASD have been published. Even with recent revisions to the clinical criteria for ASD,[2] social dysfunction and social skill deficits remain the hallmark.[3,4] Children with ASD show marked impairments in the social skills discussed in this book (see Chapter 1). These impairments may include:

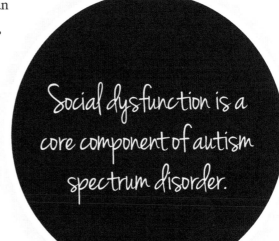

Social dysfunction is a core component of autism spectrum disorder.

- difficulty seeing a situation from another's point of view → poor perspective taking and empathy skills;
- difficulty interpreting social cues, such as trouble reading the meaning of facial expressions or tone of voice→ poor non-verbal communication skills;
- difficulty with the give-and-take of a conversation, such as obsessing on one's own interest and disregarding the other's interests→ poor verbal communication and listening skills;
- difficulty controlling obsessive or repetitive impulses, such as saying or doing things that others see as odd, out-of-place, or undesirable→ poor impulse control;
- difficulty with self-awareness of emotions→ interferes with emotion regulation; and
- awkward social behaviors, such as low eye contact and perseverative actions→ interferes with social initiation.

These impairments in basic engaging and inhibitory social skills also mean that children with ASD struggle with higher-order, solution-focused social skills, such as cooperation and social action planning.

However, while ASD is in large part defined by the presence of social skill deficits, it's important to remember that the specific presentation of deficits for a given child with ASD can vary greatly. As the word 'spectrum' suggests, children diagnosed with ASD fall along a continuum of functional ability and symptom severity. The particular pattern of social skill deficits for one child with ASD can be very different from that of another child, and the severity of these deficits can range from very mild to very severe. For example, children with ASD may have intellectual functioning classified anywhere from severely disabled to gifted. They may have no functional speech at all or demonstrate fluent speech. They may be socially aloof or highly interested in others. Therefore, it's essential to assess the child's specific symptoms and their severity in order to fully understand the social impairments of that child and thereby organize and implement effective social intervention.

WHY ARE SOCIAL SKILLS SO IMPORTANT TO CHILDREN WITH ASD?

The importance of social fluency for education, mental health, and personal well-being outcomes is clear (see Chapter 3). For individuals with ASD, the relationship is perhaps even more pronounced because of the pervasive and enduring nature of their social skill deficits. However, it's a common misconception that children with ASD do not desire social relationships or friendships. The truth is that many children with ASD strongly desire social relationships but struggle with understanding how to develop reciprocal friendships. Their behaviors are often seen as socially immature and odd by their peers. They may spend too long talking about robots, trains, or some other interest that isn't shared by the group or they may get upset if there's a change in the expected routine. As a result, children with ASD are often excluded from social opportunities with typically developing peers and experience significant social isolation.[5,6]

For children with high functioning ASD—ASD with average-to-gifted intellectual ability—these social skills challenges can be increasingly problematic. These children are typically placed in the general education

Many children with ASD strongly desire social relationships but struggle with developing them.

environment where peers and adults expect a certain level of social competence and there are negative social consequences for failing to meet this level. Middle childhood (8-12 years) is a particularly challenging time when rapid changes in socio-emotional functioning occur. Children begin to affiliate more with peers and their relationships become more complex and codified, such as with the formation of cliques[7] (see Chapter 2). In middle childhood, the social developmental gap progressively widens for children with high functioning ASD as their peer group rapidly assimilates new social skills and knowledge. They struggle to adapt to this increasingly complex social world and, as a result, the risk for peer problems such as rejection, isolation and bullying increases tremendously.[8,9]

Although bullying is a common problem worldwide,[10,11] children with ASD are at disproportionately higher risk of being bullied, with reported rates of up to 75%.[7] That is at least 30% greater than the general population estimates. Unfortunately, this statistic isn't surprising, given that bullies often target children who are socially isolated[12] and some theories suggest that bullies are particularly skilled at picking out children who might make good targets.[13,14] Put more simply, bullies often have advanced skills in social awareness, an area in which individuals with ASD tend to struggle.[15] Bullying of children with high functioning ASD also appears to be persistent. In a recent study of parents, 20% reported their child with ASD had been victimized by a bully for several months and 54% reported the bullying had gone on for more than a year.[8] These numbers are particularly troubling in light of longitudinal research on the negative outcomes of repeated bullying.[16] Over time, the social isolation and bullying experiences contribute to the development of anxiety and depressive disorders.[13,14] Without access to effective interventions to address their social impairments, children with ASD are likely to experience social isolation, peer problems, and consequent mental health disorders throughout the life span.[13]

Up to 75% of children with ASD experience bullying and teasing by peers.

SSA FOR CHILDREN WITH ASD

The traditional social skills assessment (SSA) methods discussed in Part II of this book have all been applied to children with ASD, although behavioral rating scales are most commonly used. The primary advantage of rating scales is their ability to efficiently obtain large quantities of information regarding social behavior from multiple sources and in a range of settings. However, when SSA tools include norms, these scores are usually determined with samples of typically developing children. When rating scales are used with special populations, such as with children with ASD, there can be challenges related to interpreting this normative data. For example, the level of social impairments experienced by children with ASD may place them at the extreme end of the normative curve. When the SSA is repeated again later, even if the child is actually performing better, the scores may not be able to reflect those gains. In essence, when the scores for an SSA measure are normed to the general population, there can be a **floor effect** which masks any gains made by the child with ASD.

Similarly, assessments that use diagnostic cutoffs often lack the sensitivity to demonstrate treatment effects for children with ASD, even when observers note functional improvements. In all likelihood, a child with a diagnosis of ASD will continue to demonstrate clinically significant social deficits even after effective treatment. However, it's important to assess and document that benefit even if it is not enough to bump them out of the ASD diagnostic category. Assessment measures that are not sensitive enough to detect incremental improvements could lead to unnecessary shifts in an otherwise effective treatment plan. Recognizing even small changes in children with ASD is integral to planning the next step in the intervention process.

Somewhat paradoxically, assessments of social skills can also be too 'easy' for children with high functioning ASD. Given their average-to-gifted intellectual abilities, children with high functioning ASD may have learned the 'correct' answers for questions about social situations. As such, they're able to demonstrate normative social literacy, but don't have the ability to apply those social rules in real-life situations (see Chapter 4). It's not uncommon to hear parents and providers make statements such as, *"He knows what he is supposed to do, he just doesn't do it,"* or *"He knows the answers, but can't do it around other people."* In order to detect the nuances of these children's deficits in social cognition and identify the significant impact they have in the lives of these children, it's important to include SSA tools that assess not only literacy, but also performance. It's also critical to include measurement that taps into the complexities and oddities in the social presentations of children with ASD.

Game-based SSA platforms offer that beneficial blend of social literacy and social performance assessment data. The virtual social problem solving scenarios can help tease apart the degree to which a child with ASD understands what to do in a social situation versus what she is able to actually perform in that social situation—very useful information for intervention planning. Games also provide a means of presenting social situations of varying complexity and difficulty—with the capacity to dynamically adjust these variables in response to the child's performance—so that the scores better reflect the particular pattern of the child's social strengths and weaknesses. This greater sensitivity means greater ability to individualize treatment for a given child and thereby maximize treatment benefits over time.

In addition, children with ASD have a particular proclivity for technology that makes games an excellent assessment medium.[17] Interpersonal demands during traditional SSA—such as having the child look at you while you ask questions—can make the child anxious and interfere with her performance. Games present no such interpersonal demands. Games are also inherently more engaging, increasing children's attention to task and motivation to continue, even during assessment of an area that is particularly challenging for a child with ASD. Given that many children with ASD experience learning difficulties,[18] it's also helpful that games can integrate useful accommodations, such as text-to-speech, right into the software itself, thereby alleviating some of the negative impact of literacy demands. Clearly, the use of SSA games for children with ASD warrants further research and development.

Games may be particularly well suited for collecting SSA data with children with ASD.

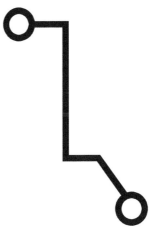

TECHNOLOGY-BASED SOCIAL SKILLS INTERVENTION FOR ASD

There's a tremendous need for social skills interventions for children with ASD. With one in 88 children diagnosed with ASD, the demand for effective interventions is greater than ever.[19] However, remarkably few rigorously tested, evidence based social skills interventions exist specifically for children with ASD. In fact, despite a dedicated effort to develop such programs,[20.21] the majority of available social interventions are simply reference books or guides that contain some useful information, but lack a rigorous evidence-base or standardized implementation methods. The majority of current evidence-based social skills training interventions for children with ASD are delivered in small groups by specially trained mental health providers.[20,22,23] While group delivery can offer tremendous benefits for children, such as modeling and real-time feedback, and offer providers an efficient way to serve multiple children, in-person social skills training (SST) faces significant implementation barriers. It can be difficult to find trained providers and challenging to assemble groups of children who are at a similar developmental level.[21,24] As a result, dissemination and use of in-person SST is limited, and families who could benefit from these interventions often face long waiting lists,[25-27] if they live in a community that offers these services at all. In addition, administration of group SST limits the provider's ability to personalize treatment to best meet any one child's individual social needs.[28]

Computerized social intervention can greatly increase access to and utilization of effective SST interventions for children with ASD. Research suggests that computerized interventions can be used as a primary or supplementary treatment modality to benefit children with ASD. For example, computer programs targeting emotion recognition and understanding have been shown to increase these social skills in children with ASD.[29-32] Computer-based virtual environments may also be effective for enhancing generalization of skill acquisition by teaching skills within realistic, interactive role plays.[33] Preliminary research supports the acceptability of this method by children with ASD and their families. In addition, children's social decision making improves after participating in a virtual social problem solving exercise.[34] Moreover, authors of a published review and meta-analysis of 11 studies that involved computerized interventions concluded that *"the use of computer based interventions to improve the social and emotional skill of individuals with ASD is a promising practice"*.[32]

> **Computerized social intervention can increase access and use of social skills training for kids with ASD.**

Advantages of Computer-based Games for Teaching Social Skills

Similar to the benefits noted in Chapter 17, computerized intervention can facilitate engagement for many children with ASD, particularly because social anxiety and apprehension about engaging with peers may make them reluctant to participate in in-person groups.[35-37] Interactive software offers a safe environment in which children with ASD can try out different social behaviors without fear, anxiety, or potentially negative social repercussions of real-life social interactions.[38]

Whereas manualized group administration of SST limits the provider's ability to personalize treatment to individual children, intelligent computer-based platforms can customize the SST experience to match the child's individual social needs.[21,24,28] For example, computer games can adjust the level of pedagogical assistance—corrective feedback, hints—as well as the pace of learning so tasks are sufficiently challenging to maintain a child's attention and motivation, but not so difficult that uncertainty, confusion, and frustration undermine mastery. This type of scaffolded training dramatically enhances engagement and learning[39] (see Chapter 17). In addition, computer platforms involve multi-sensory, active instruction, which has been found to better meet the needs of different types of learners—visual, auditory, and motor—and increase retention of information.[40,41]

Computer-based Games Extend Social Learning Into the Home

We know that parents of children with ASD experience higher stress relative to parents of typically developing children or children with other disabilities.[42-44] Among the factors associated with this stress, parents cite the challenges relating to their child's social impairments as particularly stressful.[45-47] Parents of children with ASD play a critical role in treatment both as advocates for services and as social coaches—coordinating and managing social opportunities for their child—yet many parents report feeling at a loss for how to help their child with social challenges.[48] We have heard countless parents express their profound sadness as they watch their children's painful struggle to gain social acceptance and their elation around the instances of success.

In recent years, there's been increasing recognition of the multifold benefits of engaging parents in intervention with their child with ASD.[49-51] As discussed in Chapter 19, game-based programs could be effectively used to extend social learning into the home environment. The SSA data provided through game-based platforms such as *Zoo U* can be shared with parents, along with personalized recommendations for at-home activities parents can do with their child to improve social skills. Games can also be used to directly engage parents in treatment, effectively improving parents' self-efficacy for helping their child with ASD navigate social challenges.[41] Research indicates that empowering parents with ways to intervene directly with their child can translate into improved outcomes for the child as well as positive outcomes for parents, such as higher self-confidence and lower anxiety.[52-54]

Figure 1 displays the logic model for this type of intervention. Through participation in computer-based games for social skills along with practice and generalization activities, children increase their social awareness and understanding and associated positive behavioral changes are fostered. Through engagement in online educational and skill building activities as well as through direct participation in the intervention with their child, parents improve their skills, lower their stress, and feel better equipped to help their child with social challenges. These more immediate outcomes, in turn, can result in long-term positive social, behavioral, and emotional outcomes for children and parents.

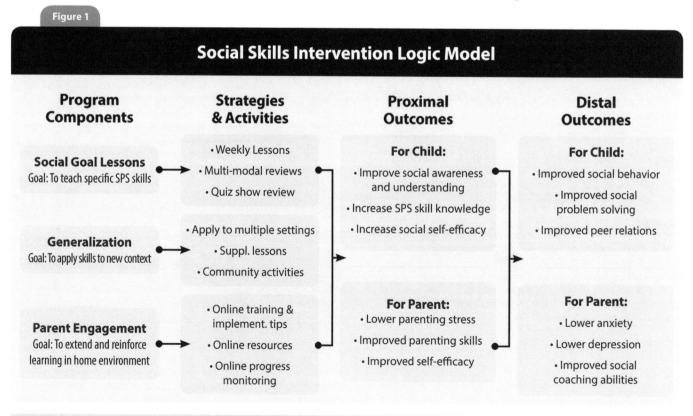

Figure 1

Social Skills Intervention Logic Model

Program Components → **Strategies & Activities** → **Proximal Outcomes** → **Distal Outcomes**

Social Goal Lessons
Goal: To teach specific SPS skills
- Weekly Lessons
- Multi-modal reviews
- Quiz show review

For Child:
- Improve social awareness and understanding
- Increase SPS skill knowledge
- Increase social self-efficacy

For Child:
- Improved social behavior
- Improved social problem solving
- Improved peer relations

Generalization
Goal: To apply skills to new context
- Apply to multiple settings
- Suppl. lessons
- Community activities

Parent Engagement
Goal: To extend and reinforce learning in home environment
- Online training & implement. tips
- Online resources
- Online progress monitoring

For Parent:
- Lower parenting stress
- Improved parenting skills
- Improved self-efficacy

For Parent:
- Lower anxiety
- Lower depression
- Improved social coaching abilities

CUSTOMIZATION OF GAMES FOR ASD

In order to maximize the utility of computer-based systems for special populations, such as individuals with ASD, there's additional work to do. Specifically, our understanding of how specific features of the user interface may impact the game experience for individuals with ASD is rudimentary at best. The unique pattern of social and cognitive strengths and deficits of individuals with autism necessitates we determine how to customize the software to optimize engagement, motivation, and learning for these individuals.[3] Developing this foundational knowledge is critically important to maximize the potential impact of games for social skills assessment and treatment with individuals with ASD.

For example, consider the role of the avatar in game play. As the representation of 'self' in the story world, the player's avatar is a core element in the game experience. Being able to identify with one's avatar has been shown to increase engagement and learning in games with typically developing children,[55] but the avatar may serve an even more critical role for individuals with ASD.[56,57] Children with ASD often experience significant facial processing deficits (difficulty deciphering facial expressions) and source monitoring errors (difficulty discriminating the source of information - self or other). Such deficits can undermine the child's identification with her avatar. When there's a greater disconnect between the child's individual characteristics—such as skin or hair color—and those of her avatar, learning and memory may suffer. In addition, individuals with ASD often experience problems generalizing learned information to real world situations. The greater the similarity between the player and her avatar, the more likely she will be able to apply what she has learned in real world situations.

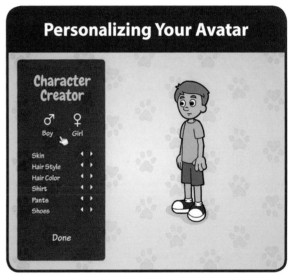

In our work developing social skills game platforms, we've observed striking differences in how typically developing children approach avatar creation compared with children with ASD. For example, children with autism will spend considerable time creating an avatar to match their own appearance as much as possible—down to matching their shoe color. One mother even noted that her son is "obsessed" with his avatar looking "just like him." In fact, when children with ASD felt their avatar was too dissimilar from themselves, they appeared anxious and this anxiety interfered with their engagement in the game. In contrast, we've observed typically developing children being just as likely to select avatar characteristics that match their own appearance as not, such as selecting purple hair or orange skin.

This example illustrates how children with autism may experience games in a fundamentally different manner. Additionally, sensory processing differences in children with ASD are common and should be considered when creating the game's user interface. Intense colors, background noises, and rapid animation that may engage some children may cause hyper-arousal, irritation, and distraction for others. It's critical that game developers are conscious of these effects and do not make conclusions about a child's game-based performance that's really the result of an unintentional user interface effect.

SUMMARY

Game-based social skills assessment and social skill interventions for ASD have shown utility in multiple domains and offer greater accessibility, individualization, and higher engagement than do traditional methods. We're at the beginning of a shift toward game-based assessment and intervention platforms. And while computer based tools will never completely replace face to face methods—nor should they—the promise of emergent technology to provide engaging and flexible companions to in-person methods is clear. Technology-based interventions—particularly games with embedded dynamic assessment capabilities—open unparalleled avenues for broad-scale dissemination and use of effective social interventions for individuals with ASD. Additionally, technology provides an accessible tool that could be easily extended for use by parents, allowing for additional opportunities for practice at home. We must conduct research to gain a better understanding of how elements within the game's user interface can be specifically keyed to the unique needs of individuals with ASD so that engagement, learning, and generalization to real-world outcomes are maximized.

CHAPTER 20 NOTES

1. Kanner, L. (1943). Autistic disturbances of affective contact. *Nervous Child, 2,* 217-250.

2. American Psychiatric Association. (2013). *Diagnostic and statistical manual of mental disorders* (5th ed.). Arlington, VA: American Psychiatric Publishing.

3. Carter, A. S., Davis, N. O., Klin, A., & Volkmar, F. R. (2005). Social development in autism. In F. R. Volkmar, R. Paul, A. Klin, & D. J. Cohen (Eds.), *Handbook of autism and pervasive developmental disorders* (pp. 312-334). Hoboken, NJ: John Wiley & Sons.

4. Saulnier, C. A., & Klin, A. (2007). Brief report: Social and communication abilities and disabilities in higher functioning individuals with autism and Asperger syndrome. *Journal of Autism and Developmental Disorders, 37*(4), 788-793.

5. Barnhill, G. P. (2001). Social attributions and depression in adolescents with Asperger syndrome. *Focus on Autism and Developmental Disabilities, 16*(1), 46-53.

6. Bauminger, N., & Kasari, C. (2000). Loneliness and friendship in high-functioning children with autism. *Child Development, 71* (2), 447-456.

7. Clark, K. E., & Ladd, G. W. (2000). Connectedness and autonomy support in parent-child relationships: Links to children's socioemotional orientation and peer relationships. *Developmental Psychology, 36* (4), 485-498.

8. Cappadocia, M. C., Weiss, J. A., & Pepler, D. (2012). Bullying experiences among children and youth with autism spectrum disorders. *Journal of Autism and Developmental Disorders, 42*(2), 266-277.

9. Rotheram-Fuller, E., Kasari, C., Chamberlain, B., & Locke, J. (2010). Social involvement of children with autism spectrum disorders in elementary school classrooms. *Journal of Child Psychology and Psychiatry, 51*(11), 1227-1234.

10. Jimerson, S. R., Swearer, S. M., & Espelage, D. L. (2010). *Handbook of bullying in schools: An international perspective.* New York, NY: Routledge/Taylor & Francis Group.

11. Due, P., Holstein, B. E., Lynch, J., Diderichsen, F., Gabhain, S. N., Scheidt, P., & Currie, C. (2005). Bullying and symptoms among school-aged children: International comparative cross sectional study in 28 countries. *The European Journal of Public Health, 15*(2), 128-132.

12. Cook, C. R., Williams, K. R., Guerra, N. G., Kim, T. E., & Sadek, S. (2010). Predictors of bullying and victimization in childhood and adolescence: A meta-analytic investigation. *School Psychology Quarterly, 25*(2), 65-83.

13. Sutton, J., Smith, P. K., & Swettenham, J. (1998). Bullying and 'theory of mind': A critique of the 'social skills deficit' view of anti-social behavior. *Social Development, 8*(1), 117-127.

14. Sutton, J., Smith, P. K., & Swettenham, J. (1999). Social cognition and bullying: Social inadequacy or skilled manipulation? *British Journal of Developmental Psychology, 17*(3), 435-450.

15. Baron-Cohen, S. (2008). Theories of the autistic mind. *The Psychologist, 21*(2), 112-116.

16. Houbre, B., Tarquinio, C., Thuillier, I., & Hergott, E. (2006). Bullying among students and its consequences on health. *European Journal of Psychology of Education, 21*(2), 183-208.

17. Shane, H. C., & Albert, P. D. (2008). Electronic screen media for persons with autism spectrum disorders: Results of a survey. *Journal of Autism and Developmental Disorders, 38*(8), 1499-1508.

18. Chen, M.-C., Wu, T.-F., Lin, Y.-L., Tasi, Y.-H., & Chen, H.-C. (2009). The effect of different representations on reading digital text for students with cognitive disabilities. *British Journal of Educational Technology, 40*(4), 764-770.

19. Centers for Disease Control and Prevention. (2012, March 30). Prevalence of autism spectrum disorders – autism and developmental disabilities monitoring network, United States, 2008. MMWR. Morbidity and Mortality Weekly Reports. Retrieved from http://www.cdc.gov/mmwr/preview/mmwrhtml/ss6103a1.htm?s_cid=ss6103a1_w

20. Rao, P. A., Beidel, D. C., & Murray, M. J. (2008). Social skills interventions for children with Asperger's syndrome or high functioning autism: A review and recommendations. *Journal of Autism and Developmental Disorders, 38,* 353-361.

21. White, S. W., Keonig, K., & Scahill, L. (2007). Social skills development in children with autism spectrum disorders: A review of the intervention research. *Journal of Autism and Developmental Disorders, 37,* 1858-1868.

22. Derosier, M. E., Swick, D. C., Davis, N. O, McMillen, J. S., & Matthews, R. The efficacy of a social skills group intervention for improving social behaviors in children with high functioning autism spectrum disorders. *Journal of Autism and Developmental Disorders, 41*(8), 1033-1043.

23. Carter, C., Meckes, L., Pritchard, L., Swensen, S., Wittman, P. P., & Velde, B. (2004). The friendship club: An after-school program for children with Asperger syndrome. *Family and Community Health, 27*(2), 143-150.

24. Bellini, S., Peters, J., Benner, L., & Hopf, A. (2007). A meta-analysis of school-based social skill interventions for children with autism spectrum disorders. *Remedial and special education, 28,* 153-162.

25. McConachie, H., Hoole, S., & Le Couteur, A. S. (2011). Improving mental health transitions for young people with autism spectrum disorder. *Child: Care, Health, and Development, 37*(6), 764-766.

26. Thomas, K. C., Ellis, A. R., McLaurin, C., Daniels, J., & Morrissey, J. P. (2007). Access to care for autism-related services. *Journal of Autism and Developmental Disorders, 37*(10), 1902-1912.

27. Montes, G., Halterman, J. S., & Magyar, C. I. (2009). Access to and satisfaction with school and community health services for U.S. children with ASD. *Pediatrics, 124*(6, Suppl 4), 407-413.

28. McConnell, S. R. (2002). Interventions to facilitate social interaction for young children with autism: Review of available research and recommendations for education interventions and future research. *Journal of Autism and Developmental Disorders, 32,* 351-372.

29. Golan, O., Ashwin, E., Granader, Y., McClintock, S., Day, K., Leggett, V., & Baron-Cohen, S. (2010). Enhancing emotional recognition in children with autism spectrum conditions: An intervention using animated vehicles with real emotional faces. *Journal of Autism and Developmental Disorders, 40,* 269-279.

30. Moore, D. J., McGrath, P., & Thorpe, J. (2000). Computer aided learning for people with autism: A framework for research and development. *Innovations in Education and Training International, 37,* 218-228.

31. Silver, M. (2001). Evaluation of a new computer intervention to teach people with autism or Asperger syndrome to recognize and predict emotions in others. *Autism, 5*(3), 299-316.

32. Ramdoss, S., Machalicek, W., Rispoli, M., Mulloy, A., Lang, R., & O'Reilly, M. (2012). Computer-based interventions to improve social and emotional skills in individuals with autism spectrum disorders: A systematic review. *Developmental Neurorehabilitation, 15*(2), 119-135.

33. Parsons, S., & Mitchell, P. (2002). The potential of virtual reality in social skills training for people with autistic spectrum disorders. *Journal of Intellectual Disability Research, 46,* 430-443.

34. Mitchell, P., Parsons, S., & Leonard, A. (2007). Using virtual environments for teaching social understanding to 6 adolescents with autism spectrum disorders. *Journal of Autism and Developmental Disorders, 37,* 589-600.

35. Sebastian, C., Blakemore, S.-J., & Charman, T. (2009). Reactions to ostracism in adolescents with autism spectrum conditions. *Journal of Autism and Developmental Disorders, 39*(8), 1122-1130.

36. Williamson, S., Craig, J., & Slinger, R. (2008). Exploring the relationship between measures of self-esteem and psychological adjustment among adolescents with Asperger syndrome. *Autism, 12*(4), 391-402.

37. Kuusikko, S., Pollock-Wurman, R., Jussila, K., Carter, A. S., Mattila, M.-L., Ebeling, H., … & Moilanen, I. (2008). Social anxiety in high-functioning children and adolescents with autism and Asperger syndrome. *Journal of Autism and Developmental Disorders, 38*(9), 1697-1709.

38. DeRosier, M. E., McMillen, J. S., & Thomas, J. M. (2011). Intelligent social tutoring system for children: Application of interactive software technology to the assessment and development of social problem solving. In A. Columbus (Ed.), *Advances in Psychology Research, Vol. 72* (pp. 99-132). Hauppauge, NY: NovaScience.

39. Pea, R. D. (2004). The social and technological dimensions of scaffolding and related theoretical concepts for learning, education, and human activity. *Journal of the Learning Sciences, 13*(3). 423-451.

40. Gardner, H. (1993). *Frames of mind: The theory of multiple intelligences.* New York, NY: Basic Books.

41. Keefe, J. W. (1987). *Learning style: Theory and practice.* Reston, VA: National Association of Secondary School Principals.

42. Dunn, M. E., Burbine, T., Bowers, C. A., & Tantleff-Dunn, S. (2001). Moderators of stress in parents of children with autism. *Community Mental Health Journal, 37*(1), 39-52.

43. Hamlyn-Wright, S., Draghi-Lorenz, R., & Ellis, J. (2007). Locus of control fails to mediate between stress and anxiety and depression in parents of children with a developmental disorder. *Autism, 11*(6), 489-501.

44. Estes, A., Munson, J., Dawson, G., Koehler, E., Zhou, X.-H., & Abbott, R. (2009). Parenting stress and psychological functioning among mothers of preschool children with autism and developmental delay. *Autism, 13*(4), 375-387.

45. Portway, S. M., & Johnson, B. (2005). Do you know I have Asperger's syndrome? Risks of a non-obvious disability. *Health, Risk, and Society, 7,* 73-83.

46. Davis, N. O., & Carter, A. (2008). Parenting stress in mothers and fathers of toddlers with autism spectrum disorders: Associations with child characteristics. *Journal of Autism and Developmental Disorders, 38*(7), 1278-1291.

47. Bode, H., Weidner, K., Storck, M. (2000). Quality of life in families of children with disabilities. *Developmental Medicine and Child Neurology, 42,* 354.

48. Tsatsanis, K., Foley, C., Donehower, C. (2004). Contemporary outcome research and programming guidelines for Asperger syndrome and high-functioning Autism. *Topics in Language Disorders, 24*(4), 249-259.

49. Sofronoff, K., & Farbotko, M. (2002). The effectiveness of parent management training to increase self-efficacy in parents of children with Asperger syndrome. *Autism, 6*(3), 271-286.

50. Sofronoff, K., Leslie, A., & Brown, W. (2004). Parent management training and Asperger syndrome: A randomized controlled trial to evaluate a parent based intervention. *Autism, 8*(3), 301-317.

51. Sofronoff, K., & Wittingham, K. (2007). Parent management training to improve competence in parents of children with Aspergers syndrome. In J. Briesmeister & C. E. Schaefer (Eds.), *Handbook of parent training: Helping parents prevent and solve problem behaviors* (3rd ed., pp. 107-128). New York, NY: John Wiley & Sons.

52. Mandell, D., & Salzer, M. (2007). Who joins support groups among parents of children with autism? *Autism, 11,* 111-122.

53. Hoagwood, K. E., Cavaleri, M. A., Serene Olin, S., Burns, B. J., Slaton, E., Gruttadaro, D., & Hughes, R. (2010). Family support in children's mental health: A review and synthesis. *Clinical Child and Family Psychology Review, 13,* 1-45.

54. Angold, A., Messer, S. C., Stangl, D., Farmer, E. M. Z., Costello, E. J., & Burns, B. J. (1998). Perceived parental burden and service use for child and adolescent psychiatric disorders. *Journal of Public Health, 88,* 75-80.

55. Baylor, A. (2011). The design of motivational agents and avatars. *Educational Technology Research and Development, 59*(2), 291-300.

56. Qian, N., & Lipkin, R. M. (2011). A learning-style theory for understanding autistic behaviors. *Frontiers in Human Neuroscience, 5,* 77.

57. Ploog, B. O., Scharf, A., Nelson, D., & Brooks, P. J. (2012). Use of computer-assisted technologies (CAT) to enhance social, communicative, and language development in children with autism spectrum disorders. *Journal of Autism and Developmental Disorders, 43*(2), 301-322.

ABOUT THE EDITOR

ABOUT THE EDITOR

Melissa E. DeRosier, Ph.D., is a clinical psychologist whose research and clinical work is dedicated to improving social, emotional, and behavioral health. For more than 15 years, Dr. DeRosier has investigated how to bridge research-proven methods for assessment and intervention into real-world settings so that youth and their families can directly benefit. She has written extensively in this area, publishing dozens of journal articles and book chapters. She has served as Principal Investigator for more than 30 federally funded grants from the National Institutes of Health, the U.S. Department of Education, and the Centers for Disease Control and Prevention. Through these funded projects, Dr. DeRosier has created over a dozen rigorously researched social-emotional interventions, which are currently used by schools and clinics with thousands of children across the United States and abroad. A particular focus of her current work is understanding how emerging technologies can be effectively used to scale up research-based programs more broadly in schools and community healthcare settings.

Dr. DeRosier obtained her master's degree in child developmental psychology from the University of Virginia and received her doctoral degree in clinical psychology from the University of North Carolina at Chapel Hill. She completed her clinical internship at George Washington University and a post-doctoral fellowship in the Developmental Epidemiology Program of Duke University Medical Center. In 2001, Dr. DeRosier founded the 3C Institute (www.3CISD.com), a research institute devoted to the creation and delivery of evidence-based tools that promote positive social, emotional, and behavioral health. In order to advance 3C's mission of integrating research and practice into real-life service settings, Dr. DeRosier founded 3-C Family Services (www.3CFS.com), an outpatient mental health practice providing the full range of psychiatric and psychological services.

Dr. DeRosier serves on the Board of the Center for Research in Emotional and Social Health (www.CRESH.org), a non-profit dedicated to helping schools and communities access effective interventions for youth and families, and on the Board of the Global Implementation Initiative (www. GlobalImplementation.org), a non-profit devoted to bringing implementation science best practices to healthcare settings across the globe.

Dr. DeRosier is also actively engaged in training research scientists. She holds faculty appointments as research assistant professor in the School of Education at the University of North Carolina at Chapel Hill, consulting associate faculty in Medical Psychiatry at Duke University Medical Center, and adjunct assistant professor of psychiatry in the Department of Psychiatry at the University of Pittsburgh Medical Center (UPMC). She serves as faculty and mentor for the Research Career Development Institute at UPMC and leads an NIH-funded project to create dynamic, interactive technology to enhance the training and career development of social and behavioral scientists.

While research and development are close to her heart, the true driving force behind Dr. DeRosier's work and life is her family. She met her husband, Dr. Jim Thomas, more than 30 years ago at the University of Virginia. Together, they have raised three wonderful boys—Jefferson, Benjamin, and Lincoln.

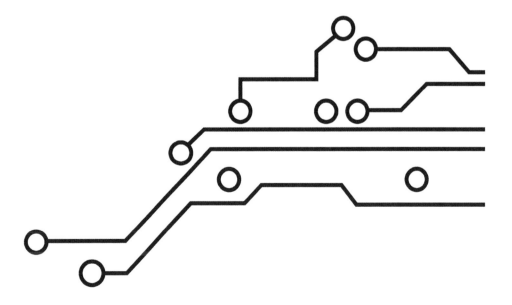

CONTRIBUTORS

CONTRIBUTORS

Chelsea Bartel (Ph.D., School Psychology, North Carolina State University, 2012) is a post-doctoral researcher at 3C Institute. Her research has focused on consultation and communication in school-based problem solving teams and on adapting a sociometric measure of depression to a sample of college athletes. She has led groups for preschool-aged children with behavioral and social-emotional difficulties; provided support and education to at-risk teen mothers; and provided consultation, assessment, and intervention services in a large public school system. Her research has appeared in *Journal of Educational and Psychological Consultation.*

Deb Childress (Ph.D., Psychology, University of North Carolina, 2008) is a Senior Research Associate at 3C Institute, with vast experience in autism research, focusing on the behavioral, personality, and cognitive characteristics of individuals with autism and their family members. She has studied the identification of early markers of autism through behavioral and imaging methodologies, and her work has appeared in publications including *Developmental Science, Autism Research,* and *American Journal of Medical Genetics (Neuropsychiatric Genetics).*

Ashley Craig (Ph.D., Lifespan Developmental Psychology, North Carolina State University, 2011) is a Research Associate at 3C Institute. Her research focuses on the social-emotional development of children, particularly within the contexts of family and school. She is especially interested in how parents' and children's socio-demographic characteristics, such as gender and culture, impact the way children experience, express, and cope with everyday emotions and stress. Her current work applies this expertise to intervention development, including Intelligent Social Tutoring Systems. She has co-authored articles in *Advances in Human-Computer Interaction, The Journal of Primary Prevention,* and *Infant and Child Development.*

Melissa E. DeRosier (Ph.D., Clinical Psychology, University of North Carolina, 1992) is the Chief Executive Officer of 3C Institute, which she founded in 2001 with the mission to bring research-proven methods for assessment and intervention into real-world settings so that youth and their families can directly benefit. Through more than 30 federally-funded projects, Dr. DeRosier has authored over a dozen rigorously researched social-emotional interventions currently used by schools and clinics across the United States and abroad. She has contributed dozens of journal articles and book chapters to publications such as *Academic Psychiatry, Advances in Human-Computer Interaction, Journal of Online Learning and Teaching,* and *Psychology in Schools.*

Kevin Leary (Ph.D., Lifespan Developmental Psychology, North Carolina State University, 2013) is a post-doctoral researcher at 3C Institute. His research interests involve the development of children's self-relevant processes within the family context and their effects on children's social and emotional well-being. He has experience with developmental research and design, including project development, data collection, and quantitative statistical analysis and interpretation, and has co-authored articles in *Psychiatric Annals* and *Psychology.*

Janey Sturtz McMillen (Ph.D., Early Childhood Special Education and School Psychology, University of North Carolina, 1997) serves as Chief Scientific Officer at 3C Institute, where she has led the Research Division since 2003, with a particular emphasis on the development and testing of web-based technologies to support effective transfer of evidence-based programs into real-world settings. For more than 25 years, she has researched the social and behavioral difficulties of children with disabling conditions, the role of technology in supporting the implementation of evidence-based programs, and other related areas. She has published extensively in journals such as *Advances in Psychology Research, Journal of Online Learning and Teaching,* and *Journal of Autism and Developmental Disorders.* She has served as a guest reviewer for publications including *Early Childhood Research Quarterly, Journal of Early Intervention, Topics in Early Childhood Special Education,* and *American Journal on Mental Retardation.*

Rebecca Sanchez (Ph.D., Cognitive and Developmental Psychology, University of Kentucky, 1999) works as a Senior Research Associate at 3C Institute. Her research experience and interests include social and emotional development, youth risk behaviors and health outcomes, at-risk populations, and mental health in children, adolescents, and adults. Her work has appeared in publications such as *Advances in Human-Computer Interaction, Journal of Adolescent Health, Journal of Abnormal Psychology, Military Psychology,* and *Journal of Clinical Child Psychology.*

Lorraine Taylor (Ph.D., Developmental Psychology, University of Virginia, 1997) is one of 3C Institute's Senior Research Associates. She has published research on parenting styles, parental involvement, academic socialization, young children's transition to school, and the impact of family economic hardship on parenting behaviors. Her work emphasizes a risk and resilience perspective and focuses on positive youth development and adaptive outcomes among at-risk youth. She has developed online parent training programs as well as online programs for promoting children's school readiness. She has published in journals including *Developmental Psychology, Journal of Applied Developmental Psychology, Elementary School Journal,* the *American Journal of Community Psychology,* and the *Journal of Primary Prevention.*

Jim Thomas (Ph.D., Computer Science, North Carolina State University, 2011) is a Research Scientist at 3C Institute, where he helps design and develop computer-based social skills tutoring systems for children. His research has focused on artificial intelligence, specifically as applied toward intelligent tutoring systems. He has presented and published extensively, contributing to *Child Development, IEEE Transactions on Learning Technologies, Artificial Intelligence in Education,* the *Games for Health Conference,* and *Problem Solving: Techniques, Steps, and Processes.*

ACKNOWLEDGMENTS

ACKNOWLEDGMENTS

If I were to claim—or even imply—that this book was all my doing, that would be a flat-out lie. Many heads and hands were needed to bring this book to fruition. In this section, I do my best to acknowledge and thank all of those who have contributed to making this book a reality.

My family

Many times I see families mentioned as the last entry in the acknowledgments section, so I'd like to change things up. Because, in fact, this book would not have happened without their years of support and guidance. My husband, Dr. Jim Thomas, has been by my side for over 30 years, never wavering in his support. He joined me on the mission to bring evidence-based social assessment and intervention into everyday use through technology, co-authoring SCAN (see Chapter 9) with me in the 1990s and contributing countless insights from the fields of artificial intelligence and computer science into the foundation of *Zoo U* and other intelligent games at 3C Institute. I'd also like to thank our three sons—Jefferson, Benjamin, and Lincoln—each of whom has helped me brainstorm ideas for 3C Institute's games, played our games to see if they could break them, and also provided honest feedback on gameplay to help me understand how to make our games most engaging.

Research participants

If you want to develop effective, accurate games, you have to conduct research and lots of it. I thank all those children, parents, teachers, school counselors, school psychologists, school administrators, and community mental health professionals who have participated in our research over the years. Your support and willingness to engage in research makes it possible for us to create effective, engaging, and highly useful technologies for health. Now children, families, and schools across the nation are benefiting from your efforts.

Funders

Research and development is expensive. And when you're trying to create games for social health—rather than for mass entertainment purposes—it can be extremely hard to obtain the funding needed. First and foremost, I thank the U.S. Federal Government for the Small Business Innovation Research (SBIR; www.sbir.gov) program, without which this book—and 3C Institute itself—would not be in existence. Though the products developed through 3C Institute have broad social and health implications, venture capital and angel investors are rarely interested in funding the research needed to establish effective social-emotional-behavioral products. The SBIR program is critical for providing small businesses like 3C Institute with the means to undertake essential R&D. It's only through SBIR funds that 3C Institute has been able to create over 30 evidence-based products that now benefit the health and well-being of thousands of children and families across the globe.

In particular, I would like to extend heartfelt thanks to Dr. Edward Metz of the U.S. Department of Education, Institute of Education Sciences. Dr. Metz is the Program Officer for 3C Institute's SBIR grants to develop and test *Zoo U* (grant award numbers ED-IES-11-C-0039 and ED-IES-12-C-0036) and other game development projects. Dr. Metz is truly devoted to improving the success of students through innovative technologies and we at 3C Institute greatly appreciate his feedback, guidance, and insights over the years. More generally, we'd like to thank the U.S. Department of Education for its willingness to take a risk on emergent technologies like *Zoo U*.

Contributors

You can't publish an edited volume without contributors, and ours are stellar. Check out the Contributors section to read about the many accomplished authors for this book. Many, many thanks for the hard work, creativity, and intellectual capital you contributed to make this book happen. In particular, I'd like to underscore the work of Dr. Ashley Craig who not only wrote key sections of this book, but also played a seminal role in the creation of *Zoo U* itself. She applied her many talents to helping me script the social problem scenes for *Zoo U* as well as create and refine the scoring rubric and algorithms that underlie the data and reports generated through the *Zoo U* assessment. This book—and *Zoo U* itself—would not be possible without Dr. Craig's immense contributions.

Developers

Similarly, if we had no *Zoo U* game, we'd have nothing to use as our example of game-based social skills assessment in this book. I would like to express how much I appreciate the coordinated efforts of all those individuals at 3C Institute who contributed to the creation of *Zoo U*. Through a unique multi-disciplinary collaboration with subject matter experts, these individuals created something completely new—an intelligent social tutoring system with embedded stealth assessment of social skills. Thank you for your countless contributions to the conceptualization of the game, creation of the underlying intelligent software engine, translation of assessment and learning objectives into gameplay, and making the user interface easy to use and highly engaging for children. Let's roll the credits for the major contributors to the development of *Zoo U*: Charles Bevan (game developer), Maurice Carter (graphic artist and animator), Stacie Cox (graphic artist and animator), James Dooley (QA tester), Matt Habel (software developer), Chris Hehman (game designer and translation guru), Jeff Jones (branding), Wes Sommer (audio engineer), Jeff Strope (website developer), and Jeremiah Weatherley (artist and animator).

Producers

And last, but surely not least (!) are the people responsible for making such a high quality, professional, and gorgeous book. Many thanks to Jeff Poe and Adger Rothwell for developing the awesome layout for this book, including cover design, color palette, and all graphic elements. I would also like to thank Steve Grothmann (copyeditor) and Dr. Rebecca Kameny (project editor) for their tireless attention to detail and fabulous editing.

Thank you all!

Made in the USA
Charleston, SC
08 December 2014